Mr Wilman's

MOTORING
ADVENTURE

TOP GEAR, GRAND TOUR AND
TWENTY YEARS OF MAGIC AND MAYHEM

Mr Wilman's
MOTORING
ADVENTURE

ANDY WILMAN

MICHAEL JOSEPH

PENGUIN

Est. 1935

PENGUIN MICHAEL JOSEPH

UK | USA | Canada | Ireland | Australia
India | New Zealand | South Africa

Penguin Michael Joseph is part of the Penguin Random House group of companies
whose addresses can be found at global.penguinrandomhouse.com

Penguin Random House UK,
One Embassy Gardens, 8 Viaduct Gardens, London SW11 7BW

penguin.co.uk

Penguin
Random House
UK

First published 2025
002

Set in 14/17pt Garamond Premier Pro
Typeset by Couper Street Type Co.
Printed and bound in Great Britain by Clays Ltd, Elcograf S.p.A.

The authorised representative in the EEA is Penguin Random House Ireland,
Morrison Chambers, 32 Nassau Street, Dublin D02 YH68

A CIP catalogue record for this book is available from the British Library

HARDBACK ISBN: 978-0-241-78895-0
TRADE PAPERBACK ISBN: 978-1-405-98351-8

Penguin Random House is committed to a sustainable future
for our business, our readers and our planet. This book is made from
Forest Stewardship Council® certified paper.

MIX
Paper | Supporting
responsible forestry
FSC
www.fsc.org   FSC® C018179

For Amanda, Martha and Noah

Introduction

When Jeremy, Richard, James and I set sail on the good ship *Top Gear* in 2003, it was with a modest ambition: make a decent car show and earn a living. What we finally brought the curtain down on, more than two decades later, was something that we never, ever dreamed of creating. There was, I promise you, no grand battle plan. Some shows have them, but we didn't.

We weren't actually skilled enough to consciously create everything we did – indeed some of our most loved elements were happy accidents. And when Fate did give us a nudge in the right direction, we were fortunately smart enough to realise it and run with it.

There were also, as we all know, some unhappy accidents, but let's not get ahead of ourselves.

The upside of this organic growth was that you saw everything happening in real time as we took our first stumbling *Top Gear* baby steps, then learned to walk, before finally breaking into a Forrest Gump run that took us all the way to the end of *The Grand Tour*. Along the way you experienced all our mistakes and our triumphs at the same time we did. And that is the best kind of relationship a show and its audience can ever have. It's lightning in a bottle all of its own.

This book then is my recollections and thoughts on how we got to where we did, how we earned our own exhibit in the Television Waxworks Museum.

What I will try and avoid as best I can is to repeat in words what you saw in the films. There's nothing I can say here that could add to the images of amphibious cars sinking or a homemade car chugging its way across the plains of Mongolia.

Also, you saw *everything* anyway. To put it another way, occasionally we were asked by TV execs: 'Why don't you make a programme showing us all the outtakes – all the bits that *really* went wrong?' And we used to reply: 'That's the show you're already watching.'

Instead, I hope you'll find what you read here as more of a companion piece. If the episodes that you saw were a car in motion, then this book aims to be a cutaway drawing of the engine, showing you all the hidden parts at work as we powered along.

There were, as you can imagine, some amazing components in that engine: directors, producers, editors, researchers, production people and camera crews – because it's a very skilled and serious job to keep three middle-aged men nine years old for over two decades, so I'll try and doff my cap to as many as I can.

In truth Jeremy should be the one writing this book. The old 'History is written by the victors' moment should be his, because he was the tentpole that held the whole marquee up. For sure we all played our parts and we played them very well, but without his extraordinary brain and his drive, absolutely none of what we did would have happened. This book would merely be a front and a back cover with fresh air in between.

Without him my own career book would be pretty slim too. In my twenties, when I was trying to find a path in life and my glass was constantly half empty because Insecurity kept knocking it over, he, like a true friend, was always there to top it up.

Students of our work may know that he and I met at school, so you'll find a bit of schooldays stuff in this book too. It's the place, I firmly believe, where our intertwined TV lives began. I don't mean we stood there filming each other with a Super 8 camera, but the *Top Gear* you saw, the spirit of it, definitely germinated there.

I'm sure also that, deep down, Penguin's accounts department would rather it were Jeremy's name on the cover. However, they've got me, and fortunately I do have one massive advantage over Jeremy in that I can actually remember what we did. He hasn't got dementia or the like, but his brain is so consumed with the present that what he had for breakfast an hour earlier quickly becomes a mystery to him; so as for what we did in Alabama, forget it. I'm pretty sure that when he reads this book he'll be on the phone saying: 'This *Top Gear* show, tell me more.'

However, having literally just boasted that I have the memory of a supercomputer, you'll notice in the book that sometimes when I talk about a person I use the phrase 'bless him', or 'bless her' after I've mentioned their name. This is because whilst I'm utterly, absolutely, unequivocally, almost nearly fairly sure of the facts as I remember them, I'm sometimes not 100 per cent on what was actually said. And I feel that if you say 'bless him/her', after someone's name, they're much less likely to sue.

One more bit of housekeeping: I sometimes jump around a bit in the timeline to try and make better sense of what we were up to. But don't worry, you won't think you're watching *Tenet*.

Finally, thank you so, so much for watching and for sticking with us. We never stopped worrying about whether what we were doing was good enough for you, and I hope we managed to enable you to take an hour off from life once a week.

Okay, I think that's everything. I guess it's time to wrap this introduction up and – I know I'm mixing my mediums now – dim the lights and let you press Play . . .

2 October 2023

'm driving along at the wheel of Camera Car 'C', across the Makgadikgadi salt pans, in Botswana. Camera Car C is my happy place. The car itself changes depending on wherever we're filming – although it's almost always a Toyota Land Cruiser – so the important elements of Camera Car C are the crew inside it, and the obligatory letter 'C', fashioned from duct tape and stuck on C pillar.

On a *Top Gear* or a *Grand Tour* shoot we always have three camera cars in the convoy – A, B and C – each carrying a cameraman, a sound recordist, a camera assistant and a driver, and the 4x4s bearing the first two letters of the alphabet are always ahead of us, doing more filming of Richard, James and Jeremy in their star cars. Consequently, to an outsider, 'C' may look like the runt of the pack, but we are in fact the 'break glass in case of emergency' camera car, because when one of the presenters' vehicles inevitably breaks down, we then stay behind with that presenter and shoot his attempts to get going again, whilst the rest of the convoy moves on. Think Hammond and his disobedient

Aston in Mauritania, with its electric windows possessed by the devil. Think Hammond again in Madagascar, with the hopeless, tangled-up wheel tracks on his Ford Focus blocking the road and holding up an entire wedding party, or him pan-frying his testicles when he opened the army rations pack. Or there's James in Eastern Europe with the unbelievably woeful Crosley that broke down every five miles, having taken five hours to do those five miles. On the plus side, Camera Car C usually gets good telly out of these situations, because comedy breakdowns have long been the main currency of our road trips. The downside, however, is that we almost always get into camp at well past midnight, long after everyone else has eaten and drunk everything within a ten-mile radius.

So that's our job: rear gunners who can break off as an independent filming unit.

Now let me introduce you to C's occupants. If we were in one of those action films about an elite Delta Force team, it would go:

Marc Wojtanowski: specialist in sound recording; amateur classic-car racer.

Joey Nutkins: specialist in being a camera assistant; irritating Chelsea fan.

Casper Leaver: specialist in being a cameraman; expert fishing enthusiast. Always photoshops the pics of fish he catches to make them look bigger.

Andy Wilman: specialist in steering-wheel-related operations, emergency director, also specialist in talking over the radio just as the presenters are finishing a long and complex three-way chat.

Casper has been with us since the *Top Gear* days but he's the most recent recruit to 'C'.

For a while his seat was taken by Steve 'Aussie' Lidgerwood, and as much as I like Steve I don't miss his Australian swearing volcanoes, which erupted whenever my driving inevitably became substandard – I'd say in our convoy of eighty, I'd come about seventy-ninth on the Competent Driver league table, and only seventy-five actually have driving licences. A memorable bad driving moment occurred at about two in the morning, when I lost control going downhill on one of those indescribably bad Madagascan roads and crashed into a tree on the verge. 'Jesus fucking Christ, mate!' Steve began. 'Where are your fucking eyes? When are you taking your fucking test . . .' etc., etc., continuing on for a good half a minute. Then, when we got out to inspect the damage and saw that the next stop would have been certain death, because the tree had actually stopped us from plunging off a cliff into the sea a hundred feet below, back out came the lexicon of Aussie insults and, understandably, another torrent was unleashed. I tried to take the temperature down by pointing out how beautiful the light from the full moon looked as it shimmered on the water below, but that just made things worse.

Steve actually lives near me in South West London and we sometimes meet up for a dog walk and a pint. On these occasions he's really nice, not shouty at all, I guess because I'm simply piloting a Labradoodle, rather than a Land Cruiser.

Anyway, Steve was now happily and safely ensconced in Camera Car B, which had a proper professional driver, and Casper the Friendly Cameraman was much . . . friendlier, whenever there was a driving mishap. In Mauritania, for example, I'd got, I suppose, a bit of rally fever when we were bombing along an empty, dead-straight dirt road, again late at night, and hit a rock which not only eviscerated the tyre but shattered the rim.

As we inspected the damage Casper, in his polite English way, did not detonate, but instead merely made a joke along the lines of 'Well I guess it's Hula Hoops for dinner again.'

But yes, back to the point of Camera Car C being my happy place. Firstly, it's because once I'm in there I can escape my role as 'The Executive Producer', the person who has to run the whole shooting match. In 'C' I can be free of that title and just do enjoyable coalface work, another cog in the machine.

Indeed, when we're filming in places where visual signs of hierarchy are important, say Africa, India or Southeast Asia, the local fixers would always try to set me up with my own separate car and driver, as befits an executive producer, because the act of driving is seen as a lowly task. And indeed again, on an occasion when Camera Car C was faced with some official who was angry at us, he would see me at the wheel and demand I get hold of the person in charge. I could then shrug and say I don't know where he is.

It's mainly my happy place though because of its crew.

Casper is endlessly funny. Marc is funny too, but also the sweetest person. He makes us all feel guilty by ringing his kids every day at teatime and enthusing about what we've been up to. He also loves it when Hammond or May break down because he can help mend their car whilst chuntering on enthusiastically with them about whatever old shit he's doing up for the race season.

As for Joey, he too makes everyone laugh and has ginger hair, albeit a sort of low-rent ginger, rather than a fiery red like Julianne Moore or Mick Hucknall. As a massive Chelsea fan Joey can talk to Jeremy about their favourite team for hours, even though, at an actual match, Jeremy sits in the Executive section, whereas Joey is proper Shed End.

And, despite his junior years, Joey always provides C with a banging road trip playlist of classic bands from the 60s to the 90s.

Finally – a small but important point – there is always harmony around the snack box, because all of us are partial to different types of nibbles and confectionery.

And so, on that particular morning – 2 October 2023 – we'd left camp after completing the usual pre-drive rituals: load film kit up, check snack box, peel off the U and the N and the T that Camera Car B had taped next to the letter

C on the side of our car, and finally, check we had fresh batteries in the walkie talkies.

We drove out of camp and conversation soon sparked into life. Marc spotted a pile of elephant dung and remarked how surprisingly small elephant craps are in relation to the size of the animal, adding that if he were an elephant, his turd pile would be the size of a Skoda Roomster. This then morphed into a discussion on the theme of: if Marc were to become an elephant, then would an elephant make a good sound recordist? We got on the radio to consult Russell Edwards, the senior sound recordist in A, who thought about it and reckoned that yes, an elephant would be tip-top at the job because it could use its sensitive and dextrous trunk to put the fiddly microphones on the presenters' shirts.

With that topic exhausted we'd normally have moved straight on to some other avenue of drivel that would never trouble the conversation around the dining table at Melvyn Bragg's house.

But today, as if our four brains were in some sort of mind meld, we all fell into silence, and stayed silent.

Up ahead we could just see Jeremy's Montecarlo, James's Stag and Richard's Capri, a blue ant, a purple ant and a yellow ant, crawling insignificantly across the vast, ice-white salt pan.

I can't remember who it was, but after a while one of us finally spoke, with the heaviest of hearts. 'Fuck me but it's been fun.'

The sadness swept through the car like one of those black clouds from outer space in a Marvel movie, that covers Manhattan.

And once settled it did not shift for the rest of the drive. Because after today the crew of Camera Car C – and A, and B, and indeed everyone in this convoy, would never be doing any of this, ever again.

The Beginning

have to start this tale in my infancy, not out of any urge to write an autobiography, but because that's where our *Top Gear* story begins. I'll make sure not to linger.

So there I am aged five, on a hospital ward, and the nurse puts the bowl of porridge on my bed. I manage to take a spoonful before the whole bowl slides off the bed and crashes into pieces on the floor. The nurse is expecting this to happen, so after some clearing up she gives me another bowl and this time I get a couple of spoonfuls in before that one too sails off the bed into pottery and porridge oblivion.

This is day one for me – ground zero – in my latest hospital, Marple Orthopaedic, and I don't know it yet but I'll be here for a year. On the plus side, by day two I'll be able to balance a porridge bowl like a seal with a ball.

The thing is, as a small child I'd been plagued by a medical condition. I didn't walk until I was three and even then made a pretty crap job of it because everything in my lower limbs was wonky, mishappen and weak, which meant I moved around like an early robot on *Tomorrow's*

World. The doctors could not work out what the problem was, but my leg line-up, relative to one another, was getting worse, so aged five I was put in an orthopaedic hospital and strapped to a metal frame on the bed in the hope that it would get my legs to straighten. The whole ward was full of kids with various developmental problems, all of us strapped to these frames. The frame itself was shaped like a drawing of a stick man with two leg bits sticking slightly outwards, then a back-shaped bit going underneath your back. The whole construction was then supported by two wooden blocks so that a bed pan could be slid underneath. Think of it as one of our *Top Gear* builds but without wheels. The bandages that strapped us down came up to mid chest, so we had full arm freedom but none of us could sit up more than a few inches, which meant we had to keep our food plate somehow balanced on our chests; hence the broken pottery initiation ceremony every time a new inmate arrived.

When I was finally released from the frame a year later, I sat on the side of the bed, stood up, and immediately fell over. All balance had gone, which meant I'd have to learn to walk all over again – not something I'd been that good at to start with. Eventually, in my later childhood years, a couple of muscle biopsies would reveal that there were underdeveloped connections between my nerves and muscles – basically a developmental job that normally gets ticked off when you're sitting on your arse in the womb, growing fingers and whatnot.

Fast forward to the age of ten, and although the basics of my problem are now known, no adult could ever seem to impart an accurate summary to another adult. Maybe parents back then didn't think it their place to ask detailed questions because the specialists all looked like James Robertson Justice, but net result, when I ended up being sent to a boarding school aged ten, very little medical information came with me. Out on the playing fields a teacher would literally say, no malice intended, 'Okay, everyone, get into two groups. Wilman, you're excused because of . . . whatever, your thing.'

But, because I was basically off games forever, I read a lot, which in turn made me good at English and History, and so aged twelve, I was put down for a scholarship to Repton, a slowly fading public school in Derbyshire.

In order to sit the exams, I had to spend four or five days at Repton itself. This in turn triggered the usual cack-handed transfer of medical information. My prep-school headmaster told my prospective new Housemaster something along the lines of: 'It's a very complicated thing; something to do with nerves and muscles; bit of an egghead job to understand it.'

I wasn't there, bless them both, but I know he must have said something like that because I was later told about the pep talk given by the Housemaster prior to my arrival at the Priory, the House I'd be joining. Mr Bryant – the Housemaster – announced to the assembled boys: 'So we've got this boy coming to take a scholarship. He has some sort of lifelong illness, apparently very rare, pretty complicated stuff, and I don't really know what to expect when he gets here. He can walk, but anyway, be nice to him.'

When I went into the House dining room on arrival, the silence was 100 per cent 'dart misses dartboard and hits pub wall'. However, once they'd seen me help myself to vegetables without my arms falling off, the other kids were pretty sociable. Then, after lunch in the corridor area of the House, where all the Priory boys congregated to talk or pick up their copies of *Melody Maker*, I stood around awkwardly, reading messages on the noticeboard over and over.

Eventually a youth approached me. He was gangly tall and had a mop of curly hair that looked somewhat out of sorts, like it had been lowered onto his head by helicopter on a windy day. Also, in the same way an Apollo space rocket jettisons its sections, the cuffs of his blazer had parted company with his wrists some time ago, such was his growth rate. The centrepiece of this schoolboy concoction, though, was his tie, which had been done up so many times that the whole tie was basically just a giant knot. I would later discover it was done this way as a particularly advanced form of insubordination, because the boy's aim was not to make the teachers angry – that was far too blunt an instrument – but instead to cause them maximum frustration. By taking this tie-knotting approach he could claim: 'Sir, the rule book says we have to wear a tie. As you can see, I am wearing a tie, but there's nothing in the rule book about *how* your tie should be done up.'

The boy who'd never model for Vidal Sassoon was clearly two or three years older than me, but was also clearly curious enough to deign to talk to me anyway. Curiosity of mind was definitely a defining feature, and the Odd Kid standing before him had piqued that. 'So,' he finally asked, 'you've got something wrong with you.' The question wasn't loaded, just . . . curious.

'Well yeah,' I replied. 'It's a muscle and nerve thing. Apparently they're not connected properly. It's really complicated, and I can walk okay but I'm always off games.' Life story in a sentence.

'Oh right,' replied Tall Boy. 'The way Bryant was talking about you, I was expecting a man in a white coat to be wheeling in a trolley carrying a fish tank, with just a brain bobbing about, wearing a school cap, with all sorts of wires connected to it. You know, like in *Doctor Who*.'

Obviously a funny image – he delivered it well – but more than that you could tell he was a bit put out that this wasn't how I'd actually made my entrance.

Still, this would not be the last time that I would frustrate Jeremy.

With a minor scholarship in the bag I started at Repton in 1975, and as with all public schools back then, there was a fagging system still in operation for the new boys.

However, the word 'fag 'was a bit *Tom Brown's Schooldays* so instead all new boys were known as Stigs. The Stigs did grunt work such as mopping the dining-room floor, cleaning the changing-room baths, sweeping the yard, etc. but strictly the communal jobs only. Personal fagging had been banned maybe ten years earlier, and if a sixth former asked you to go down to the local high street store to buy cigarettes, he had to give you two out of the packet as payment for taking the risk.

Nobody really minded being called a 'Stig'. I certainly didn't. After all, I would only be one for my first year and then the name would be out of my life forever . . .

As for Repton School itself, let me set the scene.

The school was in Repton village, with its various Houses – nine of them, holding fifty boys apiece, scattered throughout the village. On top of that there was the usual assortment of classroom buildings and sports pitches, plus another House where the bachelor teachers lived. The main feature of the village was an ancient stone cross-type affair, at the top of some pretty shonky ancient stone steps surrounding it in a circular fashion. It was called 'The Cross' and it was of great importance to historians because it signified that the village of Repton had once been the capital of Mercia, one of the great Anglo-Saxon regions in the country.

Opposite The Cross was a bus stop flanked by two red phone boxes, which was where you went once a week to phone your parents. This in turn put you on the radar of the local village lads who hung around at the bus stop, and who would sometimes beat you up for being a scholar and a poof. Then, if you managed to snog a local girl, you were beaten up for *not* being a poof. Diplomatic relations were complex.

In its day Repton had been one of the Great Public Schools. But that day had been a great many days ago, back when cars still had starter handles and women were still called Daphne. The last famous pupil had been Roald Dahl, and he hated the place so much he'd even written a short story to say so.

Actually I'm wrong. The last famous pupil had been the Paul McCartney of Formula 1 car design, Adrian Newey. But he was still technically a schoolboy – about to leave as I arrived, and therefore yet to be famous.

Now, if you think public schools and the people who go to them should be burned alive atop a bonfire of their own entitlement, I'm not here to try and persuade you otherwise. Judge away. All I'm saying is that the school had dropped down the ranks until it was now in the equivalent of the Vauxhall Conference League, and all of us there kind of liked it that way. Over at Eton or Harrow every pupil was expected to become the Prime Minister or solve time travel, but at Repton you could happily mooch about in the Careers Room, looking at the pamphlet on 'How to be an Estate Agent', and think: 'Blimey, tough gig.'

As for the Houses within Repton itself, there was a ranking for those too, with the Priory firmly cemented to the bottom. Academic achievements and various inter-House competitions for school cups for football or cricket, etc. decided a House's place in the table, but the Priory's most consistent achievement – and we were utterly untouchable in this field – was being the House with the biggest annual bill for the most broken windows.

Yet again, this approach to life made for a happy environment. I mean what teenage boy wants to burden his day having to worry about coming second, when you can put your feet up and come eighth? As someone whose biggest physical achievement so far had been to learn to walk – twice – I loved the Priory from the get-go.

When I arrived I was technically two academic years below Jeremy, but because my scholarship classified me as clever I leapfrogged a year, which put me in the Upper Fifth, now just one year behind Jeremy's Lower Sixth. Think of it as like one of our Car versus Train races, but with schoolboys and Geography books.

The big side benefit of this stratospheric academic rise was enhanced smoking privileges. The Fourth Form and Lower Fifth had to take their chances out in the wilds, nabbing a tab in whatever alleyway they could, at the mercy of marauding, vindictive schoolteachers. But as an Upper Fifth person I could now smoke in the same places as Jeremy's year. The star location was the outside lavatory block, which in Derbyshire in January, with its broken windows and a smorgasbord of unflushed turds floating in various cubicles, gave off full Gulag chic. To us though, it was Studio 54. We would congregate in there, spark up a Gold Leaf or a No. 6, and talk about the new Genesis album, safe from any prowling teachers. Then at some point Jeremy would turn up and – I know you'll probably be amazed by this – immediately start talking in huge, Olympic-gold superlatives. Nothing for him was merely 'good' or 'quite good'. He would walk in brandishing the Stranglers album *Rattus Norvegicus* and announce it to be 'literally the single greatest album ever made'. Then, next week, Supertramp, with *Even In The Quietest Moments*, were now responsible for 'literally the single greatest album ever made'.

I swear if Jeremy had been presenting *Top of the Pops* back then, it would have been a six-minute programme. The show would have gone: *Top of the Pops* theme tune, nur-nur-nur-nurrr-nurr ('Whole Lotta Love' riff), camera swoops over applauding audience to Jeremy standing next to Dave Lee Travis, and there'd have been none of that 'up ten places to number seventeen . . .' nonsense; he simply wouldn't have had the attention span to worry about what Brotherhood of Man were doing in the lower regions. Instead it would have been BLAM – straight down to the main order of business – 'This week at Number One, it's Electric Light Orchestra with 'Evil Woman', literally the greatest song . . .' – cut to ELO playing song, roll credits.

Alongside this distinct lack of grey in his opinions he was also extremely bright, but chose not to waste any of that brightness in places like, say, classrooms, on teachers.

He also did important Community Work. It was he alone, for example, who persuaded the local corner shop, Mace, to stock Marlboro Reds, so that we wouldn't have to go around smoking No. 6 or Gold Leaf anymore, like shop stewards at a Trade Union meeting.

The pair of us may have been two birthdays apart, which in teenage years is normally a gap the width of the Atlantic, but the gap was bridged a little by the fact that we shared some important traits.

Firstly, there was an inability to play sport. Of any kind. Obviously I had an excuse, what with my Triple A, Platinum Plus off-games chit for life, but Jeremy didn't have medical privileges so the lack of communication between his limbs was there for all to see. He would gangle around the football pitch like a giraffe connected to a firehose, with everyone else on the pitch just wishing he would go home. If you'd been standing on the touchline and were asked to 'Point to the schoolboy who, thirty-five years from now, will be holding a Corvette ZR1 in a graceful powerslide around the *Top Gear* track', your finger would not have come to rest on him.

Being shit at sport, though, was an important connector for us, because if you weren't scoring goals or taking wickets the only way to be admired by your peers – and boy were the pair of us hounds for that – was to get into trouble.

That wasn't without risk though because the penalties for transgression were not sophisticated: get caught in a pub or smoking, you get beaten with the cane. Get caught again, you get sent home for two weeks. Third strike, and you go home for good; basically a bit like that film *Cool Hand Luke*.

I got beaten twice, the second time by the headmaster, and that session was definitely one to remember. Our headmaster was about the same size as Hagrid and he had a wooden leg. Legend has it that in the Second World War a grenade landed near his platoon and he threw his helmet over it and then stood on it in order to absorb the blast. You get the picture: a man of integrity, a man with very little patience for dandruffy oiks slithering into Burton-on-Trent to try and get served in a pub. When his massive arm came down with the cane . . . Jesus, Mother of Mary.

At least he had the decency not to use the line: 'This will hurt me more than it hurts you', but when he finished he did fire out the other cliché: 'I hope that teaches you a lesson.'

It didn't though, because it just couldn't. Jeremy and I weren't getting into trouble as something to pass the time; it wasn't a hobby. It defined us, it was our currency.

On the plus side for the school, we always tried to transgress with a bit of style, a soupçon of panache. Not for us the braindead activities of breaking windows or spraying graffiti. Instead Jeremy would be involved in, say, manhandling a teacher's car up the steps and into the assembly hall the night before Parents' Day. The little extra kicker then was to stand just behind the apoplectic teachers crowded round the car the following morning, throw in a bit of empathetic tutting, then offer to help them move it back down the steps again.

Or, in the early hours of Sunday morning, we would climb the ancient, revered Viking monument in the middle of the village with a bundle of the Housemaster's wife's clothes we'd found in the attic and spruce up the monument with a nice twin set, matching skirt and hat. Five hundred boys would walk past this later that morning on the way to chapel and, mindful that we needed to keep it a secret that we'd been the perpetrators, we would be careful to brag about it to only 490 of them.

Equally important for us, the cut and thrust of avoiding being caught by the teachers was always at its best when it had a bit of a Bond/Blofeld air to it – the way Blofeld gives Bond a tasty candlelit dinner before opening the shark tank. When a teacher said: 'I know it was you two putting all those women's clothes on the Cross the other night' but had no proof so would simply smile, then we'd smile back and all go our separate ways. That moment was as rewarding as the doing of the deed.

Now I'm not saying any of the above qualifies us for the Bad Boys Hall of Fame, Outlaws of the Century. However, it is about context. If you're an inmate in one of those prisons in Central America that are so scary even the warders dare not enter, then you have to behead every other person on your wing in order to get some Lad Points. Jeremy and I were in a 1970s public school in

Derbyshire where there was chapel every Sunday, a retired Navy sergeant inspected your shoes for shininess and the highlight of the week was being allowed to watch *The Professionals*. You didn't have to try that hard.

More importantly, although neither of us were to know it yet, this natural synergy for buzzing like a wasp around authority's stern head would, I'm utterly convinced, be there to offer a helping hand when we made a car show many years later.

Bedder Six

Although these foundations of mischief were being laid, we had absolutely no clue that we would actually end up working together – none of that Bill Gates and his mates in a garage malarkey for us. That's not to say, though, that we didn't discuss endlessly and whimsically how we wanted our lives to turn out. The dormitories in the Priory were called Bedders – don't ask why, I don't know. None of them would have scored well on Tripadvisor because in winter all of them had ice on the inside of the windows, but one term Jeremy and I found ourselves in Bedder Six, and that was a real win.

Bedder Six's main attraction was its horsehair mattresses, which were so old that a sort of deep valley had formed in the centre of them, and if you lay down in this pit bit with your blankets over your head, the Housemaster, when doing his rounds to make sure everyone was going to chapel, wouldn't notice you were there.

Once he'd gone and the House had fallen silent we'd open the windows, fire up the Marlboro Reds, and then have a bit of a careers meeting about our prospective futures. Jeremy wanted to be either Keith Moon or – I guess because he already had the haircut – Jody Scheckter.

I wanted to be Keith Richards. Neither of us were bothered about the fact that the jobs we wanted were already taken by the people actually doing them. What we didn't realise, though, was that as we lay in our respective beds, pretending to have other people's jobs, our fate was already in the process of being written. Because at the same time, in a galaxy far far away – 46 miles away in Birmingham, to be precise – at the BBC's Pebble Mill Studios, a new car show was being launched, called *Top Gear*.

But for now, all that was Mystic Meg stuff for the future. To us, Bedder Six was, at that moment, the place where we talked shit until we'd literally composted ourselves and where we became friends, with the glue being the fact that we instinctively talked the same shit and liked the same kind of mischief. Many years later, when we formed our first company around *Top Gear* and were asked to think up a name for said company, we immediately called it Bedder Six. The papers thought it was some crass pun on 'better sex'. I mean, please. Bedder Six was quite simply us honouring that crappy little dormitory with the hollowed-out mattresses. Likewise in future years, whenever we both experienced a pinch-yourself moment, such as standing in a Syrian desert at sunset, or finding ourselves talking to both Cameron Diaz *and* Tom Cruise, one of us would turn to the other and say: 'Bedder Six'. It was the ground zero where all our unknown dreams had begun. I'd have loved to have called this book Bedder Six, but again, the accounts department at Penguin would take a dim view of that.

The Eighties and Nineties – A Dress Rehearsal

'll try and canter through these two decades as briskly as possible to get to the *Top Gear* bit, but I do need to spend a page or two laying the groundwork. Basically it goes like this:

1978. Having racked up one misdemeanour too many, Jeremy is asked to leave the school by a fed-up headmaster and gets a job on the *Rotherham Advertiser*. His journalistic career is under way. This also marks the point of my first car experience with him, when he comes back to school in his Ford 1600E.

Notable recollection: he'd replaced the Ford badge on the steering wheel with a Debbie Harry badge. I guess subliminally there was already a man in a white coat somewhere in his head, offering him a gold envelope with the challenge: 'You will now modify your car so that everyone knows it's owned by a teenage boy who wanks too much.' We then lose touch for a good couple of years.

As for me: 1979, despite being on my last warning,

I manage to go the distance, finish my A levels and get piss-poor results. But that's okay because I'm going to London with mates to form a band and be a rock star. The music on offer at that time is absolutely stellar. In the space of about three months I saw a deluge of new bands: The B-52s, Stiff Little Fingers, Joe Jackson, Joy Division, Graham Parker, Elvis Costello, Siouxsie and the Banshees, The Undertones, The Police and the Two Tone tour – Madness, The Specials, The Beat. You literally could not move for musical wonderment and once I got to London me and my mates were going to become part of that Hall of Fame.

Four weeks later our band has broken up and I'm wearing a paper hat, working in McDonald's as a French Fries Dispersement Executive. But once again: that's okay, no worries, I'll go to acting college to be a film star. In between audition rejections and drama school rejections I do the night shift restacking the shelves at the Sainsbury's in Paddington. They actually did like me there and one evening the night manageress, one of life's good people, asked me whether I wanted to join the Sainsbury's trainee management scheme.

'Thanks but no, you're alright,' I replied. 'Thing is I'm going to be an actor so, you know, eye on the prize and all that.'

'Right you are,' she said, trying to hide her disappointment, but persisting anyway: 'Well look, why don't you do the entry test that we ask people to do to see if they're right for the scheme? Come on, Andy, just do that, then let's take it from there.' I couldn't say no, so I said yes.

With the hook now in my feeble mouth she then outlined how my career path would go – pass entry test, work my way up by running the various areas – fruit and veg, meat section, bakery section and so on, until one day, maybe three centuries down the line, I make store manager.

My brain immediately fired off a distress flare: 'Shit! I'm being sucked into Sainsbury's World. How the hell am I going to work with Al Pacino if this carries on?' But there was no way I could hurt the manageress's feelings, so I decided there was only one option for escaping the gravitational pull of this black hole: fail the entry test.

I'm guessing not many of you have done the 1980s Sainsbury's Trainee Management entry test but, no disrespect intended, it's not hard. There were multiple-choice questions such as: 'You find a tin of salmon on the shelf, it's punctured and there's rust around the hole. Do you A) reduce it in price and leave it on sale B) stick it at the back of the shelf behind the other tins or C) remove it from sale?

Obviously the answer was C but I had to sit there, watching the pain on the manageress's face as I circled B.

On to the next question. 'You are loading your cart to take out onto the shop floor to restack the shelves. What is the correct way to load your cart?' The options were: A) a picture of a cart with one box on it B) a picture of a cart loaded up like the Leaning Tower of Pisa, with smashed bottles and fallen boxes all over the floor, or C) a picture of a perfectly stacked cart with just the right amount of neatly arranged boxes.

With a heavy heart I circled B. I could literally hear her wince.

And so it went on. By the time I'd finished, the manageress was clearly wondering how I managed to dress myself without help. She told me I'd failed, I drew on all my De Niro skills to look suitably pained, but at least I was now free to carry on failing to become an actor.

Eventually though, at around the age of twenty-five, I threw in the towel on the thespian dreams, bit the bullet, packed all my stuff into my 1.3 Nissan Sunny (5 speed) and did what I was supposed to do at eighteen, which is to go to university; Keele, in Staffordshire, to be precise, where I read American and Russian Studies.

Bedder Six Reunites

While I'd been busy getting nowhere, Jeremy meanwhile had moved to London and become a freelance motoring journalist. He soon made a name for himself with his fearless, pithy reviews and his laterally delightful column in *Performance Car*.

Then one night on a car launch he gets drunk and, emboldened by the free Châteauneuf-du-Pape, goes over to tell the team from *Top Gear* that their show needs a kick up the arse. They duly give him an audition, hire him, and he then makes it his mission to try and liven up the content.

Now if you've only ever seen our version of *Top Gear*, with its race track and amphibious cars and space shuttles and tyre smoke, you might be quite surprised at just how much of an uphill struggle that was for him, but yes, it truly was. The BBC's philosophy for creating content is underpinned by three principles laid down by its first Director-General, Lord John Reith, way back in the 1920s: 'Inform, Educate and Entertain.' Early *Top Gear* only really served up the first two of those three, with endless information about fuel economy, the workings of a diesel engine and boot space.

Jeremy was determined to fight Entertainment's corner, quite simply because he wanted Britain's biggest car show to reflect what he himself would like to watch: some gratuitous fantasy in amongst the verdicts on glove boxes.

Consequently he made a film featuring a line-up of Lamborghinis tearing up the tarmac on an airfield. Much smoke, much speed, much power, much excitement. And on seeing this finished cut there was much worry amongst the bosses in the *Top Gear* office. In fact it caused such a disturbance in the force that it had to be looked over and considered by the big BBC bosses in London. Would such a film incite reckless imitative behaviour? What's the point of showing cars that only Rod Stewart can buy? And so on. That, then, was how far things were from where we took you. Mercifully, the late BBC supremo Alan Yentob had the casting vote and as a lover of good television above all other considerations, gave it the thumbs up.

Whilst Captain Tyre Smoke was fighting his crusade at Pebble Mill, I meanwhile arrived back in London in 1990 with my degree in American and Russian Studies and sod all idea of what to do with it. Assuming the Russian bit would be a calling card I apply to join the Foreign Office, but I fail the Intelligence Test (and with this one I really *did* try my hardest) you're required to pass before you *even* get an interview.

So there I am, making beer money by doing unskilled building jobs and I'm at my wits' end.

Jeremy can see this. He can see that I'm still, after a decade, effectively rudderless, without any sort of plan, and he knows that I can't see a way out. And so he comes round one afternoon and, like the bestest of mates, he tries to help put my life on track. 'You know what you need to do,' he says, 'you need to be a journalist.'

I protest that that's an impossible hill to climb: thousands of graduates apply for a mere handful of jobs on newspapers. I have neither the skill nor the self-belief to get there.

'Nonsense,' he replies. 'Don't worry about all that. You're funny, you can write, just start writing.'

Having ten times more faith in me than I ever did, he then went and convinced a chap called Howard Walker, a renowned motoring journalist who was currently editing the newly launched *Auto Express*, to give me a shot.

'Write something for Howard and send it in. He'll read it,' Jeremy said.

'But I don't know anything about cars!'

'Doesn't matter! *Auto Express* is a weekly newspaper. They're chewing through stories over there. Just write something to do with motoring.'

I eventually wrote a feature on how people smuggle stuff through customs . . . in their cars. Howard Walker, bless him, duly read my piece with a nudge from Jeremy and then said I should call him.

I will never forget that telephone interview. The launch of Mr Wilman's motoring career.

I rang Howard from a phone box and optimistically thumbed in enough ten-pence pieces to see us through a good long chat:

HW: 'That's actually quite a nice piece, I can use that. So Jeremy says you're looking for a job?'

AW: 'Absolutely.'

HW: 'So what other outlets have you worked for?'

AW: 'Well, to be honest, none.'

HW: 'Okay, no problem, everyone's got to start somewhere. What training have you had?'

AW: 'Well again, if you mean *training* training, none.'

HW: 'Right. No matter, self-taught, that can work. So what other pieces have you written for other papers, you know, freelance?'

AW: 'Well as of now, that one you've just read.'
HW: (bit of a silence)
Then beeping as more 10ps go in.
HW: 'But you like cars right? You know about cars?'
AW: (lying through both back and front teeth) 'Yep.
    Love 'em.'

In the end Howard was wonderful. He gave me a three-month trial and crucially promised not to tell the news editor or any of the other reporters that I had literally not a fucking clue what I was doing. I had my own desk, my own phone, my own Tandon computer with keyboard, and when the news editor dropped a press release on my desk and said 'give me a couple of pars on that' I would use my phone to call Jeremy, ask him what a par was (turns out it's a paragraph), whisper the contents of the press release, and he'd tell me what to write.

In this one-sided and furtive way, our legendary partnership began.

Mirror, Signal, Manoeuvre

Actually, not quite. It didn't begin properly for another three or four years. In the interim I'd found my feet in motoring journalism and become Features Editor at *Top Gear* magazine. Jeremy's onscreen *Top Gear* career, meanwhile, had rocketed to the point where the BBC gave him his first solo show: *Jeremy Clarkson's Motorworld*. The aim here was kind of as it says on the tin – go round the world, looking at the motoring culture in various far-away countries. And although I'd never worked in TV before, when the BBC asked Jeremy who he wanted to help him make it, he said firmly: 'Andy.'

This begs a substantial question – why me? Yes, sure, we were friends, but his first shot at his own solo show was a pretty damn critical moment career-wise. Why would he trust me, who had never worked in television, to be his wingman?

It wasn't for my driving skills, that's for damn sure. Basically, when I finally got round to taking driving lessons in my early twenties, my lifetime off-games chit and all the years of never having learned to throw a ball, catch a ball, kick a ball or hit a ball came home to roost. I was a man whose co-ordination skills maxed out at pressing a lift button, so trying to master the simultaneous use of a clutch, a gear change and indicators whilst at the same time looking through a windscreen – I mean, that was literally fighter pilot shit. That's what the Red Arrows did.

Luckily though, I had just the driving instructor for the job. I won't say his name here in case he's head of the AA or something now, so let's call him Barnabus (my book, my made-up names), but yes, fortunately for me, Barnabus had about as much interest in teaching me to drive as I did in learning to drive. On a typical lesson, for example, if by some miracle I managed a successful parallel parking manoeuvre into a space outside a pub, we'd then celebrate by spending the rest of the lesson in that pub. I mean – shoot me. How was I to know Fate had reserved a space for me as part of the greatest motoring show . . . in the world? Barnabus certainly didn't know that either. So instead we wasted away the rest of the lesson watching Tina Turner on the video jukebox while he told me how shit my driving was.

The irony here is that I have a brother, Stephen, and he isn't just competent at driving – as in he has a driving licence – he was actually a British Motocross Sidecar Champion. He has completed the Paris–Dakar on a motorbike – the most hardcore of two-wheeled achievements – several times. How did a pair of siblings end up so shit and so good? It's almost like when God was making the two of us, He accidentally tipped all the Driving Skills Powder meant for both of us into Stephen, then when He realised His mistake said: 'Oh, bollocks! Oh, wait a minute, hang on, if I just loosen these nerve and muscle connections in his legs a bit, everyone will think that's the problem. Nothing to see here!'

Anyway, Barnabus and I managed to squeeze in more lessons in between pub visits, and eventually I passed . . . after just five attempts!

Jeremy adores this statistic. It's one of his favourites. And months down the line, when he sat in the passenger seat of my Nissan Sunny, watching in bafflement – but politely not saying anything – as I once again changed up to fifth in order to accelerate, I do think part of him believes they'd been generous with the marking.

But like I say, I wasn't his wingman because of my driving. No no no. The reason for that was because of my innate, complete and utter . . . love of story.

How I Learned to Tell a Tale

The power of story has been ingrained, and I mean absolutely soldered into me, since the year dot. Let me take a moment just to lay out the landscape. I was born in 1962, in a place called Glossop, a town in Derbyshire that has some varied claims to fame. Let's start with the Snake Pass. This is a road much loved by bikers, connecting Glossop to Sheffield, where the drummer from Def Leppard crashed his Corvette and lost his arm. Glossop claims that one. Notable people from Glossop include esteemed author Hilary Mantel *and* esteemed pornographer Paul Raymond. That's some serious bookends. What's less trumpeted, though, is that Glossop was also the stomping ground of Moors murderers Myra Hindley and Ian Brady.

So yes, the type of town that Wikipedia is waiting to be invented for. But my crushingly dominant memories, as a young child, are of the brutal violence I witnessed at home. During the first five years of my existence, before my stepdad came along – and with him the means for me to go to a school such as Repton – life was dark. Behind closed doors it was an endless litany of violence and domestic abuse – not towards me, I must add, but to my mum. As a toddler I had a ringside seat – ringside being the operative word – so I had to live it and watch it. As soon as I was old enough to have conscious memories, in went the images and the sounds.

This wasn't an era when social workers stepped in, but luckily my great-uncle John was in the picture. Seeing how frightened and distressed I was, Uncle John and his wife, Auntie May, would make sure I stayed with them when things got really bad.

My uncle John was Irish and physically he was quite small, about five foot four. By contrast, Auntie May towered over him and wore the same glasses as Roz, the formidable administrator lady in *Monsters, Inc.*

It wasn't until I became an adult and a parent that I fully appreciated the wonderful pick 'n' mix of qualities and traits that went into the makeup of Uncle John. He worked as a navvy on the railways, but adored opera. In the Second World War he was a humble corporal in the infantry but whilst in Italy he didn't see that country as just somewhere to fight, but also as a place where he could teach himself Italian.

The inherent goodness in his heart could have made a hot air balloon rise, and he was determined to suck some of the poison out of my hellish four-year-old existence.

The way he did that, for me, was by unleashing his hands-down greatest skill: telling stories. He would pull up the anchors that held us attached to real life, and then set sail into Nonsense World.

Jesus were his tales tall. If you've ever seen that magical film *Big Fish* – that's him.

He had, for example, two tiny pockmarks plumb in the centre of his forehead, and he would look me straight in the eye and tell me they were from when the Germans shot him twice through the head in the war, right through the middle of his brain. Likewise he had a sort of purple birthmark on his chest and with the same conviction he told me how another German had bayoneted him straight through the heart. Obviously I believed him, such was the brilliance of the delivery.

It wasn't just the tallness of his tales though; that was kind of easy to do. What was special to me was his imagination, how he improvised. On one of those days when I was over at their house to escape the violence at mine, he and I would lie in front of the fire once Auntie May had gone off to bingo, and with the two of us using his dog, Lassie, as a pillow, I'd ask him to tell me a story. And straight out of the traps he would conjure up the most amazing tale from thin air. I still remember one about how all the fish and the chips and mushy peas in the chip shop came to life after the chip shop had closed, and then went down into the underworld to fight some evil goblins trying to take over the world. There were huge battles with wooden chip forks being fired like arrows, boiling cauldrons of curry sauce, and salt and vinegar bombs being dropped on the goblins. It was literally *Lord of the Rings* set in a chip shop. I mean, Pixar, if you're reading this, get drawing.

So yes, this incredible man was the catalyst for my love of story. His ability to make tall and wondrous tales an escape from reality – and doesn't that sound familiar – soaked my DNA.

Then at the age of five came my year in hospital strapped to the frame, and now, looking back, I realise that time had not just an effect on my legs, but also on developing my love of story even further.

The point is, if you put a bunch of five- and six-year-olds together and take away their ability to move, they actually very quickly adapt. They soon build, as near to it as they possibly can, their version of a normal five- to six-year-old's world. We still had the same impulses to show off, form gangs and throw our weight about, but we just didn't have the normal tools to hand, such as winning a fight in the playground or building a den or blitzing a running race. And so we swapped out arms and legs for the only element of our body that didn't need movement – our imaginations. Whenever a new kid was wheeled onto the ward, we'd want that kid to join our gang, but the only way to entice him was to literally pitch, verbally, why your gang was the best. You just made up absolute bollocks about the perks of being in your gang, even though it was clear that your gang wasn't physically going anywhere.

Having graduated from the Uncle John Academy of Nonsense, I was really good at pitching our gang. It also helped that, come visiting time, the one adult that *all* the kids wanted to see the most was my uncle John. The vast majority of parents would arrive and talk to their child, and maybe the one in the next bed, and although, yes, it was nice to see a mum or a dad, it was hardly a visit from Jimmy Carr.

Uncle John, however, was the headline act. He would arrive from work, sometimes a bit drunk cos on a hot day he and his co-workers would usually have a bucket of beer on the go while they were working on the lines, then he'd pull his jacket over his head, stick his false teeth out like a sort of pissed Irish early prototype for the monster in Ridley Scott's *Alien*, and career round the ward making monster noises. The kids were nearly sick from laughing and the nurses loved him because he was giving their pint-sized, strapped-down patients something they couldn't. And on that ward he was now showing me, rather than telling me by the fire, the value of escapism. I had no idea that was happening of course, but it was germinating inside me.

Sadly, as lovely as he was, my stepdad Harry was absolutely not cut from the same cloth as Uncle John. I'll never forget watching *You Only Live Twice* on the telly with Harry; it was the moment when the giant fake volcano opened and a space rocket that had swallowed another space rocket was lowering itself into the arms of Blofeld and hundreds of baddies on monorails. Harry turned to me and said: 'This is all just made up, this is.'

That . . . was a bit of a digression. But I want to pay tribute to Uncle John because if you believe that I played any meaningful part in making the shows you loved, well, without him, I don't think there'd be any me.

Cutting My Telly Teeth

Anyway, back to the 1990s and *Motorworld*, the first TV that Jeremy and I would make together.

Between 1994 and 1995 we shot twelve episodes of our globetrotting celebration of other countries' car culture, and it was an extremely lean team bringing the viewers the goods. You had Jeremy doing the writing and presenting, supported by Dennis the director, Keith the cameraman, Murray the soundman and then me on forward reconnaissance, flying out in advance to find stories and set them up.

Today my memory of those *Motorworld* episodes is like one of those photo collages that people make of their kids growing up – random moments all stuck haphazardly together in my head.

Japan: standing on a mountain road above Tokyo late at night, watching the fledgling Drift culture come to life as kids opposite locked their 200SXs around corners.

Texas: Interviewing ZZ Top in a boiling-hot Houston diner and giving the bass player, Dusty, a handheld battery fan so he could cool himself down, and then having to stop filming when it became completely entangled in his ZZ Top beard.

Iceland: picking up my jaw as one of their offroaders defied gravity as it climbed a vertical cliff and spewed volcanic dust in triumph.

Detroit: being engulfed in engine roar and tyre smoke from an impromptu street race we'd sparked, then having beers with Bob Seger in the evening and Guinness with Martha Reeves in the morning.

Dubai: standing in the desert looking up at a working Dodge pickup truck so large that it contained bedrooms and a living room.

Cuba: persuading the government to let us bring Che Guevara's cherished car out of its museum retirement, and then us accidentally setting fire to it while trying to get it going.

Equally joyous were some of the moments when I was out on my own, doing the recces. One time I was in Texas, driving on an arrow-straight completely deserted road through a classic *Thelma & Louise* landscape, and got stopped by a Texan police patrolman. Given the emptiness of the road and the driving tunes from Rock Station FM, my speed had climbed up to near 80 mph. In the eyes of the Texas lawman, this was a big contravention and he was seriously considering taking me back to town to put me before the judge. Sheriff Pepper asked to see my UK driving licence, which back then were still in paper form and carried a record of any penalty points one might have gathered along the way. Studying the licence carefully, he pointed his huge gnarly cop finger at my penalty points. I had at least nine on there for speeding, but it didn't say 'speeding', it just said 'SP' next to each offence. 'What are these here?' he demanded. I looked once again at the remoteness of our location, and just prayed that the furthest this guy had travelled in his life was to a baseball game in the next county. It was worth a shot.

'Those,' I said, with as much conviction as I could muster, 'are Reward Points. If you drive really responsibly for a certain period of time, the police give you Reward Points as a sort of . . . reward.'

Silence.

'The SP stands for Safety and Precision.'

I then realised as I finished speaking that if he went back to his car – like they do in the movies – and got on the radio and asked someone to check up on this drivel, then without question by the end of the day I'd be doing some hard time in the local penis-tentiary. There was a long, painful moment as he studied my licence some more, and then he finally spoke:

'Well, son, if you've got this many Reward Points, then I guess you're a law-abiding kind of person and you must've just got carried away on these big empty roads. So I'll let you off this time.'

Before he could change his mind I drove away. At 40.

*

When the *Motorworld* shows came out they were, luckily, hits. I think Iceland got more than 7 million viewers – excellent for a BBC Two show in 1995 – and a 'beyond your wildest dream' type number in 2025. Those viewing figures were certainly the short-term reward, but on top of that, *Motorworld* had laid some foundations for both our TV futures. Jeremy had taken his writing and presenting skills beyond the confines of a six-minute *Top Gear* car review and I had started to develop my skillset as a producer. More importantly though, the lean operation that was *Motorworld* had been the best boot camp for making the two of us self-sufficient. We had instinctively decided that, to make TV, we didn't really need much else beyond each other. Give us a camera and some petrol and we'd be fine.

After *Motorworld* we continued our licence-payer schooling by making a series called *Extreme Machines*, about the world's most . . . extreme machines. I'll tell you about just one of those moments, on an oil tanker called the *Jahre Viking*, because not only was it by far the most extreme machine on earth, it also put us in extreme peril.

First though, let's get the stats out of the way. The *Jahre Viking* was quite simply the biggest manmade moving object ever built. At 1,504 feet in length it was longer than the Empire State Building and the Petronas Towers; or in pub-quiz measurement, four and a half football fields.

Its weight, fully loaded with crude oil, was just shy of 650,000 tons, or nearly a quarter of a million Range Rovers piled on top of one another.

With that kind of dimension and heft it needed a 50-ton propellor to move it and a 230-ton rudder to turn it. Put the brakes on and it would take 5.5 miles to stop.

Naturally the *Jahre Viking* was a prime candidate for our TV show and Jeremy, our film crew and I landed on it by helicopter as it was trundling past the southern tip of South Africa, bound for Texas.

The plan was for us to spend a day and a night on the tanker and then once our filming was done another helicopter would fly out from the South African coastal town of Port Elizabeth and whisk us back to dry land.

This good plan remained a good plan right up until the morning we were due to be lifted off, when a huge storm enveloped us and tore it all to shit. Captain Mohan, the ship's boss, informed us that the weather was too bad for a helicopter to fly out and pick us up, and nor would any boats venture out to ferry us back. And obviously, *the Jahre Viking*, being that bit bigger than an Uber, couldn't just 'drop us off'. In fact, it wouldn't be stopping until it anchored at the Texan port of Galveston in about ten days' time.

We all stared at each other on the bridge. It was one of those moments when the problem is so huge and so binary that you can't really get in a flap. There were no angles, no solutions to work.

Jeremy then pragmatically pointed out that although this diary change was a pain, we did have warm cabins, plenty of food and beer, and the recreation room's TV cupboard was rammed with enough 80s action movies and porn to see us comfortably round the globe. So, that being the case, next stop: Galveston. As the saying goes, worse things happen at sea.

Keith the cameraman then pointed out that if we didn't get off the boat, worse things would absolutely happen on dry land, because he was due to get married this coming Saturday and today was Tuesday. Also, the wedding was in the Midlands, England, not Midland, Texas.

I don't know whether Keith was more perturbed about the fact that he faced missing his big day, or the fact that we all seemed to have forgotten we were invited, but nevertheless the Chuck Norris and porn marathon now suddenly looked like a very bad option.

The lovely Captain Mohan then added that our only hope of rescue was if the weather eased enough for a tug boat to feel brave enough to venture out. But, he added – he was no stand-up comedian, bless him – in less than twenty-four hours he'd be far out in the Atlantic, beyond the reach of any tug boats.

Up on the bridge it was actually quite hard to process that we were in the grip of a severe storm. For sure the sky was a heavy deep grey, the wind was fierce and the rain was lashing against the bridge windows, but the ground beneath our feet was as steady as a Surrey living room. The *Jahre Viking* was so immense and so low in the water with its cargo that it just pushed through the sea like scissors through silk. Every so often a huge – and I mean tower-block high – wave would break over the bow and then roll its way down the deck before slamming itself to death against the bridge's superstructure. And on the bridge the coffee in our mugs would merely react with a slight ripple.

In the radio room, as I burned up a small town's licence fees in satellite phone bills, asking the Port Elizabeth authorities to help us find a boat, the same answer kept coming back: too rough to come out.

Clearly though, Mother Nature likes a wedding, because come late afternoon we finally did receive a message that a tug boat felt brave enough to sail out of Port Elizabeth to pick us up.

Jubilantly we packed all our film kit and Captain Mohan explained that, because the *Jahre Viking* couldn't stop, we'd have to do a boat-to-boat transfer on the move once the tug boat came alongside. The five of us all understood his words, but since none of us had ever done what he was describing, we couldn't really turn them into useful thoughts. In the end that was probably for the best, because ignorance gave us a few more hours' bliss.

From memory it was around midnight when the lights of the tug boat appeared out of the darkness. On deck the rain and wind had clearly lessened so us landlubbers were relatively calm of mind. Perceptions, however, deceive, and it was only when the tug boat came alongside that we realised what we were in for. The point is, when you're on the *Jahre Viking*, the waves undulating alongside its hull look like something a toddler would create in a bath. But once a normal vessel joined the picture to provide some scale, we suddenly realised how big the waves were. One second the deck of the tug boat was five feet below our noses, the next, twenty-five feet, as it rose and plunged at the whim of the sea. We then saw the rope ladder we'd have to climb down. Instead of hanging free, like you see in the movies, this one was fixed firmly to the hull. The ladder steps were wood, but so thin that you could at best get two inches of toe on them. Either side of the ladder there were lengths of rope to hold onto, but because the whole construction was so tightly fixed to the hull, you could barely close your hands around them.

Murray the soundman's face was death white. He looked like he was going to have a heart attack. 'This isn't right,' he kept muttering as we watched the tiny tug boat rise up to greet us and then plummet down again. On top of the rollercoaster surging, the little boat was also getting slammed against the side of the *Jahre Viking*'s hull every time a wave decided to be a prick. Like Murray, the rest of us were shitting ourselves. By contrast the crew of the *Jahre Viking* busily tied ropes around our filming boxes and lowered them into the hands of the tug boat sailors each time a wave brought them up close. Then, with all the inanimate objects transferred, it was our turn.

I won't say my imagination ran riot because frankly it didn't need to. The facts were terrifying enough. Each of us had to climb over the side and then, clinging onto the ladder with the tips of our fingers and toes, descend the wet, rain-lashed rungs . . . but only to a certain point. Climb down too far and when a big wave slammed the tug into the tanker's hull, your legs would be the meat in the sandwich. But don't climb down far enough, and when the tug rose up on a wave, the jump you had to make onto the deck would be too dangerous a leap.

The trick, then, was to cling onto the ladder, wait for the tug boat's deck to be just a few feet below you, and then let go. And once you committed you really did have to let go, because the deck – your landing platform – would only be in that position, atop the wave, for a couple of seconds. Prevaricate and jump, and you'd be falling over 20 feet.

One by one we found ourselves on that ladder, rain in our faces, waiting for the tug deck to rise up, tensing to jump, then bailing out with fear and clinging to the ropes until the next chance came. One by one we committed to fate and let go, and all of us landed into the waiting hands of the tug boat crew. With the transfer finally done we moved away from the *Jahre Viking* which, like a giant steel whale, lumbered into the darkness impassively, already having forgotten we had ridden on its back.

In the end we made the wedding, all except for Murray, who genuinely did have a heart attack as a result of our escapades on the ladder. Luckily though he's a tough old soundman and was back at work with us a few weeks later.

So, two things for me as I recall our *Jahre Viking* moment:

1. Jesus what an adventure. It wasn't like being in a car that's going too fast – you can try and slow down, there are airbags if you can't. On the side of the hull of that ship, Fate could have easily taken one of us two before we even got close to creating our *Top Gear* opus.
2. We never filmed our hairy moment! It's a measure of the TV nursery slopes we were on back then that our mindset was to only shoot what we'd set out to shoot. 'Our' *Top Gear* would change all that, but Lord above I wish we'd had the nous to do it at the time.

You Had One Job . . .

In between working with Jeremy on *Motorworld* and *Extreme Machines* I also tried my hand at being a *Top Gear* presenter. To be honest it wasn't like joining the SAS. You'd suggest an idea for a film to the main producer, Jon Bentley, and then while he was ruminating one would throw in the idea of perhaps presenting it, and then Jon would ask you to film yourself talking to a handicam, have a look at it, and say yes or no. I was always a 'maybe', as in only if my story was good enough would I be allowed to present it.

The one film that defines – actually make that 'crowns' – my presenter era is the Nude Car Show. This event was held every year in Wisconsin and consisted of – spoiler alert – a classic car show where all the participants were naked. Think Sid James and Barbara Windsor in *Carry On Camping*, with Mustangs, and you're kinda there. Knowing this would be a shoe-in for a *Top Gear* item, possibly my big break, I hurried to find the organiser's details before anyone else could nick the story, rang them and asked if I could film the event. Sure I could, replied the man on the phone, but on one condition: my camera crew and I would have to be in the buff too. No exceptions.

'Absolutely,' I immediately replied on everyone's behalf, 'that won't be a problem, see you there.' I put the phone down thinking: 'Shit!' The Brummie film crews at Pebble Mill didn't exactly have a background in French experimental art house cinema. They made *Gardener's World*. Who the hell was going to get their cock out for this gig?

As it turned out, once the director, David Leyton, said he was in, we soon had a soundman and cameraman. I then told *Top Gear* magazine about the event and they said they'd take the story too. 'You'll need to send a photographer who'll get his kit off,' I informed them. The next day Marcel, the art director at the magazine, phoned to say a photographer called Ben, a good reportage guy, was up for it. With just over three weeks to go I was feeling pretty pleased with myself because everything was green for go. TV piece – get famous, magazine piece on top, earn double bubble.

All was good except for one thing . . . my back. I guess there's no pressing delete on the keyboard now; I've done the foreplay with this anecdote, so you may as well know that the feature I most disliked about myself was my hairy back. And it's not just me. You read any 'Top Ten Least Attractive Things About a Man' survey in any woman's magazine at that time and right there at No.2, just one place below 'child murderer', is 'a hairy back'.

Up to this point in life I'd prided myself on not being vain. I'm from Glossop. But now, suddenly, faced with the prospect of millions of people seeing my rear-facing stair carpet on BBC Two, I crumbled.

In urgent need of grooming-based advice I asked my wife, Amanda, what was to be done. 'Well, you need to get your back waxed,' she said, a tad too eagerly. Then added:

'When are you filming this thing?'

'Just over three weeks' time.'

'Okay, well you need to start getting it waxed now.'

This absolutely baffled me.

'Now?'

'Yes. Now. There's a lot of hair there. You'll need a good few waxing sessions. You can't do *all that* at once.'

'Yes, but surely whatever bit I have done first will start growing again by the time I get to the last bit?' I protested and queried simultaneously.

'No, it doesn't work like that. It'll be fine. But honestly, trust me, you need to start getting it done now. You'll need at least four sessions.'

I then weighed up our respective depths of knowledge regarding all matters waxing. Amanda: probably at least sixteen years. Me: the conversation we'd just had. It was an absolute no-brainer. Ignore her and get it all done in one go.

And then, to add insult to stupidity, I got it into my head that doing it as close to filming as possible would be the best move.

And so, the evening before I was due to fly to Wisconsin, the bell over the door of Ace Waxing in South West London duly tinkled as I walked in. The Waxing Solutions Executive, bless her, was lovely and welcoming.

'If you could just pop your shirt off so I can have a look at what needs doing, and don't worry, if it's your first time there's nothing to be alarm— oh, goodness . . .' From the involuntary exclamation, followed by the silence behind me, I knew she had instantly made her assessment, and her assessment was that this job needed some South American deforestation equipment.

'Erm, okay,' she finally continued, having composed herself back to professionalism. 'That's going to take a bit of work. I would recommend at least four, maybe five sessions to do your whole back. So if we start now . . .'

'No, sorry,' I interrupted. 'You need to do it all tonight. It's all got to come off now.'

Her face looked like someone who'd just been asked to kick a lion in the face and then stay there. 'There's no way I can do that,' she protested. 'The pain will be off the scale.

Honestly, it'll probably make your body go into shock. No, I can't.'

In return I explained the situation – Heathrow in the morning, film shoot, on camera naked, *Top Gear*, blah, television conquers all, yadda yadda, no choice, and eventually she gave in.

As I lay face down on the bed she prepared enough hot wax to defend a castle in the Crusades. She then placed the hot wax, in strips, over my back, with lots of saying sorry as she did so – clearly she was getting her apologies in before I lost consciousness, but I just lay there thinking – and I know Jeremy had yet to invent the phrase – an early version of 'How hard can it be?'

Then she started to pull the strips off and I got my answer. I remember screaming, I remember my vision exploding with white light, and I remember thinking after she'd pulled off two strips: 'Oh fuck, there's still four to go.' I could only hope the pain would lessen but it didn't. As the fifth strip was ripped away I thought she was tearing my actual back from off my skeleton. The Waxing Solutions Executive clearly had her own issues, because she had to judge the pain management. Logic said: 'go fast, don't stop, get it over with', but if she went *too* fast the tidal wave of pain would be so great that I'd have a coronary, so she had to leave a few seconds between each rip – just enough time for my pain receptors to recharge for the next one.

Eventually, mercifully, it was done. I drove home, my

back a good six inches from the car seat, and that night developed a feverish temperature – presumably my body's way of calling me a twat.

The next morning, however, I felt surprisingly good and headed off to the airport to meet the film crew and also the magazine photographer, Ben. I'd never met him before but tried to imagine what sort of chap would, on his very first job with a load of strangers, agree to get his kit off. What I didn't imagine was that Ben would be a girl, which she was.

Not only was she a very skilled reportage and portrait photographer, she was also game for a laugh, and during the flight she got on with me and the crew like a house on fire. On top of that, my back felt pretty damn fine so I went to bed very much looking forward to the shoot. Also, as a vanity bonus, Ben the girl, when photographing events tomorrow, would now never know that I once possessed the rear section of a woolly mammoth.

All that changed in the morning, however, when I woke up to discover that my whole back had, overnight, erupted in a huge rash of red spots. Having solved the hair problem, I would now appear on camera looking like a medieval plague victim.

I sat at breakfast, wondering what to do. Filming was due to start in a couple of hours. I looked at the film crew. They were all blokes from Birmingham hammering the buffet. The chances of dermatology being in their skill sets was nil. There was nothing for it but to ask for help from

Ben the girl. And now, not only would I have to tell her that my back was covered in the Black Death, but also the reason it had got like that in the first place.

When she'd finally finished laughing, she took David the director and me to a chemist and bought some super-strong pancake stuff – I think it was foundation – that old ladies use. Then she instructed David to smear it across my back until it set like some sort of Golden Girls concrete. The finished result wouldn't win an Oscar for Best Make-up, but it would do. We were back in business.

Eventually we arrived at the Nude Car Show, which was held in the grounds of a nudist camp. All around there were scores of naked people doing nudist-camp things such as barbecuing, with an assortment of Stingrays and old Corvettes dotted around. Granted, not Pebble Beach, but a lot more volleyball.

Our plucky crew disrobed and, once they'd casually positioned whatever piece of film kit they could over their Brummie todgers, we set off to film.

By lunchtime I thought everything was actually going okay. We'd got some nice interviews and shot some lovely cars, but what I hadn't logged, being a make-up virgin, was the effect of it being a nice sunny day. In fact it wasn't until I sat on the white vinyl bench seat of someone's classic car that we all realised the old lady's suit of armour on my back was starting to melt. Apologising profusely to the owner, we finally got the pinky-brown imprint of me cleaned off his car seat, then we tried to apply another layer to shore up what was coming away. In the heat, though, it was hopeless. In the end I couldn't go near any owners' cars – kind of the point of a car show – and for the rest of the day I just sort of walked around sideways like a crab, so that the camera wouldn't catch my back.

When the finished item eventually went out on TV I watched it from behind my hands. But on the plus side, I thought, that was the only time anyone would ever see it. At least nobody would ever invent some sort of popular amateur channel where anyone could upload whatever they liked, so that things remained on there for all time, for everyone to see.

I also thought that my Nude Car Show film, on account of it being quite a noticeable and unusual piece, would at least cement my position as a proper *Top Gear* presenter. That assumption, however, was a bit wide of the mark, because one day Jon Bentley the producer invited me to the pub for lunch, saying he wanted to discuss my future. As it turned out it was quite a quick chat, because soon after we got sat down Jon fired me. There were no more Jeremy solo series in the pipeline, and as for me presenting, the verdict was that I had the onscreen charisma of junk mail. Now I actually quite like Jon, but hand on heart I can't say his firing technique is of the highest calibre. Once he'd delivered the bad news he then picked up the pub menu and cried with enthusiasm: 'Right! Lunch!'

A Disturbance in the Force

My enforced retirement from presenting troubled absolutely nobody. But the same cannot be said of the moment when, towards the end of the 90s, *Top Gear*'s Ronaldo decided to quit.

According to Jeremy, the moment of throwing in the towel arrived when he could no longer think of anything interesting to say about yet another mass market car (I think it was a Renault) rolling off a production line, so to the extreme consternation of the *TG* office, he handed in his gun and his badge.

Soon after he left, the show itself pretty quickly started to go downhill. To be fair, it was not the fault of the remaining presenters. The real problem was the show itself. There was now a new wave of Factual Entertainment programmes filling the airwaves, such as *Changing Rooms* and *Ground Force*, where all the presenters went about their business in a completely relaxed manner, chatting to each other as if the cameras weren't there. Then alongside those you had Jamie Oliver whizzing about on his scooter in Hoxton, glugging olive oil over everything and making cheeky quips to the producer off screen. Next to these newcomers the decades-old format of *Top Gear* – with its presenters all alone, all doggedly presenting long pieces to camera full of consumer advice – looked like it belonged in the Bayeux Tapestry.

And so in 2000, Jane Root, the Controller of BBC

Two, saw in the millennium by bringing the axe down on the show. It would remain off air, she said, either forever, or until someone made it into a show worth watching.

Without question Jeremy and I had a moment's silence for Pebble Mill for its loss. Birmingham's BBC outpost may have looked a bit parochial with its pebbledash exterior and offices full of middle-aged women who knocked off at five, but it had schooled us both to an immense degree. With its roster of low-budget fast-turnaround shows, Pebble Mill taught you how to work quickly and made you park any editorial preciousness at the door. It was akin to a well-oiled local newspaper turning out a daily edition to a deadline. When our version of *Top Gear* was at its grandest and fanciest with its films, a power test at the track would take more than a week to cut together. At Pebble Mill you had a day.

Yet despite the hammer-down work pace, the place was also a lot of fun. The studio cameramen recording the daily live regional news show, for example, had worked out that they could get from the Pebble Mill bar to their positions at their cameras in the studio in less than a minute by going over the roof of the bar, through the window of the main building and then dropping down into the studio itself. Better than that, if they timed it just right they could have another drink and get through the window, to their cameras, just seconds before the show went live. Nobody's teaching those skills at Amazon or Netflix.

But yes, despite it being a great building that had taught us so much, including what it felt like to be fired, its version of *Top Gear* was no more. As sad a moment as it was, you could not blame Jane Root for one second: the execution needed to be carried out. But as for her mandate that the show would stay dead until it could be made into something worth watching, fortunately someone had been listening.

A Star is Reborn

A Stormy Brain

Sometime in 2000 I got a call from Jeremy mid morning, asking me if I was free to meet him in the local pub near his flat in Notting Hill. I knew from the tone that he wanted to talk shop but had no idea as to what.

When we got sat down with our pints he dived straight in: *Top Gear*.

'I reckon,' he announced, pulling out various bits of paper full of Beautiful Mind scribbles, 'that if Jane says it's up for grabs, we should take *Top Gear* back.'

'Back? We never had it. We only worked on it.'

'Yes yes yes,' he said impatiently, 'you know what I mean. Take it, redo it, whatever.'

He had clearly spent a lot of time picking over the bones of the show that had made him, and although he kept insisting these were early thoughts, I reckon at least 70 per cent of the show that would eventually go into the *Guinness Book of Records* for its audience size was already laid out on his messy bits of paper.

Obviously there was no Richard and James, no Stig, no Tom Cruise on two wheels, no what one might call 'magic dust', no ambition whatsoever to make a car show that would transcend the needs of car fans and enthral families, but what became clear as he talked was that he'd cracked the problems that were suffocating the existing show. Instead of five disparate items presented by five separate people, the new show would be anchored from 'a place'. Maybe an aircraft hangar rather than a conventional studio, with three presenters all together in the hangar at the same time, actually talking to each other.

Outside, he continued, there could be a race track where the fast cars could be tested at full red-meat speeds. There'd be no more driving along in a Ferrari at 59 mph on a 60 mph road, shouting: 'and once unleashed, the speed will rip your eyes out . . .' then accelerating to 61.

'Then once the test is done we can do a lap with the cars, they set a lap time, and we put the times on a board. It's Nick Hornby – *High Fidelity* – that dweeb in the record shop. Blokes love lists, and the track means we can have a big list.'

For emphasis he then started sketching out a race track, but because he can't draw he gave up once he'd reached his drawing limit, which was an oval.

'Guests!' he proclaimed next. 'We'll have guests, and . . . we'll get a shitty car and they'll have to set a lap time round the track.'

'What, like Bryan Ferry in a Hyundai?'

'Exactly!'

'Ah,' I then countered, 'what if the guest refuses to do the lap?'

'Well they don't come on the show,' he replied firmly.

'Jesus, that's gonna reduce the pool somewhat,' replied this pragmatic producer.

'If we give in once, we're bollocksed; word will get round,' he shot back. 'Celebs take the piss whenever they can unless you hold firm.' He must know, I thought, what with being one.

He then moved onto his next idea: a news section where, in front of the studio audience he and the other presenters – TBD – would discuss the new cars that had gone on sale.

'This will be properly useful. The new Volkswagen Golf is launched, we all know it's a very important car, one of the biggest sellers in the country, but boring as shit to film. Why bother making a seven-minute piece on it when we can just say in our news section: "There's a new Golf on sale, we've driven it, it's excellent, it costs this much, buy it if you want one." Bish bash bosh. Then we can save our films for cars that are more interesting and quirky.'

I liked that idea a lot. But I didn't like his next one. 'I also reckon,' he said, 'we don't feature a car on the show until it's on sale in the UK, in the showrooms.'

At this point I crapped my producer pants. Everything he was saying was flying in the face of established motoring journalism logic: namely, you use your clout to feature the car before anyone else, to get the scoop. However, he was ready for my comeback.

'You're right, absolutely' – then a pause for dramatic effect – 'as long as you're a car magazine read by nerd petrolheads. But we're a TV show and we're watched by people who are just casually interested, maybe thinking about buying a car. What's the point in us showing them a film of a left-hand drive BMW that won't go on sale here for a year?'

'Okay,' I countered, 'fair point, but what about the supercars – the Lamborghinis and the Ferraris – the car porn? Viewers will never forgive us if we're a year late showing them those.'

'Relax. We'll be fine,' he replied. Not the most detailed of answers, but in truth he had already made many thrilling, albeit frightening, points.

I then realised, as we drank and talked, that the show would never be reinvented to the level that was needed with my sort of cautiousness at the helm. Here was a moment when someone needed to smash the vase against the wall with total force, so that there was no chance of it being repaired. Then, a new one would *have* to be ... moulded, pottered, whatever, because there would be no option for going back.

Job one, though, was to convince the BBC that we were the men for the job.

Green Light

Convincing the BBC, in reality, meant convincing Jane. Quite a few people had pitched her ideas for *Top Gear* rebirths, but with none of them having hit the spot, any new idea landing on her desk was definitely guilty until proven innocent. But, as soon as Jeremy started talking about the hangar, her face lit up. 'You mean *Top Gear* has a home? I love it,' she, erm, squealed. The rest of the pitch zipped along and we came out of the meeting basically in business. Jane wanted us to cast the cast, find our hangar, then shoot her a pilot and if that passed muster, we'd be on air in 2002. She also wanted an audience of at least 3 million. That was our survival target.

However, she didn't trust Jeremy and me completely with the keys to the castle, and assigned us one of her senior exec producers, Gary Hunter, along with another senior senior BBC exec, Andy Batten-Foster.

We set about looking for a location and after a search of various air bases we alighted upon Dunsfold – and it was a slam dunk. The place had been owned by British Aerospace, it had a sterling military pedigree courtesy of the Harrier jump jet being developed there, and just before BAE upped sticks they'd very thoughtfully re-surfaced the runway. On top of that one of the hangars could be made to work as the studio, and the whole shooting match was conveniently about an hour from London, just off the A3.

Next we needed a team: researchers, producers, direct-ors and what have you.

Jim Wiseman was an early hiring. I'd worked with Jim before and I loved that –maybe because he's dyslexic – he always looked at things from a different angle. It was Jim, for example, who mused: 'Everyone always goes on about how many buses can a motorbike jump; nobody's asking how many bikes can a bus jump?'

Maybe one in five of his ideas was usable, but boy was he persistent. I came into the office one day to find him watching one of those Discovery documentaries about a man who lives with a tame grizzly bear. Ten minutes later he was on the phone to a zoo, asking them about the possibility of teaching a bear to drive. My desk was opposite his so I could hear the zookeeper becoming more irate: 'Okay, maybe not a bear but what about a monkey?' Eventually he put the phone down, sighing heavily.

'How did it go?'

'Not brilliant. She says she's going to report me to the police. You might get a call.'

The other notable hire was Rowland French. Rowly loved *Max Power* magazine and car modding and doing doughnuts in the B&Q car park in his MR2. The only element clashing with this roadman picture was that his mum had made him wear a suit for the interview – one that he'd clearly outgrown a couple of years back – so he looked more like an apprentice undertaker than a twoccer.

However, he was too bright and infectiously joyful not to hire.

Then we come to directors. Nigel Simpkiss. Nigel, bless him, had a balding head and the most intense, slightly unnerving stare. Think Steven Berkoff's baddie in *Rambo 2*. When I asked him a question – it really wasn't a tricky one, something like: 'Did you manage to park okay?' he massaged his head in a rather pained manner, remained silent for a long, long moment, then eventually: 'Sorry. I'm not good at interviews.'

Just as I was looking around for a number for security, Nigel took out a VHS tape, indicated the little telly on the table, leaned between Gary Hunter and I and slotted the tape in. On it were samples of small car films he'd already shot and clearly what he lacked in word power he made up for in pictures, because although he'd been working for some underfunded shows, his tape contained some of the most inventive stuff we had ever seen. This was talent in search of a budget. Nigel was duly deputised and given his gun and badge.

The other key hire was Richard Porter. Richard was a motoring writer, a researcher on old *Top Gear* and a complete nerd, bless him, on old Rovers. But we weren't interested in any of that. Porter had also created a website called Sniff Petrol which took – I have to use the words, I'm sorry – 'an amusing sideways look' at the motor industry. It was very funny and very spikey, and instinctively we knew his Sniff Petrol brain would be valuable in helping set an editorial tone for our new show, even though we were still shifting the big building blocks into place, and hadn't yet got round to anything as complex as nuance. Or even words coming out of mouths. Jeremy was well known for his wit and pithiness around cars for sure, but he couldn't be everywhere all at once. The show would need its own energy supply of 'attitude'.

Casting

Jane Root was pretty adamant she wanted a clean break with the old *Top Gear*, which meant in terms of onscreen talent the only component that could be retained was Jeremy. This being the case, we decided to throw the net wide and invite any member of the public who thought they had the chops for the job to send a tape in.

Cue Band Aid-level sackloads of VHS tapes arriving at the office. Some of them were sublime in their crapness. The one that sticks in the mind for me was of a salesman-type gentleman with a BMW 3 Series, trying to do a handbrake turn on a piece of waste ground. This, if you've been given this book as a gift but didn't actually want it, is the manoeuvre whereby through use of steering and application of the handbrake, you turn a car around very quickly, well within its own diameter.

You don't have to be Max Verstappen to do one, but clearly it seemed beyond the skillset of the chap who'd sent the tape in. Whoever was recording him on the handicam definitely must have died of old age as the driver made attempt after attempt after attempt after attempt. After attempt. Nonetheless it became hypnotic viewing. Nobody dared walk off, not even Jeremy with his meagre patience levels. Finally the chap managed to execute something close to a handbrake turn. Phew! Now we could see what his presenting skills were like once he started talking. But no. He got out of the car, shut the door with a flourish and walked off without looking back. His whole audition, his transformation from photocopier salesman to TV superstar, he'd decided, would rest on half a handbrake turn.

Highlights like handbrake-turn man aside, sifting through the tapes became, for the poor sods involved, what it must have been like to have to answer the Beatles' fanmail in 1964. Bundle after bundle arrived without any let-up.

Then one afternoon a producer called Kate Shiers, chief tape sifter, called us into the tape-sifting room.

'Have a look at this one,' she said. 'It's a bit shit what he's doing, but there's something there.'

It was indeed a bit shit – we were watching a man in a party-shop Batman suit jump off a wall and then, upon landing, attempt to morph from comic-book hero into reviewer of the car he'd fetched up next to.

'Why is he wearing a Batman suit?'

'Fuck knows.'

She wasn't wrong. It had absolutely nothing to do with anything he was saying about whatever the car was.

'It seems he's on *Men & Motors*.' (A car show of the day that was low budget but absolutely made the best of cutting the cloth it could afford.)

'You're right, though, there's definitely something about him.'

Kate looked through the accompanying letter. 'Richard Hammond.'

'Okay, let's put him on the list.'

Britain's Got a Bit of Talent

The 'list' may not have been up there with Schindler's List, but in its final iteration it meant a lot to us. On it were the candidates that would make up two days of auditions with Jeremy in a studio in West London, during which they'd talk a bit about a car – in this case the newly launched mentalist that was the Renault Avantime, and then sit at a desk and run through some news stories with Jeremy.

We powered through the screen tests and chirpy second-hand car expert Jason Dawe went onto the 'very likely' list.

Established motoring journalist James May also came and did a turn, but we thought he didn't quite fit, so passed on him.

Then, it was the turn of . . . Richard Hammond. He'd

arrived in an old left-hand-drive 911, which confused Jeremy, Porter and me.

'It means he could be a real hardcore petrolhead,' opined one of us.

'Or a twat who'll do anything to be seen in a 911,' suggested another.

No matter, it was time for the Budgens Batman that we'd all liked to step up. Twenty minutes later his screen test was over and he'd been . . . okay. But no more. In fact a few of us were disappointed because this guy had been our secret little hope. He'd said some okay stuff about the Avantime, but nothing memorable, and likewise his news biffabout with Jeremy had been fairly good, but no rockets had gone off.

Sitting next to Jeremy at the pretend news desk, Hammo shuffled the press releases about a bit, then suddenly said: 'I've fucked this up, haven't I?'

'No! Good God no! No!' exclaimed Jeremy in a tidal wave of British drinks party politeness.

'No, I have; I've properly bollocksed it,' insisted Hammond.

'No it was great, absolutely fine,' insisted Jeremy back, knowing full well it hadn't been.

'This happens every time,' continued Richard. 'Get the big break, bollocks it up.'

He then launched into this soliloquy, relating various examples of past career failures, and it got funnier and funnier. It had that Frank Skinner deadpan delivery.

Everyone started laughing, and then he wrapped up with his big closing number: the story of how the peak of his radio DJ career had been the night shift on Radio Cumbria, reading out a twenty-five-minute long list of the names of lambs up for adoption. By this point we were in tears of laughter. Jeremy could barely speak. Who gave a shit what he thought about the Avantime? We knew there and then we had a keeper, but my God does Fate twist on a small thread. No speech from him, and we'd have moved on.

By the end of the auditions we'd made our choices. It would be Hammond and Dawe.

Birthing Pains

We'd decided throughout the audition process that the magic number for the line-up was three, on the basis that two is a TV pairing whereas three is more of a natural gang. We had Jeremy – road tester; Jason Dawe – used car expert; and Richard Hammond – job description TBD. However, that still left the problem of 'a Tiff', a driver with unquestionable steering-wheel pedigree who could *also* talk to a camera. Tiff, back then, was a rare beast. But even if we found a Tiff, the other problem remained: four was not a good number.

I was alone in the new *TG* office one evening, wrestling with this problem when Jeremy dropped by. On one wall there was this huge, and I mean Coldplay video screen size, whiteboard, which was now covered in Oppenheimer-type scribbles, outlining options for how the presenters' workload would be divided up during a show.

'None of it works,' I moaned. 'We have film 1, news, film 2, guest, then film 3, then end of show. We still need a Tiff, which makes it four presenters, but we've only got three films, so each week one of you is sitting there with your thumb up your bum.'

I threw the whiteboard marker down in frustration. 'We need a Tiff, someone who can drive and string a frigging sentence together. Mind you, it's not like we've had any joy with that anyway.'

'With what?' asked Jeremy.

'Finding a driver who can speak.'

Clarkson stared at the board, looking for an answer that wasn't there in the maths. Then, after a long moment, the lightbulb went on.

'Hang on a minute!' he exclaimed. 'Why does he need to speak?'

'Eh?'

'The racing driver – why does he even need to speak?' Then the lightbulb brightened by a couple more watts.

'Look, I'm good enough now to do the slidey stuff round the corners,' he said, 'the smoking tyres for the camera and so on. But what I can't do is precise lap times. I can't hit the same apex in exactly the same spot, lap after lap, like racing drivers can do.

79

'So . . .' he continued, now fully on a roll, 'we film a new Lambo or whatever down at our track, I do the main test, and then we only need the racing driver to set the lap time for the lap board, and he doesn't need to speak!

'Oh wait a minute, hang on! Hang on . . .' The lightbulb was now about to explode. 'Never mind not speaking, we make sure he *never* speaks and we never say who he is! We'll get him a suit made, full face helmet, and he's completely mute! He'll become a character. People will even start trying to work out who he is!'

I was genuinely excited: 'OMG. This is brilliant! He's going to need a name though.'

Jeremy thought some more: 'Hey, I was watching *Pulp Fiction* the other week. Why don't we just call him the Gimp?' And on that note, we went to the pub for a celebratory drink.

After that things happened quite quickly. To fill the Gimp suit we needed a racing driver who was quick enough to be in demand, but not so in demand that he couldn't be available every Wednesday – the day we'd decided studio record day would be. We found that very chap in Perry McCarthy, who in half a morning down at Dunsfold (we were paying him by the day) mapped out a workable version of a *Top Gear* track. We also told him his new name would be the Gimp, and he told us to go fuck ourselves. Jeremy, presumably scrolling through his mental Rolodex, brought it to rest back at the Repton pages, then said: 'Okay, fair enough. Let's call him the Stig.'

The Pilot

The next job for Operation *TG* Resurrection would be to make a pilot. I'm sure everyone not in TV knows what one of those is – it's like a dry run, a show that you don't broadcast, to help you iron out your mistakes.

Now as the God of Diaries would have it, the day before we were to shoot the pilot, Jeremy and his wife Francie were hosting a charity go-kart event and naturally we – me, Hammo, Jason and Perry – all went along. Also present would be their friends and some celeb chums, such as Rob Brydon, Steve Coogan and Brian Conley. The go-kart track was an indoor one on an industrial estate – I can't remember where exactly, but what I do remember is, when we arrived, Francie telling us in a complete panic that the go-kart company had gone bust and the go-kart operators had been locked out of their track.

Obviously we couldn't just pack up and go home, what with money needing to be raised for poorly kids so, given that the operators still had the actual go-karts, an outside track was hastily laid out around the roads of the industrial estate.

As everyone high-fived each other on a wave of Churchillian spirit, I noticed Perry standing watching as cones were laid down and hay bales positioned on bends, shaking his head.

'This,' he said to me in a knowing and unhappy way, 'is a fucking death trap.'

'Right. Do go on.'

'The surface has got oil and shit all over it cos it's a road on an industrial estate. That means there'll be no grip. Then see where they're putting the hay bales.' He pointed at some hay bales being positioned at a corner by a friendly farmer. 'They're sitting on top of the kerb, they're not covering the kerb, so when you do spin off your kart will hit the kerb and bounce you straight up into the hay bales. And hay bales – why does everyone think hay bales are soft? They might as well be concrete.'

There was absolutely no sense of 'maybe' in his delivery. It wasn't so much a verdict as a prophecy. But the fact remained we were there for charity, so we chose to hope for the best, and began karting.

One of the celebrity guests taking part was Dr Mark Porter, a daytime TV medical guru, but by about lap ten he was no longer at the wheel of his kart, and instead was busy single-handedly manning a field hospital hastily fashioned out of a vacant Portakabin.

Sure enough, as Perry had predicted, drivers were slewing about everywhere and slamming mercilessly into the kerbs, before being flung upwards into the rock-hard hay bales. I can't remember how long I lasted, but given my driving skills it can't have been long, and the pain knocked me sideways when I barrelled into the concrete straw. Unsurprisingly there was a bit of an 'A&E on a Saturday night' queue outside Dr Mark Porter's hospital, but when I finally saw him he made me breathe in and out, saw the pain as I did so and told me I'd definitely busted a rib or two. That was me done, but amazingly the uninjured stoically carried on karting, until it was time for the dinner and raffle.

That evening I sat at my table, wincing with every intake of breath, knowing that whatever happened, I would definitely not be doing any laughing at tomorrow's pilot record.

As it turned out I needn't have worried, because the last thing anyone at all did that day was any laughing.

Let me set the scene. The filming would take place in a hangar at Dunsfold. There would be an audience of around a hundred. The aim of the pilot was to make sure that the studio part of the show worked and the checklist comprised:

1. Try out the studio set to see how it works
2. Interview a guest
3. Introduce the Stig
4. Do some studio links around some static cars to see how Richard can handle a roomful of people
5. Do a second-hand car news slot with Jason to see how *he* copes.

With regard to the set, we'd consulted some set designers and opted for a sort of metal coliseum affair, circular, with the audience standing around it on the top area, looking down onto the studio floor. The three presenters would move around on the floor or sit together in a cordoned-off area, along with the guest. Off to the side was a covered-up cage. We would uncover this to dramatically reveal the Stig, residing within.

With regard to lighting, we'd gone big: spotlights and what have you, all over the set. In our heads I guess it was a kind of *Mad Max* Thunderdome meets Pink Floyd vibe that we were going for.

The first sign that all might not go well was when the audience trotted in and took up position. It was a hot day, they were in a metal hangar, and the Pink Floyd lights were relentlessly making it hotter. Jeremy tried to make light of it by saying: 'Everyone, take your last breath,' as the hangar doors were pulled shut.

Soon, the temperature was the same as Alec Guinness's tin box in *The Bridge on the River Kwai*. The 'guest' was David Ginola, but none of us had actually told him that he was just a guest, so he sat alongside the other three presenters, assuming he was also a presenter.

Then came the moment to unveil the Stig. Jeremy spouted some over-the-top intro, cue dry ice and enough strobe action to induce a dozen epileptic fits, and then the Stig started to emerge from his cage. It wasn't actually Perry in the suit – he wasn't around – I think it was a friend of ours from *Top Gear* magazine called Nik Berg; but as with David Ginola, nobody had briefed him on what to do, so he, understandably playing to the whole dry ice and thunderous music vibe, started to march about like a *Doctor Who* robot. The audience members who hadn't yet passed out were now completely baffled. The last time they'd seen *Top Gear*, William Woollard had been standing with his foot on the bumper of an Astra diesel saying: 'See you next week . . . and drive safely.'

Richard and Jason did okay with their bits but honestly, with the blood in their veins now the temperature of lava, the audience didn't really care that there were some sharp bargains to be had on used Citroëns. It was a terrible, excruciating evening, and once we'd edited the pilot we just wanted to seal it in a lead box and drop it in the Mariana Trench.

Instead, as is custom, we had to send it over to the woman who'd paid for it, and once it had gone off to Jane we sat there, waiting to be fired. But to her credit, when she finished watching this massive TV turd she remained remarkably calm, and just said: 'Oh, that wasn't what I was expecting.'

Then she added: 'What's with all this fancy set and showbiz lighting? When you said it was in a hangar I thought we'd be seeing hangar walls and the cameramen in shot and all the cables on the floor and people walking around with cups of tea.' Not only was she not showing us the door, she was also showing us the way. She wanted a much earthier show.

*

And so, we threw away the set and went back to work. Over the following months we shot some films – mostly road tests – and went round the manufacturers with a begging bowl, asking for one of them to provide us with the car for 'Star in a Reasonably Priced Car'. The motor industry is a conservative and penny-minded business and consequently door after door was shut in our faces. I could understand their position because the financial commitment was hefty, and for what? Given the pounding it would take in the hands of daytime TV stars, if the car broke down regularly in front of millions of *Top Gear* viewers, what manufacturer would fund his own crucifixion on national television?

I was ready for this question and had a good answer: 'Well, in that case can you give us *two* cars? I know that would be double what you already don't want to spend, but there's your safety net right there: a backup car waiting in the wings.'

Eventually, plucky little Suzuki, never a big player, never front of anyone's mind, but with a wonderful Head of Press who had enough mischief in him to realise this was worth spinning the dice for, agreed to give us a 1.6 litre Liana.

Now we just needed guests to put in it. A couple of friendly petrolhead celebs such as Jay Kay and Steve Coogan said to count them in, but the problem was there were ten shows that needed filling, and despite endless phone calls by the guest booker, we had nobody for show 1, the recording of which was now only a couple of weeks away.

This guest drought was not a surprise. Firstly, when celebs do a chat-show slot such as Jonathan Ross or Norton, it involves sitting on a sofa in a London studio, banging out some anecdotes, trousering a good few grand, then into a car, back at the bar in Soho House by ten. By contrast we were asking people to give up their whole day to come down to Surrey, learn to drive round a track, sit around whilst their lap is edited, then do the interview, all for £2,000 – less than half of what the established shows were offering, and which would have to be split with their agent and Tommy Taxman. Why do that? Also there's a sort of unwritten celeb rule that nobody goes on a new chat show in its opening episodes. What if it's shit? You let others test the waters first.

Finally, what if you're a TV tough guy, known for doing tasty driving while chasing after baddies? Why would you go on national television if there's a chance that in real life you're slower than Mary Berry?

This Show 1 guest-slot black hole was the grave topic of conversation as Jeremy, Porter, Hammo, Jason and I gathered for a drink in the pub near Jeremy's flat after work. After we'd done that man thing of pointlessly listing everyone who'd already said no, we fell into troubled silence. It was at this very moment that two men walked past us on their way out of the pub. Unfortunately for one of them, he was Harry Enfield. Harry was right in front of us without the protection of an agent or manager. He was defenceless. We fell on him like jackals. By the time he left the pub – I remember that as a sweetener we'd agreed on Volvo's behalf, although they didn't yet know it, that they would absolutely definitely lend him an XC90 for his holidays – one of Britain's most revered comedians was signed up! Show 1 was ready to go.

2002
A Stuttering Start

On 20 October 2002, at 8 p.m. on a Sunday evening, the sound of 'Jessica' once more filled the living rooms of Britain.

If our new *Top Gear* was an aeroplane, we'd spent a year designing and building that plane, strapping the wings on and slotting the engines in, and that night it taxied down the runway and lumbered into the air. Our job now – and who knew how long that might be – was to keep it up there and more importantly, find out how high we could climb and how far we could go.

If episode one was the initial climb though, my god was it a bumpy ride. The opening film, Jeremy testing a Citroën Berlingo, was a ballsy call. A review of a French utility van that had been converted into a budget passenger car, being driven to a Calais supermarket for a booze run on a wet overcast day, is not how TV logic says you should come out of the traps. Logic says you open the show with an Italian supercar, but we felt that would be a yawn in its predictability, that it would say that this show is for petrolheads, and we knew we didn't want to do that.

Having said that, we did then move on to a supercar double-helping with a Zonda and a Murciélago, but the Berlingo had to come first, as a sort of disrupter.

As for the studio, we'd followed Jane's orders and turned the hangar back into a hangar, but as for what was going on inside it – that was still a shitshow.

The first problem was the size of the audience. We'd shipped in about fifty punters, which we thought would be just enough to give the *Top Gear* base some atmosphere, but not so many as to turn the show into a Light Entertainment Ant and Dec affair. However, once everyone was in, that number barely touched the sides. On camera it just looked like some people from the industrial unit next door had wandered in for a look round.

Also, *because* we were insistent that we didn't want to come across as a Light Entertainment show, we'd told the audience not to applaud at the opening, which added immensely to the completely dead atmosphere. Then, when Jeremy did a link around a car and said something funny and in turn made a few people laugh, he was like: 'No, please don't laugh there. This is the car show bit. You can laugh when the guest is on.' So now we were telling people when to find things funny and when not to: literally unheard of in television, or indeed life. Luckily at this point our studio director, Brian Klein, veteran of many a shiny floor show, pointed out firmly that you cannot fight one of the fundamental dynamics of television, which is that whenever you get an audience in a room, your whole impetus is to make them laugh. So we gave in and the studio audience were – radical move – allowed to enjoy themselves at moments of their choosing.

Regarding the cars dotted around the studio, the Mazda 6 we were featuring was not exactly positioned where Brian the director wanted it to be. That was because whilst driving it down to the studio, Jim Wiseman had backed it into a post at a petrol station, stoving in the boot. Luckily we weren't featuring Rowland French's own Toyota MR2 which, on his exuberant drive down, he'd put into a ditch.

The recording continued on. And on. And on. We'd started at about 3 p.m., but by 6 p.m. we still hadn't finished and the audience, who'd been on their feet for all that time, had literally died of boredom. Harry Enfield's slot had briefly acted like one of those defibrillators that restarts your heart, but soon afterwards everyone's vital signs went back to flatlining. To make matters worse, we'd left Jason's Used News segment until the very last, and Jason, bless him, as banterous as he normally was, could not for the life of him deliver links down the barrel of a lens. We would do take after take of him telling the viewers there were tasty deals on used Micras to be had and as he struggled on, members of the audience started to leave. Given we didn't have that many in the room to start with, I barred the exit door, pleading with people to stay. 'I'm sure you've got babysitters but pleeeeeeaasssse will you stay until we've done Used News.' When that didn't work

I even started paying people, literally putting tenners in their hands to make them hang around and listen about a second-hand Fiesta they were never going to buy.

We finished that first record too tired to be shell-shocked, just knowing with dread that we were going to have to do it all over again next week.

Mercifully, the second show was a much more sprightly affair, in part because Jay Kay was the guest. Unlike Harry, whom we'd kidnapped from his local, the space cowboy came down with his best driving trousers on, full of vim and vigour to attack the track. Naturally he beat Enfield's time, which meant with two names on it we now had the makings of a leaderboard. Then, after he'd snarfed all the screwtop white wine and Jaffa Cakes in the Green Room, he stayed around in the studio, just basically being part of the crowd who, we were starting to realise, it was no crime to entertain.

That's not to say that our amateurishness didn't keep popping up elsewhere. One Tuesday – the day when the presenters would come in to write their links and news stories for the following day's studio – Richard Hammond arrived with a corker of a black eye. It turned out he'd been in the pub with one of his West Country yokel mates and the two of them had got into a fierce debate about which was the best Subaru. This in turn, aided by lashings of beer juice, had developed into a full-on fight in the road outside the pub. It simply hadn't occurred to him that being on national television now came with certain responsibilities, such as the need to schedule your pub fights for when we were off air. Still, the make-up lady did sterling work and at least the subject matter of his fight – Subarus – was on brand.

Elsewhere though, more upbeat things were happening. Firstly, the juvenile segments – how many bikes can a bus jump, can a granny do a doughnut, a shootout to find the Fastest Faith – were all hitting the spot with the viewers, and more importantly giving our car show a point of difference. Those little films were setting our tone of mischief and also putting out the message that you didn't have to like cars to watch *Top Gear*. That point, by the way – seeking to entice non-car fans – was not part of our thinking. It was more that we were amusing ourselves with what kind of malarkey we could get up to.

Secondly, the Stig was well received, and as Jeremy had hoped, viewers were now having fun on the internet trying to crack his identity. Mostly the votes were going to Damon Hill.

Also, there was a huge stride forward with the quality of our films. Nigel the director had more than made up for being the world's worst interviewee by literally reinventing what our car tests looked like, especially when shot at the track. For Nigel and his main cameraman, Ben Joiner, Dunsfold was a blank canvas. Every trope and style that Jeremy and I had been weaned on at Pebble Mill was thrown away as Nigel and Ben took us to school. On old *Top Gear*, the presenter would typically do a piece to camera outside the car, then be filmed getting into the car, putting the seatbelt on, shutting the door, starting the engine, saying something like 'Okay, let's find out' before, a fortnight later, finally driving off. It was known as 'preserving the continuity'. With Nigel it was a case of fuck continuity, it's taking forever. Thus the whole bit between Jeremy finishing talking and driving away was sacked off and cars were either stopped or moving. Then, in the edit, Nigel and the editor worked more magic with all those little treats for the eye – the sky going backwards, artsy shots of blades of grass or runway lights or puddles, etc. The visuals were also helped by a thorough purge of Pebble Mill music. Into the bin went the Bachman–Turner Overdrive CD, to be replaced by Unkle and Mercury Rev.

Nigel would eventually be joined by other magnificent directors as the series rolled on, but he started it all. He gave me and Jeremy something we hadn't even thought to ask for.

Alongside the cinematic film work and the dough-nutting grannies, Fate also threw us the odd bone. In our main office back at BBC White City, the humungous whiteboard where Jeremy had conceived the Stig now displayed a grid for the series. There'd be boxes for each film, for studio items, etc., plus one containing the name of that week's guest. We even had a little running joke of writing 'Tom Cruise' in the guest box, then sighing wistfully, before rubbing him out and replacing him with Rick Parfitt.

So far, sometimes by the skin of our teeth, we'd managed to fill each weekly slot. However, the box for episode eight remained stubbornly empty. I was even starting to think about ringing Michael Winner.

Then, literally a couple of days before we were due to record the show, Jeremy entered on the crest of a wave of lunch and evident relief: 'I've got us a guest, and you'll never guess who.'

'Who!?'

'Guess.'

This panto went on for a minute or two until even he realised there was no more milking to be done:

'We've only gone and got . . . Michael Gambon!' This was indeed a moment. Nobody got Gambon. Gambon had no interest in doing any chat shows, even with his new wave of fame as Dumbledore swirling around him. In fact, the great chat-show king himself, Sir Michael Parkinson, always said that Gambon was his biggest regret as 'the one that got away'.

Sir Gambon, however, loved engineering and mechanics. He had a workshop at his country home where he tinkered, and the idea of coming on *Top Gear* tickled his fancy. Obviously we didn't know what to expect as to how he'd be, and the thought of his arrival suddenly made us all realise how shit our Green Room was. How could we expect a legendary thespian knight of the realm to sit on that sofa? However, when he did turn up, he made himself completely comfortable and waved away our apologies. Maybe he was acting – he was good at that – but we'll never know. What he certainly had in spades was mischief. He told us how, on the *Harry Potter* press junkets, he taught all the kids – Rupert Grint, Emma Watson, Daniel Radcliffe – that the best way to get through these excruciating ordeals was to try and come up with the best lie you can think of and slip it into the interview. His particular favourite had been when he'd told an interviewer that he'd been secretly gay but given it up because 'it made my eyes water'. As for his renowned 'intense stare' on camera, that, he confided, was definitely not method acting. 'The thing is, I can't be doing with learning all the lines anymore, so I have an earpiece fitted, and someone reads the lines to me, and then I say them. That stare is me just listening while the lines are read to me.'

If you've seen the show you'll know his main contribution to *Top Gear* folklore was his lap, when he powered into the last corner too fast and took the corner on two wheels, which we immediately named after him in his honour. When you look at his two-wheeled moment now it's actually quite a mild up-ender compared to Tom Cruise's, but back then, in Series 1, it was what we needed. The sheer incongruity of it – a knight of the realm in a suit, tie and helmet – wilfully risking his neck in a 1.6 Liana, was the sort of moment that was starting to give our show its identity.

Indeed as our first series approached its end, we felt we might actually be able to pat ourselves on the collective back: we'd got through it, there were green shoots of promise in the content, and we'd filled every guest slot. The only person not sharing this optimism was our production manager. Production managers look after the money and one morning she told us, with stern face on, that we hadn't got any left. Although I now regretted giving so many audience members cash handouts to stay to the end – we'd established a discreet slush fund of licence-fee money to finance this – Jeremy and I nevertheless struggled to be cross with ourselves. We'd never made ten shows in a row before, we'd never made ten of anything, how were *we* supposed to see that far into the fiscal future?

That logic, though, didn't help solve the problem that we still had one more show to make and no money to shoot all the films. There was nothing for it but a bit of wartime make do and mend, which is why we gave you . . . the '*Top Gear* Awards'. This handy – and unashamedly lengthy – segment, was cheap enough to eat up the required airtime minutes.

Series 1 came to an end just before Christmas, in 2002. We'd got through it, we'd got better, and most important of all, we'd hit Jane's magic number of 3 million viewers. However, there were problems that needed sorting before we came back on air, the most pressing being that Jason, sadly, had to go. We'd gone into this reinvention believing that an element of the show needed to keep its feet on the ground by telling viewers how to find a bargain and save a few quid. But now that grannies were doing dough-nuts and knights of the realm were driving around on two wheels, it was clear that advice on second-hand Kias had no place on the menu.

However, much to Jeremy's and my shock, the BBC high-ups also weren't sure about Richard. It wasn't a definite decision, as with Jason, but axing Richard was definitely on the table. I told Richard he was safe, he'd be fine, but in truth I did not yet have the kind of clout to back that promise up, and he knew it. Then, to top it all – I guess duty of care was still in its infancy – a senior exec told Richard just as we broke up: 'So it's not definite that we're going to keep you, but let's pick this up in the new year. In the meantime you relax and enjoy your Christmas.'

The Name's May . . . James May

Richard's late Christmas present from the BBC, given to him in the new year, was that he kept his job. This meant we only had to seek out one new presenter, but we had to do it quickly.

Luckily at that time Jeremy, despite now helming *Top Gear* outright, was still going on car launches, like an old-school motoring journalist. A car launch, may I remind you, is when the car maker launches a new car to the press by flying a . . . I don't know what the collective noun is for motoring journalists so let's say 'a lot of them', to a nice country with nice driving roads, where they can test the car then stay in a nice hotel and get bongoed on even nicer food and drink.

Upon returning from one of these trips, Jeremy rushed straight over to the *TG* office with his best 'I've had an idea' trousers on.

'Hey, new presenter,' he began. 'James May.'

'James? We've auditioned James already. We know he's good but we said then he wasn't right.'

'Well sure, yes, but now I think he is,' Jeremy retorted. 'I just shared a car with him on this launch and the thing is, we fundamentally disagreed on just about every aspect of the car. And he knows what he's on about too. He'd be a good counterpoint to me and Hammond.'

Recalling this conversation today makes me chuckle, because it reminds me just how clueless we were about what our show would become. All we discussed was James's ability to deliver a verdict on a car, whereas with a functioning crystal ball, we would have probed him about converting a Triumph Herald into a sailing boat. All that stuff, for now though, was hidden from sight in the waiting room of our collective futures.

We floated the idea of James to our superiors in the executive play area, and immediately received some BBC management logic by way of reply:

'Hmmm. James. The thing is, that would make the line-up three white middleish-aged males.'

'And?'

'Well, wouldn't we be better off with some variety? A bit of chalk and cheese?' said the execs. Today that response would probably be a lot less opaque, more in the vein of: 'Why don't you hire Alison Hammond or Clare Balding?' Back then, it was 'chalk and cheese'.

Luckily Jeremy and I could counter with evidence that 'cheese and cheese' also works really well. Trinny and Susannah, for example: two poshos whose joint chemistry had made their show one of the most popular on television. Or the Two Fat Ladies, both of whom cooked everything with double cream and lard, and both of whom were indeed fat.

Our argument won the day, and enter James Daniel May, from the London Borough of Hammersmith.

James, I would say, had a broader intellectual spectrum than us three. For starters he'd studied music at university, which meant he could play the flute and the piano to, I guess, university level. By contrast Hammond had done a photography course at somewhere like his local Jessops, and although Jeremy did have a doctorate, it had been given to him for free, without him having to actually learn anything. James also didn't just possess a degree, he'd studied metalwork and worked as a civil servant. More important though, he was a very good writer in the columnist vein, which meant that, like Jeremy, he could come to work with witty and lateral opinions – be they in front of a camera testing a car, or in the studio. Whatever he said was the product of him, not the show. Also, he'd known Jeremy for years, which meant they weren't strangers pretending to be TV friends on camera. He and Hammond also got on a storm. In fact too much of a storm. I remember calling him one day around the time of the early series, asking him whether he was coming in for an editorial meeting. 'Bit tricky, I'm afraid,' he replied. 'I'm on a train up north. Can't get out of it.'

It turned out that he and Hammond had started playing a game they called 'eBay Roulette', which had quite simple rules: you both get drunk, you bid on a car you like the look of that hasn't got many hours left, you go to bed. If when you wake up, you discover that you now own it, you obviously have to go and buy it. Even if you're so drunk that you didn't realise the car is in Blackpool.

The other advantage with James was that when we asked Rover if we could road test their new CityRover and they gave us a flat 'No', we could in fact best them. It was pretty inevitable that Rover would refuse our request: the car was based on a small Indian Tata and had a dismal reputation. However, we had James: his face was not yet well known to the public.

'*Bowfinger*,' I said.

'Yes. *Bowfinger*!' the office replied.

Students of cinema will know this is the film where a struggling film maker, played by Eddie Murphy, tricks a

Hollywood star played by Steve Martin into starring in his low-budget movie by secretly filming him when he doesn't know he's actually in it.

Likewise we wired up James with some of those hidden cameras used by *Watchdog* when they go undercover to record wrong 'uns, and sent him off to the Rover showroom, posing as an innocent punter who wanted a test drive. If you've seen the film you'll probably recall that our James could never be confused with the one whose surname is Bond. By the time he'd finished fiddling with his jacket the secret cameras were filming the ceiling tiles, the floor, everything except the car. But, the cameramen in the secret tracking car and the ones dotted along the test drive route *were* up to the job, and we got our film.

2003-2004
The Plane Climbs Higher

After the hand-to-mouth organisational shambles that defined the filming of Series 1, we vowed to be slicker for Series 2. Certainly we were more on it, but there was definitely still room for improvement, with the Talon being a fine example. The Talon was a huge armoured riot vehicle that we'd been loaned, and we thought a good way to demonstrate its prowess at riot-quelling would be to drive it through yet another old Portakabin of which Dunsfold seemed to have an endless supply. And, given that we had all the camera crews already on site to shoot the guest laps, we thought it financially logical to film this sequence on a Wednesday, when we recorded the studio segments.

As ever though, rehearsals ran over and other fuck-up fairies landed here and there as they always did, so that by the time we got round to filming Hammond driving the Talon through the Portakabin, we were minutes from starting the studio record. In fact, as he climbed into the driver's seat and strapped himself in, Brian the studio director was already warming up the audience and Jeremy and James were waiting for him outside the hangar door, moments from stepping in.

Now, okay, as stunts go this wasn't Tom Cruise running down the side of the Burj Khalifa, but the Portakabin the Talon would drive through was a big sturdy beast and a bit of health and safety stuff was still required. However, Hammond gunned the engine, shouted a cheery 'Sorry, can't stop!' to the stunt coordinator trying to give him instruction through the window, floored the throttle and lunged forward.

The Talon, when it hit the Portakabin, absolutely obliterated it. On the internal cameras you can see the shockwave of the impact as it rocks Hammond in his seat. Fortunately, he was well strapped in with harnesses and the like. The same couldn't be said, however, for the director and his cameraman who, unbeknown to us, were still in the back of the Talon when it had set off and on impact they had themselves a full tumble-dryer moment. As for Richard, he had no clue. He was already running across the airfield and skidded to a halt next to Jeremy and James as they walked in to take the applause.

Age Before Beauty

Moments like this aside, over the next few series we got our act together in much more important ways; in particular with the films.

The most significant breakthrough came when we realised that old, knackered, cheap cars provided much more entertainment than new metal sent over by the manufacturer.

The first such film was the £100 Car Challenge, but the one that properly revealed the enormity of the rich editorial seam we'd accidentally discovered was the Cheap Porsche Challenge. The premise was quite simple – can you live with a Porsche that costs less than £1,500 – and once the three of them had made their purchases they met up at the start point, the Porsche heartland that is the financial City of London. Their first challenge was to drive to Brighton, an extremely modest distance of under 70 miles.

By the time they'd travelled less than five – I think they'd managed to reach Elephant and Castle at best – Jeremy's 928 had broken down in a petrol station, steam was pissing out of the radiator and motorists at the other pumps were there on camera, trying to help get it going again. And then, for me, came the key moment, which didn't happen on camera. In the midst of all this comedy chaos the director – very much a petrolhead but definitely more old school – came up to Jeremy and said: 'Shall I break the crew for lunch while you get all this stuff sorted out?' Jeremy shot back: 'No. This, this what's going on here, this *is* the film.' You couldn't blame the director because in the past his call would have been right. On old *Top Gear*, if a car broke down you rang the office and said: 'The shoot's off.'

The culture of achieving what you'd set out to achieve was still strong in telly back then, which was why a show such as Denis Norden's *It'll Be Alright on the Night*, a programme dedicated to showing bloopers and mistakes, made such an impact. Now though, we started to make these blooper moments the meat of the actual show.

Alongside that penny dropping, with the £1,500 Porsches, we had reached another important landmark, because the heroics of underdog old shitters – in smaller films and eventually the Specials – would become a bedrock of our new *Top Gear* and eventually the *Grand Tour*, right through to the very end of our motoring adventures.

I mean, pick your favourite old cheap shitter moment. You'll struggle, given the choices, but I guess many would vote for the Toyota Hilux film. I threw the idea for this one in the pot, having watched the news coverage of million-mile Toyota and Nissan pickups being used as the go-to transport in every conflict in the Middle East, with their suspension somehow supporting the weight of twenty fighters plus a .50 cal machine gun thrown in for good measure. We bought our old Toyota at random from the classifieds, then Jeremy set about putting it through its gauntlet of destruction tests, with all of us expecting the film to end with him saying: 'Okay, so it survived drowning and crashing, but in the end we killed it by . . .' At first we thought the death knell would indeed be drowning, because when the tide broke our Hilux from its moorings in the Bristol Channel and swept it away – that was definitely not part of the plan. Then, when it survived that and all the other challenges, we were absolutely certain that parking it on top of a tower block due for demolition would be a fitting execution for such a toughie. But as you all saw, the four-wheeled cockroach amazed us again by surviving the fall, and it was then that we decided: 'You deserve to live, amazing machine. You shall sit in splendour on a plinth in the studio.'

Gentlemen, Start Your Engines

The next important strand we hit upon was the Big Races. These took shape when we were brainstorming and came across an article about Bentley Boy Woolf Barnato racing the Blue Train from Cannes to Calais in his Bentley Speed Six. We updated the weaponry to a modern-day Aston Martin DB9 versus the Eurostar, and in the hands of our three this 1930s upper-class Bertie Wooster challenge became a thrilling populist drama for families across the land.

In the next series we upped the stakes for the car and put a Ferrari 612 up against a plane, for a race to the ski resort of Verbier. This race had easily the closest finish of the lot and James throwing his suitcase at the car as Jeremy drives past – that is not a man doing it for camera. That is a man who thought he had it in the bag. These films quickly became pure drama, not just because of the tension one gets from a good race, but because the respective machinery had come alive: the car was the goodie, the public transport the baddie, and every time we upped the stakes, the car became more of a hero.

But Seriously . . .

Elsewhere, the acorn of 'nonsense' films that we'd planted in Series 1 with grannies doing doughnuts soon grew into a veritable oak tree of cocking about, with nuns driving monster trucks, Richard and James playing conkers with caravans and, having borrowed the cannon that fires cars in the movies and painted a huge dart board on a quarry floor, Car Darts.

What made these films just that bit more entertaining was that we presented each juvenile vignette with a mock gravitas normally reserved for the most serious of investigative consumer shows. Richard would look straight down the camera and, with his most serious *Watchdog* face, say: 'We've had a letter from a viewer asking: what is the best car to be in if you're driving behind the engines of a 747?'

Cue excuse to drive different cars behind a 747 with its engines on thrust, and watch each one get blown away by the jet wash.

We also employed military-grade nonsense to say goodbye to Black Suit Stig, because sadly the time had come for Perry and us to part ways. I can't remember the full details of the whys and wherefores, but it would have been about money, and Perry wanting to promote himself as the secret racing driver. It was kind of inevitable: racing drivers are also businessmen with a short shelf life, and it would have been frustrating to watch the character you make real growing into a potential Mattel toy, and you can't earn any coin on the back end. Perry had been great at getting the character off the starting block and his departure, as the mafia say, was nothing personal. Thus we all agreed he should have a spectacular send-off – literally – when he tried to reach 100 mph in a modified XJS on the deck of the aircraft carrier HMS *Invincible*. His untimely death then paved the way for the arrival of White Suit Stig, inhabited by Ben Collins, an excellent racing driver and, although we didn't know it yet, accomplished novelist.

Broad Church

So, cheap old cars, Big Races, more cocking about, new Stig. These editorial leaps across 2003 and 2004 were now bringing in a bigger audience. What we absolutely hadn't expected, though, was how broad that audience was becoming.

The most noticeable newcomers were the people who'd say: 'I'm not interested in cars but I do watch *Top Gear*.'

I think one important reason for their attendance was because we were smart about the way we shaped our car content. We made casual viewers like cars without them realising it. As I said earlier, by turning the cheap cars and the cars in the Big Races into either plucky underdogs or superheroes, we were humanising them.

On top of that we also managed to bring more everyday models to life by crafting an engaging film around them. Jeremy trying to get a Discovery up a mountain is a good case in point. There, up there, was the mountain top. Jeremy's attempt to reach the summit kept you engaged, even though he could have actually tested the car on the same terrain by driving round a tough offroad course. But that option would have been a story with no ending, and we wanted to give you a story with an ending.

Actually – and I know Jeremy's written about this so apologies for the *Groundhog Day* moment – the Discovery up a Mountain film did have a little extra ending that never made it on camera. Once he'd reached the top, Jeremy hopped in a helicopter to fly back to the airport, leaving Nigel and the camera crew to pick up the vital extra shots they needed. It was only when Jeremy landed, switched his phone on and watched it explode with texts that he realised he'd flown off with the Discovery keys in his pocket.

Car key theft aside, Jeremy's tabloid brain had now realised that we were organically morphing a car show into an entertainment show, which in turn meant all problems were now in fact just opportunities. A great example of this was the Albania Road Trip. (Memory jog: best boot for carrying a murdered fat man; bank robbery with James going over cliff.)

Our desired car line-up for this road trip was a Mercedes S65 AMG, a Silver Ghost and a Bentley Mulsanne. Unfortunately, Bentley management, having become sniffy about us, refused to provide a car. In the office we were more than a bit panicky because there was simply no other car that would fit the bill. When I rang Jeremy he was initially likewise downbeat. 'Oh shit ... etc etc.' Ten minutes later, though, he was back on the phone, now elated: 'I've got it. Roy Hattersley, *Have I Got News For You*.'

I hadn't seen that episode. Where was this going?

'He was due to come on their show but pulled out at the very last minute, so the *Have I Got News* lot just replaced him with a tub of lard. That's what we do.' Jeremy's tub of lard of choice was an absolutely fucked old Yugo, and in the film he simply referred to is as a Bentley Mulsanne. Even if Bentley had changed their mind and agreed to provide us with a car, I believe we would have stuck with the joke of the Yugo, such was the pendulum swing towards entertaining our viewers.

Another problem that we, and indeed every car show and magazine had, was the fact that most modern cars were absolutely fine. They had their foibles for sure, but nothing that would stop you buying one, nothing for motoring journalists to get their teeth into like they could have in the 70s. And so we deliberately added extraneous bells and whistles. For a test of a bog-standard Peugeot 207, James would pit it against a team of parkour experts around the streets of Liverpool. Along the way you got the necessary car info: price, comfort, how it drove, but in between you also got to watch some gymnastic loons hurl themselves out of a multi-storey car park. It was all basically smoke and mirrors.

Richard too had a sweet way of demystifying a car. One time he was driving a small Citroën and his pronouncement to the viewers was: 'If you like little French cars but you're put off by all these stories about them being badly built, don't worry. After a few thousand miles, when all the bits that you don't really need that were always going to drop off have dropped off, then you'll be left with a nice little car that's fun to drive.' No other motoring journalist was giving out *that* kind of advice.

On top of all this, Nigel and the other directors were making our films ever more ravishing to look at. Nigel's shots of the Phantom cruising imperiously over the Humber Bridge were as sumptuous as the car itself. The Mercury Rev music – 'The Dark is Rising' – was the perfect accompaniment. I remember the studio audience watching in stunned silence as the film came to an end, and then bursting into thunderous, quite emotional, applause. Nobody had ever seen car films presented with this much . . . theatre.

The Kids Are Alright

Then, of course, there were the kids. We didn't need BBC market research to tell us that they were now watching in droves. Our office, for example, was getting plenty of letters from teachers asking us if James would stop saying 'Oh cock!' because all the children were now copying him in the playground.

Certainly I was witnessing this firsthand at home. Our daughter, Martha, aged about six, would sit there on a Sunday night, fidgeting her way through a Ferrari in a cloud of beautifully graded tyre smoke on full opposite lock, then turn to me and ask: 'When's the funny film on?' For her, our show would peak when Richard fell over on a ski slope in the Winter Olympics. Nothing could possibly follow that.

Obviously the kids loved all the nonsense films like car darts and were excited by the races, but Jeremy, Richard and James themselves also held much appeal. My theory is that most kids know they will never be David Beckham or Lewis Hamilton, but they do stand a chance of being a badly dressed Peter Pan who gets paid to build a boat out of a car and then fall out of it.

Life for children is also a constant litany of being told to do your best, be your best, win the whatever. We, by contrast, let them enjoy the celebration of failure every week. They spent an hour watching literally nothing being achieved. If we needed to feature an expert we would deliberately avoid seeking out the best. There was so much more fun in announcing: 'He is Wales's *fifth* best rally driver . . .'

Our younger viewers also adored the Stig. They loved not just his mysterious weirdness, but also his unfriendliness, case in point being when the Scouts came down to give him an award for being a good instructor and by way of thanks he set about attacking them. This was playground stuff, but on telly on Sunday night.

I got a firsthand demonstration of how much kids love him when my son Noah had his sixth birthday party. He and his mates all went karting in these tiny electric kiddie karts – the little sods were all over the place, everywhere but the track – and I asked Gavin, one of the new researchers, if he wouldn't mind dressing up as the Stig and coming along to hand out the trophies. 'You betcha,' said the excited Gavin. 'I get to wear the Stig suit. Count me in.'

And so, on the Saturday, just as the karting had finished, he strolled into the venue and marched towards Noah and his mates. What none of us adults had realised was that the first thing six-year-olds want to know is whether the Stig is human or a robot. And the only way they can find that out is by touching him. Consequently they all charged forward, off their tits on sugary drinks, and whacked him in unison. And . . . because they're six they were the perfect height for hitting him in the nuts. Stand-in Stig doubled over, with all the kids quite shocked that:

a) he spoke, and

b) his words were a strangled 'Fuck me . . .'

Ladies' Night

It's usually quite a chore having to listen to BBC market research findings, but one day they hit us with a bombshell: our audience was now not far off 50 per cent female. That stopped us in our tracks, not because women aren't interested in cars – plenty are – but because when you see Jeremy, Richard and James you don't think: 'Oh look, Brad Pitt, George Clooney and Henry Cavill are testing three hatchbacks.'

But there were several logical reasons why women liked watching the show.

Firstly, women got that our three may have been male, but they weren't macho. There was no rugby lad/stag night vibe about them. In those polls in women's magazines all three of them won the *Heat* Weird Crush Award and were voted the guys 'you'd have a fun night out with and be delivered safely to your door', rather than the 'most like to go to bed with'.

I think girls also liked the fact that 'grooming' was simply not a word in their dictionary. They liked that, four days into a Bolivian special, they all looked like shit. They liked that Jeremy had zero dignity and would happily show his face contorted into a House of Horrors mask at the wheel of a high-speed Ariel Atom.

The show also celebrated women at the wheel. When Jodie Kidd and Ellen MacArthur went top of the board we were ecstatic. Whenever the wonderful and much-missed Sabine Schmitz, the Queen of the Nürburgring, took our guys to school on the track, we worshipped at her feet.

I believe also our show was a charming way of getting an insight into the male brain, a place where, as all men know, absolutely nothing is going on. I imagine a woman's brain to be like a set from *Game of Thrones*, with loads of fantastical scenery and characters and machinations and emotions and dragons all whizzing hither and thither. Whereas in a bloke's brain there is just this vast, dark, empty room the size of Wembley Stadium, with a small rubber ball bouncing in the corner.

Jeremy, Richard and James illustrated this contrast in an entertaining way. They had the charm and wit and self-deprecation – without the looks – of the guys from *Friends*.

Finally, our time slot: 8 p.m. on a Sunday night, was a gift. Unwittingly we'd made a Friday night 'start the weekend' show for the most downbeat evening of the week and everyone wanted a piece of that. Kids get to watch *Top Gear* before bed. The dads want to watch it too. Mum walks in and she sees one of the things that pleases her more than anything: her brood all together, doing the same thing. So she thinks, 'Sod *Call the Midwife*, *Top Gear* it is.'

Chemistry Set

Our *Top Gear* could never have been made in America. Over there when a show goes on air it needs to hit the ground running, with its ideas fully formed and the hosts instantly displaying a ready-made onscreen relationship.

Our three, however – and BBC, we will be eternally grateful to you for this – were never pressured into a speedy relationship, and thus the building blocks of their friendship grew organically. James, for example, was never called Captain Slow as the result of a meeting. It was just a name that Hammond came up with one day during a news segment.

And what wasn't an accident was genuine, particularly when it came to their characters. Jeremy really was a bombast who struggled with complex machinery such as cutlery. I once watched him attempt to open a ketchup sachet and you'd think he was trying to build a matchstick cathedral. James really was so much in his own world that he'd go back inside for a dump just as the whole filming convoy was in the car park, engines running and ready to go. Likewise Hammond really was an accident-prone chav.

Collectively, their individual skills complemented one another very nicely. Jeremy was the tip of the arrow, no question. He was the creative driving force without whom there simply wouldn't be a show. Richard had easily the fastest wit of the trio. In their three-way chats his off-the-cuff comments had everyone behind the camera in stitches, and his sharp brain knew exactly how their dynamic should work. 'Jeremy is the tall poppy, and he also has zero dignity,' he reasoned. 'It's our job to feed that TV beast, help him make his nonsense work.'

As for James, I loved his off-kilter logic, his musings on how the driving position made everyone look completely undignified, and so on. But to me he was also a bit more everyman than the other two; like a viewer who'd won a prize to take part in the show. Viewers thought: 'If I could be any one of them, it would be him.'

As for humour, luckily they all shared the same funny bone. This came out in lovely moments such as when we filmed the Search for the Nile Special. There was a point midway in the journey where they'd modded their cars so they could sleep in them, and we shot a sunset scene with them all sitting atop their cars, enjoying a beer and the view. Once the cameras had cut, us crew all went back to our tents a few hundred yards away, and that night hardly got any sleep, because of the constant laughter from Jeremy, James and Richard as they drank late into the night, clearly on a roll. The next morning they had their whole riff worked out about how Victorian explorers were all charlatans who pretended they were lost and suffering from malaria, but in fact were partying with the locals and just couldn't be arsed to come back to listen to poetry readings in stuffy drawing rooms. It's a small moment, I know, but when people ask 'Was it scripted?' you can look them in the eye and say no.

I think also that, even if we weren't the best at it, laughter for us trumped everything. One time, a BBC senior person, congratulating me on a good show that week, suddenly asked: 'Something that puzzles me though; why do they do those introductions?' I knew absolutely what she meant. You'll remember it too. Each week, top of the show, theme tune, then Jeremy's voice: 'On tonight's show, Richard struggles with his coat zip (shot of Richard doing just that), James closes a car door (shot of that), and I point at a mountain (shot of that).' These deliberately lame and bland introductions were not part of any master plan. They were simply done just to wind me up. If you're the exec producer, you're a bit Lord Sugar. You want to sell. Sell your show, grab the viewers from the get-go: 'On tonight's show, we max a Veyron, we try to cross the Channel in amphibious cars, we blow the world up, etc.'; get your best fruit and veg at the front of the stall. And because they'd rather wind their mate up than big up their show, that is what you got.

This organic development of their friendship, which viewers saw unfolding and therefore felt part of, was definitely worth the time it took, because soon we found ourselves with three motoring journalists who had turned into proper TV stars.

The evidence of this fame would present itself in unusual ways.I give you, Hammond and fish.

Basically, on one of their shoots – it was a dinner or lunch scene – the other two had taken the mick out of

Richard for being a bit of a Karl Pilkington in his Brummie aversion to anything different, and he'd gone along with that by saying he didn't like fish. Lots of laughter between the three of them, then onto the next scene.

Then, a week after the film had gone out, Hammond comes into the office in a complaining mood:

'I was out for dinner with Mindy the other night,' he began. 'I ordered fish, and the waiter said, "I thought you didn't like fish."' Richard told him it had been a bit of a joke and ordered his fish.

'Then, later on, I'm eating it, and another diner comes over and says, "Richard, I thought you didn't eat fish."'

He was fairly indignant that his eating habits were now being scrutinised, and to be fair, he had a point. For me the solution was clear. And it was the only solution.

'Mate, from now on, you can't be seen in public eating fish.'

'What?! Oh do bugger off.'

'No, I'm sorry. You know how Brian Epstein wouldn't let the Beatles be seen out with their girlfriends for fear of upsetting their fans, that's where we're at here.'

'The Beatles. You're saying we're the Beatles?'

'No, I'm saying it's the same principle. With them it was girlfriends, with you it's fish.'

W1A Strikes

Even though the public were clear about their feelings for Richard, James and Jeremy, sometimes the BBC senior management appeared not to have got the memo. This fact reared its head often in the most *W1A*-type ways. If you've seen the show *W1A*, you'll most likely know exactly what I mean. For those who haven't seen the show, *W1A*'s schtick is to poke fun at the more ludicrous aspects of BBC senior management, particularly their ability to tie themselves in knots by overthinking what is the politically correct thing to do or not do.

This very thing had happened the last time I'd been in a meeting with some management when I'd mentioned that we might be doing a film on a form of banger racing called Siamese Banger racing.

'Jeremy and I did it once,' I explained. 'It's when you chain two banger racers together and then you've got two cars being driven by two drivers at the same time and you're in a race, and it's hilarious.'

Silence. Then one of the execs said: 'Well surely in that case it should be called Conjoined Banger Racing.'

'Probably not. Shall we just forget it, eh.'

This time, however, when I was asked to go over for a W1A meet, they kicked off by saying they had tremendous news for me.

'The thing is,' began one of them, 'BBC Two normally struggles to attract young black and Asian viewers, but our latest research shows you guys are cracking it. *Top Gear* is pulling them in! So a massive well done.'

'Well that's great news,' I said. 'Thanks for letting me know. I'll get back and tell everyone in the office.'

A silence then broke out, a BBC silence, which meant there was more to come.

Eventually the words popped out of the exec's mouth and, like a mortar shell, arced elegantly over the desk and landed with a plop on my head.

'So the thing is, now you're doing so well at pulling in this demographic, how about replacing one of your line-up with a young . . . black or Asian presenter.'

My impulse was to do the *W1A* thing and say: 'Well that's certainly given us food for thought and we'll get back to you,' knowing I never would. There was no need, after all, for an outburst over class 1 idiocy of this level.

But I couldn't let the logic of it go.

'So hang on, you've got young black and Asian viewers who have chosen, seemingly quite happily, to watch three white middle-class, middle-aged men doing what they do, and in response to that, we should now break that team up – the one they enjoy watching – and give them something they're most likely not asking for? Isn't that sort of patronising to . . . young black and Asian viewers?' I knew this was checkmate. I'd managed to get patronising and ethnic diversity into the same sentence.

At that point the Awkward BBC Meeting Life Raft automatically inflated. This is the device that allows a meeting that's going nowhere to reach dry land. Its emergency kit contains sentences like: 'Well, yes quite, that's food for thought, so you have a think about it and let's pick this up another time.' And then, you all go your separate ways.

Lionel Richie's Big Day Out

As the show gained traction with the viewers it became easier to book guests. Simon Cowell was a great moment, both for him and us. At that time he was the biggest TV star around so his status helped our guest-slot status rise considerably. In return, the nation saw another side to him, because the prickly talent judge on a shiny floor ITV show was actually extremely self-deprecating in his wit, and he could *really* drive. Likewise we were feeling pretty good about ourselves when Sir Patrick Stewart readily said yes to coming on. Old Jean-Luc was a big Jaguar fan, and it appealed that he could come on a chat show and talk about something different and personal to him, rather than his latest adventure in outer space.

As for the Stig, he was extremely excited about tutoring two famous characters with petrol in their veins; this was a good day at the office for him.

Then . . . along came Jimmy Carr. Now, bit of housekeeping first. On the day of Jimmy's appearance we didn't have Ben, the usual Stig. He was away on another job so another racing driver, Julian Bailey, deputised for him. Julian is extremely accomplished at the wheel, having driven in F1 for Lotus and Tyrrell, and in Touring Cars for Toyota. He is, however, the polar opposite of Ben in that he's grumpy, and struggled to deliver the Stig Concierge Service that's often required to coax a lap time from a celebrity. From the Portakabin window we'd seen Jimmy doing his practice runs, and there was a fair bit of spinning and foraying onto the airfield grass going on. After a while I thought I'd better drive down to see what was what and passed Julian coming the other way in his own car. 'Where you going?' I asked. 'Jimmy hasn't finished his laps yet, has he?'

'I've had enough of that cunt,' came Julian's diplomatic reply. 'He just won't fucking listen. He's doing my head in. And the stupid thing is, he's actually quite good, but he's just pissing about.'

I asked him to stick around and went and found Jimmy. When I repeated what Julian had said about him, I got the famous Jimmy Carr laugh – the one that sounds like a seal with hiccups.

'I don't blame him,' said Jimmy. 'But I'm not here for lap times. I come down here, I come to entertain. That's what I do.' For Jimmy that meant crowd-pleasing lairy driving and spins, but when I told him we already had those in the can, and that Stig reckoned he could do good things, he agreed to apply himself. Grumpy Stig returned, Jimmy listened as best he could, and bugger me if he didn't go top of the board.

So yes, overall the Star in a Car slot was trucking along nicely, but one thing still eluded us . . . a big American guest. This was a nut that had to be cracked, because until we got at least one American star watching Jeremy scribble their time on the lap board, the Los Angeles agents wouldn't even take the time to tell us to fuck off.

Week after week went by as we watched in frustration as Norton and Ross welcomed on the likes of Matt Damon and Harrison Ford to thunderous applause.

Then finally – cue choir music and heavenly beams of celestial light – Lionel Richie said 'yes'. In truth the carrot that had lured him across the pond was the chance to perform to millions on *Children in Need*, but that minor detail was quickly forgotten as we high-fived round the office.

Job one, clearly, would be to look after him properly. To date, the Star in a Reasonably Priced Car guests had been allocated, as their celebrity Green Room, a tiny partitioned-off cell in our breathtakingly shit production office Portakabin. What can I say about that room? It definitely lacked, without sounding sexist, 'a woman's touch'. There was a sofa from Poundland, a floor lamp from Two-Poundland, and a carpet held together by bacteria. We weren't in the chat show business, we needed money for crisps and explosions, so none of our budget was going into this place. Consequently the guests had to sit in this room, blissfully unaware they'd be going home with fleas.

Even we knew, though, that this would not do for Lionel. Lionel would definitely need his own motorhome. I asked Roger the production manager to hire one and went off to tend to other matters, completely forgetting that Roger is the tightest human being ever to switch on a calculator. On shoots he would cut four-finger KitKats in half, insisting he'd always intended to buy two-finger ones but that they'd arrived in faulty packaging. Roger would watch one of those *Blue Peter* stunts on the telly where thirty-eight people try and get into a Mini and nod approvingly, assuming it was commuters from the same street trying out a car share. Our penny-wise finance guru thumbed through the *Yellow Pages*, called up Triple A Motorhome Hire and the instant the voice on the other end said: 'Our prices start at . . .' Roger cut him off with 'We'll take one of those,' and went back to snapping KitKats.

Come the big recording day at the *Top Gear* test track, none of us really paid the rented motorhome much attention. I made a mental note to have it moved a bit further away from the Portaloos and then Jeremy and I, like British consuls in a far-off place greeting a member of the Royal Family, prepared to welcome Lionel as he stepped out of his chauffeured car. It only took a few seconds of exchanges to know that Lionel was lovely: charming, relaxed, also good at pretending that he'd heard of the show and that this would be the highlight of his trip. His manager, though, less so. Basically he was a tough American, not given to wasting his time on small talk, and wanting to get his star back to London and a shiny floor BBC studio, where life made more sense.

As Lionel started his laps in the Suzuki Liana, the rain came down. Hard. Then the wind started to deliver the raindrops, like soggy stinging nettles, into the eyes of the manager and me, as we stood by the side of the track, watching Lionel go round and round.

The Stig came and stood next to us. The manager asked him how Lionel's tuition had gone, but because the Stig took his job of anonymity seriously and would only speak to the celeb in the car, he just stood there, completely mute. That's fine when you know the Stig's schtick but when you don't, as was clearly the case with Lionel's manager, his silence just added a veneer of rudeness to the miserable, piss-wet conditions.

The manager spoke again: 'So people say this is a pretty popular show, right?' Just as I was telling him that indeed it was, and therefore a worthwhile experience for any guest, there came the almightiest graunching sound, as the front suspension of the Suzuki completely collapsed whilst Lionel gamely pushed it round a fast corner. The worn-out car must have been doing at least 60 mph as it nosedived, in a shower of sparks and tortured metal, off the tarmac and onto the grass, heading, as luck wouldn't have it, straight for a bank of runway lights.

Lionel's destiny was now most definitely in Lionel's hands, and somehow he managed to avoid the runway lights and bring the runaway car to a juddering halt.

Thankfully, the manager's silent fury was balanced by our singing superstar's perkiness, as he walked across the wet field to join us. Lionel would tell me later about having to endure the hard racism of the Deep South when touring with a band in his pre-fame days, so by contrast a collapsed suspension at high speed was a breeze. Seeing how cheery he was as he joined us I drew breath to say: 'Bet you thought you'd be dancing on the ceiling', but then saw the manager's face and went with 'Everything okay?'

So, what to do next to get back in the manager's good books? The motorhome! We had a motorhome!

'Gentlemen, if you'll follow me, let's get you out of the rain and into our nice warm VIP motorhome,' I announced.

Upon arrival at the motorhome I opened the door, ignored the pent-up wave of mildew aroma that rushed forth and, with a full Basil Fawlty flourish, gestured for the two Americans to step inside. Up the steps and in they went. Package delivered. Then I heard the manager exclaim: 'What the fuck is this?!'

I poked my head round the door, expecting to see Lionel engulfed in rotting, mice-infested velour, but no, that was absolutely not the issue. I immediately saw the issue, and it was worse. The fact is, the walls were completely bereft of all decorations, except for one cheaply framed poster that the manager was now pointing sternly at.

And, to this day, many years later, I still have absolutely no idea why a motorhome hire firm near Guildford thought the appropriate décor for a visiting American star would be . . . a poster of the Twin Towers.

Andy the Producer

It's logical that, when writing a book like this, one has to think about what oneself brought to the party.

Firstly, I found that I could run a team. Given that I'd spent most of my career working as a twosome with Jeremy and a tiny crew I came to the *Top Gear* job with no experience of wrangling a sizeable office, so I took inspiration from the most famous office manager in Britain: David Brent.

Obviously he was insufferable in so many ways, but I also believe he got some things right. He intrinsically knew, for example, that it's a slightly weird world where capitalism has managed to arrange things so that we spend the best hours of the day not with our friends and loved ones, but with colleagues at work. And if that has to be the case, then give the place a bit of theatre. So in the best way I could, I became a theatrical boss. Once, when faced with a mountain of CVs, I even copied David Brent's efficiency tactic of tipping half of them in the bin, arguing that we shouldn't employ unlucky people.

Secondly, I like to think I was good in the edit. I'd initially just gone in there out of necessity, to help cut the films when our whole operation was completely arse over tit during Series 1. But once there, I knew I'd found my happy place. All those vivid coloured moments of my early life: Uncle John, the stormy waters at home, the hospital incarceration, had marinaded me in the art of storytelling, and now here was my outlet. I knew when to be slapstick and when to be dry. I knew how to put in misdirects to set up the presenter failures. Then as the films got longer and more ambitious and the storylines became more complex, my brain sort of set up a washing line in my head, so that I could hang up all the separate parts of the story and then move them around, *Minority Report* style, without getting muddled.

Another area where I earned my wages was in helping to protect the office, building a force field around it.

The fact is, there's often a simple equation to be found in television whereby the less the senior executives know about a show's subject matter, the more they feel compelled to dabble. The vast majority of TV bigwigs, for example, are quite into their food, so they are more relaxed about leaving a food show to do its thing. Jamie knows his onions so leave him be, etc.

When it comes to cars, though, literally nobody on the top floor of a TV building knows anything about them or cares about them. And so, according to the rules of the equation, the opinions then come forth. For Show 2 of the first series, for example, we the *Top Gear* team said we'd be celebrating fast Fords, because we knew it was a popular topic. Blue collar, white collar, dog collar:

mostly everyone inclined to watch *Top Gear* liked fast Fords.

'Hmmm, does anyone actually *like* fast Fords?' came the exec response, based on no information whatsoever.

At times like this you have to proactively make moves to protect the kingdom. We could sense we were getting into our groove and we needed to stay there by keeping everyone else out of it.

One tactic was quite binary, in that we fastidiously ensured the office remained a total shit hole. Once something arrived in it – e.g. props from a shoot – they never left. In 2005, after the 'Two Door Coupé That Isn't A £1,500 Porsche' shoot, a set of rally tyres were temporarily piled next to someone's desk, and they were still there ten years later. Likewise a gift shop Darth Vader helmet with a photo of Jeremy and Mrs Thatcher at a drinks do stuck inside it: the more left-wing members of the team had told Jeremy to make sure he came back with a picture so that the party-shop helmet would have a purpose, and that two-day joke stayed there for a decade. Traffic cones, flags, Communist Stig's red helmet, the door from Jeremy's British Leyland car, a framed photo of Will Young – everything just wandered in and never left, and over time the office became a giant kid's bedroom.

Another pillar of our independence came in the shape of us insisting we gave our own responses when the papers kicked off about something we'd done. Every big broadcaster has their own press department and the established protocol is that they are the ones who respond to media enquiries. There's a logic to that because not every TV maker is trained to deal with journalists' crafty questioning and a naïve answer can end up making a situation worse. The downside, though, is that big broadcasters prefer to bland things out when tricky queries come in and as such have a set of stock responses. 'Whilst the BBC acknowledges that X did Y, our editorial standards ensure that blah . . .' 'No offence was intended . . .' was another stalwart and the one that would be used when Jeremy said something like there needed to be snipers positioned on motorway bridges so that they could shoot motorists in the face who hogged the middle lane. I hated this response most of all. Of course we meant to offend or else we wouldn't have said it. We would have just been having rudderless thoughts otherwise. We got the logic behind the bland responses but we didn't want any of it for us. Instead we wanted to protect our right to have an attitude.

A good example of this was the Caravan film, where Jeremy, Richard, James and *Top Gear* dog went away to experience a caravan weekend. As you'd expect, given the subject matter, it was a pretty gentle film throughout, so we decided it needed a rousing full stop and duly made sure the caravan caught fire, but pretended in the film that it had happened by accident. After the film had gone out the press office got a call from one of the tabloids saying they'd spoken to a fireman who'd been booked in advance to put the fire out, and therefore we were guilty of fakery. The press office were ready to go with a: 'All shows are required to comply with the editorial standards laid down by . . .' stock answer, and I asked Tara, our amazing press officer, if I could do the responding, and very graciously she let me. I then rang the journalist, who asked me if we'd deliberately started the caravan fire.

'We absolutely did,' I replied.

'What?! You're admitting it?'

'Yes. We had a half-hour film that was nice and gentle, so we thought we'd give it a lively ending.' I then explained that since our show was in the Factual Entertainment category, it was up to us what was Factual and what was Entertainment.

The journalist thanked me for my straight answer. I knew that despite the civility of his farewell he'd still be duty-bound to give the show a kicking, and the next day he duly did. However, he also printed my response in detail, and that was all that mattered to our show.

The other reason we wanted to control our dealings with the press was that we knew some papers were extra keen to make us targets. The fact was Jeremy wrote for the *Sun*, which meant that the *Mirror* and the *Mail*, as rivals of News International, would automatically be double gunning for us. It was sport, school playground high jinks with a Fleet Street budget, and one day we handed the *Mirror* a gift from the gods.

The problem started when we realised that the audience in the hangar was no longer the right fit for the show we were making. Although the people watching *Top Gear* at home were now this broad church, with more and more kids and women joining the congregation every series, the studio audience was still mainly comprised of the hardcore car nerds with beards and Subaru fleeces. And as much as we loved their dedication, they were there mainly for the horsepower chat. Best will in the world, even Ricky Gervais would struggle to make them laugh. The comic *Viz* then poured salt on our wound by printing one of their made-up letters which asked the question: 'When did the *Top Gear* hangar become a moron storage facility?' Funny as it was – *Viz* even sent us the artwork so we could get T-shirts printed – we knew action was needed. And so, in order to mix up/liven up the hangar crowd, we made it a condition that audience tickets (which are free) would only be issued in pairs, and that each pair attending had to be one male and one female.

This tactic duly did improve the atmosphere in the hangar, but then one day I got a call from the *Mirror*. A fan of the show had applied for tickets, and on being told the male/female rule replied that he was gay and wanted to bring his partner. The ticket people said sorry but the rule is the rule, so the man duly rang the *Mirror* to complain.

I told the reporter we stood by the decision on the grounds that the audience members are an important part of the show, that they help provide the atmosphere, and consequently we had a right to curate them.

It was, I thought, a good answer, and the *Mirror* likewise was glad I stood by it, because the next day, there was the front page they'd dreamed of: 'Top Gear Bans Gays!'

I knew the *Mirror* editor quite well and rang him, and boy was he loving the moment: 'Aww, mate,' he said, 'what an own goal. Magic.'

The BBC, fearing an impending homophobia storm, were in a bit of a panic, but Jeremy insisted that he, Richard and James would take care of the response in the coming week's show, and they handled it masterfully. Jeremy began by stating directly to the camera: 'It's been reported in the *Mirror* this week that we don't allow gays in the studio.' Then instead of saying anything more, he just let his face, with its expression of *I mean . . . ?* carry the room, and the audience died with laughter.

So yes, protecting ourselves on our terms was an important piece of business, and we would remain adept at doing so for many years, until eventually, we didn't.

2005-2006

Maximum Revs

With five series now under our belt we powered through 2005 and 2006 in fine fettle, and our *Top Gear* plane continued to gain altitude.

For starters, alongside cheap-car films and Big Races, we added a new string to our bow: 'Car Sports', kicking off – literally – the first show of 2005 with two teams of Toyota Aygos playing car football. On the surface this was pure nine-year-olds' entertainment at its best, but for us as a show this film was an important indication of how much power we now had in relation to the car companies.

Two years earlier at one of the manufacturers' annual gatherings in London, some executives had lobbied a motion that since we were now no longer a serious car show, there was equally no longer a need or obligation to provide us with cars. I suspect this was a trojan horse for neutering Jeremy, whose scything verdicts on bad cars had upset many of them in the past. Fortunately some manu-facturers had spoken in our defence, arguing that we were at the end of the day providing a much bigger, overarching service, of making it okay for people to like cars, to enjoy cars, to celebrate cars.

And sure enough, here we now were, offloading a dozen or so small Aygos that we had permission to bash and crash at Toyota's expense.

Meanwhile Jeremy was continuing to make Britain vulnerable to foreign invasion by singlehandedly burning his way through Britain's defence budget. Having gone toe to toe with an Apache gunship in a Lotus Exige the previous year, he now did the same with a new Range Rover Sport against a Challenger 2 tank and then, four episodes later, dodged thousands of bullets in a real-world consumer test to see which out of a Porsche Boxster and a Mercedes SLK had the best handling to avoid sniper fire.

These films marked another shift in our status, but this time within the BBC. Basically, and there's no other way of saying it, we'd fucked over *Blue Peter*.

The thing was, when *Blue Peter* had been at its peak as a kids' show, there had been an unwritten contract between it and the armed forces whereby the military would put jets and warships and what have you at the disposal of John Noakes and Valerie Singleton and the other bloke, because the screentime was an effective recruiting tool. Show the kit in action with an eager telly civilian, and youngsters would head off to the recruitment office as soon as their balls dropped.

Now though, it was *Top Gear* that was attracting the kids, and the army knew it.

I felt really sorry for the *Blue Peter* team, who were a lovely, modest bunch. At one point they actually asked me to come and give them some advice as to how to attract kids back to their show, and I thought hard about it and realised I couldn't help them.

'I think the problem is,' I said to the main producer, 'when you think about it, what are kids? They're unfair, they're mean, they're naughty and they're often really funny. That's Jeremy, Richard and James. The kids see them as bigger kids. They leave each other behind when someone's car breaks down. They cheat in races by using the Stig and pretending it's James. With respect, *Blue Peter* is always about kids doing the right thing: making good use of their time, playing nicely.' He not only graciously accepted my TED Talk babble, but thanked me by making me a member of one of the most select clubs in the world, whose roll-call includes Beckham, Lewis Hamilton, the late Queen, Spielberg, JK Rowling, Attenborough, Marcus Rashford, Ed Sheeran and Paul McCartney. Yes, he gave me a Gold *Blue Peter* badge. When it fell out of the package onto my desk, my guilt level needle shot up to 8,000 rpm. But what could I do? Hopefully, if I waited long enough, it would become lost in the office's Pit of Eternal Mess.

In this period we also shot my favourite Cheap Car film, the snappily titled 'Can You Own An Italian Mid-Engined Supercar For Less Than £10,000?'

To save you going on Wikipedia, let me remind you of the cars: James had a Lamborghini Urraco, Jeremy a Maserati Merak and Richard a Ferrari 308 GT4. You can read on the classic car websites how the Urraco marked a shift for Lamborghini away from V12s to V8s, but that didn't make the one we bought any less shit. Jeremy's Maserati came from the Citroën partnership era and had Citroën hydropneumatic bits in it, or to put it another way, time bombs. Also all these cars were built in the 70s, so had three decades of wear and tear apiece under their belts when we bought them – as the film title says – for less than ten grand. That may sound a fair bit for a cheap car challenge but to give a bit of context, a properly spruced-up one at that time would have cost you about £80,000, and even in that condition you'd be crossing your fingers.

Cars purchased, we set out with high hopes that the cars would provide a level of comedy. But this, however, was one of those occasions when the cars themselves just took over the film and said: 'Lads, we're thirty-year-old Italian supercars. Fifteen-hundred quid Porsches? Fuck off. You want breakdowns? We'll give you breakdowns.'

The start point for the road trip was Bristol, and the finish line was a Spearmint Rhino gentlemen's emporium in Slough: a less than taxing distance of 96 miles. James's Lambo immediately set the reliability bar by arriving at the start line on the back of an AA truck, fizzing with electrical issues. Eventually he got it going but whilst trying to beat the lap time set by the Stig in an Astra diesel at Castle Combe, it broke down again on the first corner. Jeremy hoped to vanquish the Astra's lap time in his Maserati but amazingly his Citroën-designed brakes completely failed him.

In a mere day and a half, all three belligerent cars somehow made it from Bristol to the market town of Marlborough, an eye-watering distance of 49 miles. After that it was a straight 40-mile drive to Slough and the finish line at Spearmint Rhino. On an easy stretch of road like this Jeremy reckoned the Maserati would be quids in, because although his whole car had cost around £7,000, the previous owner had at some point spent at least ten grand on rebuilding the engine. In Jeremy's head, that investment would now pay off. But the Merak instead thought: 'Hang on, I'm in a cheap-car challenge on *Top Gear*, I know the form here,' and then duly shat that very engine's innards all over James's windscreen.

Several miles further on, the other two gave up the ghost. None of the cars made it to Spearmint, and secretly we were extremely relieved. For sure a lap dancing bar was an appropriate destination for a deconstructed 70s supercar owner, but what would any of our three actually have done had they got there? We're talking about three *Heat* Magazine Weird Crush winners here after all. James would have asked where the rhino was.

S-S-S-Studio

Alongside the films, the studio also went up a notch. On camera it now looked like a fun place to be, and the demand to be part of it reflected that. There I'd been in Series 1, literally giving audience members their licence fees back in bribes, and now the guy in charge of ticket allocations was telling me we would have to record shows for another twenty-one years in order to get through the waiting list.

Nevertheless, I really didn't like studio. I was never any good at it and it kept me away from the edit. Luckily, my aversion to it was equalled by Jeremy's love for it.

On Tuesdays, when we wrote the content for the studio up in the London office, and on Wednesdays, when we recorded, he was an absolute pig in shit. It wasn't hard to see why. As I've said before he's a tabloid journalist at heart; he absolutely loves the pace and energy and drama that newsroom deadlines give and Tuesdays and Wednesdays was the closest he could get to his newsroom fix.

On Tuesday morning he, Hammo, May and Porter would go through all the news stories and work up their news items. Then, come about 3 p.m., all the office would gather round them whilst they did a run through of their offerings. If nobody laughed, back to the drawing board they went.

The thing was though, he actually preferred it when there were problems, because for him they have the same effect as Red Bull. One Tuesday, Brian the director came into the office in a considerable flap.

'Fuck me fuck me,' he spurted in his panicky voice. 'The warehouse where we keep all the studio props, there's been a fire! We've lost your sofa and chair that go on the stage!' Brian, as a director, is anal. He likes anal. He does not welcome disturbances in the force. Jeremy, however, was doing back flips. 'Ohhh this is epic!' he said. 'Brian, get us some shit old chairs, all mismatched, like you get in those clearance junk shops. We'll use those on the stage, and then we'll say *Fifth Gear* burned all our stuff.'

This sort of moment would give him the perfect tabloid buzz, but if the day had gone well, with no need for rewrites and everything coming together neatly, I actually swear the little sod would start looking for problems, just so he could get another slug of newsroom adrenaline. There was a particular Tuesday when things had gone surprisingly well for scripting the first show of our new series and the prospect of an after-work pint was looming large. Jeremy then suddenly said: 'Hang on, if we're back on air this Sunday, we need to create a bit of publicity.'

(To be clear, the BBC were showing trailers and all the papers had covered our return in the TV listings, but his hands were now idle after an annoyingly smooth day.)

'Got it!' he suddenly said. 'Buses! Let's get arrested!' His genius plan was that the three of them should go down to the big bus station in Hammersmith, handcuff themselves, Greenpeace-style, to a bus, and then protest about buses. The police would come, they'd be arrested, tons of newspaper coverage, we're back on air this Sunday, job's a good'un. A researcher went to Ann Summers and purchased three sets of handcuffs with pink fake fur on them, and off they went for their date with outlaw destiny.

I've just googled it now, and can only find a piece in *Hammersmith Today*, so not quite the Greta moment he was after, but you get my point. A human daily-tabloid newspaper-editor cyclone in action.

On Wednesday morning we would all congregate early at the studio for run throughs and rehearsals. TV protocol says that the studio director is nominally in charge at this point, but Brian's authority was somewhat diminished by the fact that he had absolutely no spatial awareness. This was bad news for his car because he was endlessly crashing into the alabaster lions and Greek urns in his driveway. We were like: 'Brian, just remove everything. Turn your drive into a runway.'

It was even worse in the studio gallery though – the place where all sound and mixing technicians sit at the desks full of switches and knobs – because he would, pretty much like clockwork, sit down in his director seat in front of all his screens, lean forward to shout: 'Camera One, action' and knock his orange juice all over the mixing desk.

We wouldn't have any other director, though, for three reasons:

1. We loved Brian and it somehow felt on brand that a show like our *Top Gear* should have a clumsy director pouring fruit juice all over the equipment.
2. He was a very kind man, great with people, much respected and actually did know what he was doing.

3. He was smart enough to give Jeremy his head, because the studio, with its immediacy and pressure, was the sort of place where he wanted control.

Wednesday's pace was frantic. Whilst the rehearsals were going on we'd shoot the Stig laps, then the guest laps and cut them together on site. Always it was to the wire. You had to get the laps into the machine and play them to the audience on time, because the audience were standing for too long as it was, and once their energy dropped, you never got their energy back.

And no matter how tiring it was for the audience, it was worse for Jeremy, Richard and James, because we never used a warm-up man. If you've seen a studio show being recorded you'll know this as the person who comes out before Graham Norton or whoever, and literally gets the crowd warmed up with a bit of a routine. Our three, though, did it themselves. They just intrinsically knew that putting a warm-up person out before them would be too 'starry', so they did that job too.

With the studio wrapped, all of us, presenters and crew, would retire to our shit Portakabin (outside in the summer) and treat ourselves to beers and a buffet made up of every 'Reduced to Clear' brown food Sainsburys had to offer: mini scotch eggs, mini pork pies, mini sausage rolls and for some vitamins, cheese and onion crisps. Then Brian would come in, everyone would swoop their drinks up off the carpet before he started beer bottle skittles, and we'd finally breathe.

As glad as I was come the completion of every studio record, those after-work drinks were special. We were far from London and the BBC, and in our own little kingdom.

Surely No Higher?

As for the rest of 2005 and 2006, my memories are filled with words like 'more' and 'bigger'.

We shot two monster races, the first being the one to Oslo, with Richard and James on train and boat, versus Jeremy in the McLaren SLR. Two moments stick out as memorable to me: the breathtakingly beautiful sequence where the SLR drives over the Øresund Bridge connecting Denmark and Sweden, and Richard puking everywhere in a Rib with a broken engine on a choppy sea. The first was down to the work of Nigel and the editors, the second was down to Richard not, as it appeared, suffering from sea sickness, but having got absolutely bladdered the night before on the ferry.

As for the second race, the Bugatti Veyron versus James and Richard, with James flying a Cessna light aircraft from Italy to London, that film became so big that it took up most of the show. Certainly it hit the jackpot for the record number of speeding tickets we amassed in one shoot: even if you made me listen to Belgian techno all day and all night, I will never reveal the number. In truth though, like the speeding tickets, the finished film actually had got out of hand. It was a bit of a bloated prog rock album, and as a result we parked the Big Races until we could get our mojo back.

Elsewhere in the blossoming world that was our show, some of the more prestigious film-score writers were now proud to be associated with us using their work: Craig Armstrong even had a *Top Gear* section on his website.

Other musicians were, quite amusingly, more conflicted. I enjoyed reading an interview in *Q* magazine with Guy Garvey from Elbow, who in the space of the same article criticised us four for being posh public school twats, and then several paragraphs later made appreciative noises about the fact that we were using Elbow's music. That was fine by me. He could character assassinate away so long as we could borrow 'Grounds for Divorce'.

The gongs started coming our way too. We won the first of four National Television Awards and even an Emmy. As for Baftas, some parts of the internet say we won them, but some parts of the internet also say Jeremy models swimwear for Gucci. We were actually nominated around four or five times for a Bafta, but always ended up the bridesmaid. The first time we lost it was to *Wife Swap* and we went: 'Yep, that's fair. That show is a mould-breaker.' Next time round though, when you lose to a cooking show, you're like – okay, we are clearly not the sort of programme that Bafta committees are interested in. No worries, we'll make do with Richard's Heartthrob Award from Ann Summers, which was a giant dildo mounted on a plinth. Now if you're worried that that might have looked distasteful in the trophy cabinet, relax: it was spray-painted in gold.

Then came the final series of 2006, where we premiered yet another strand of car-based malarkey: the *Top Gear* builds. In a previous brainstorm James May of Hammersmith had come up with two memorable ideas. One: buy a dog. Two: try and build a successful amphibious car.

Top Gear dog was lovely, but refused to accept that she was now a TV star and kept getting up to wander about whilst we were recording the news. This made editing the stories impossible, as obviously, one second she was there, the next she wasn't, so we fired her and she enjoyed a comfortable retirement at Hammo's rural menagerie.

As for Amphibious Cars though, that was one of the most successful films we ever pulled off, and indeed ushered in an era of ludicrous builds.

In 2001 Jane Root had given us our survival target of 3 million viewers. Now, in 2006, we were pulling in 5 million viewers on the overnights, closer to 6 million when the consolidated figures came in: extraordinary figures for a car show. In our minds, we had surely peaked. Our *Top Gear* plane had reached maximum altitude. There was simply no way we could get any bigger.

And then Richard walked into the office one morning and said: 'Right, chaps. Next series, I want to go really fucking fast.'

The Crash

'What do you mean fast?' we all asked. 'An F1 car?' 'No, sod that,' came Richard's reply. 'REALLY REALLY fast. I mean, what would that sensation be like?'

The office search led us and him to the Vampire, a dragster powered by a Rolls-Royce jet engine, with quite astonishing figures attached to it: 0–272 mph in six seconds, 5,500 lbs of thrust with the afterburner on, but fortunately very economical, as it only used 10 gallons of fuel per mile. Also it had set a land speed record of 300 mph, which then satisfied the 'REALLY REALLY fast' requirement.

The checking out and preparations were made, and the date was set.

The weekend before Richard drove the jet car, he and Mindy came over to our house in South London for lunch with Amanda and me. We ate and we drank and the Hammonds also said hello to the kitten we'd got off them. They'd had a litter a while back and we'd taken one, May had taken one, Ben the Stig had taken one, and every single cute little one of the fuckers turned out to be a complete psychopath. Each Wednesday down at Dunsfold, James, Ben and I would compare cuts and scratches and share stories of how terrifying our lives had become, like some Kitten Abuse Survival group.

Our kids, Martha and Noah, had acquired so many scratches they'd stopped bothering yowling and just thought a small cat clinging to your scalp was part of growing up.

Richard, however, was a different matter. The kids were chuffed to see *Top Gear*'s Norman Wisdom, their favourite nine-year-old.

Also, for some reason Noah, who was about two and a half, always addressed him formally as Richard Hammond. He would stare up at him, his head decorated in kitten scratches, and pronounce: 'Richard Hammond, come and look at my car.'

It was a lovely, sunny lunching-type day and someone suggested we should do this again soon. I then quipped: 'Well we'd better not hang about because by the end of next week Richard will probably be eating through a straw.'

There then followed a Richard and Mindy moment where she asked what I was on about. Richard said he was driving a 300 mph jet car, and she said something like 'Oh bloody hell' in an eye-rolling, 'you're an idiot' type of way. She wasn't cross; it was the daredevil Richard she knew.

*

The filming took place on 20 September and I guess if you're reading this book there isn't much you won't know about the crash because so much has been written already, so I'll just add my few threads to the patchwork quilt that exists.

On the day of the shoot, up at Elvington airfield in Yorkshire, I was in our edit suite in London. Pat, the series producer, was running things on location and we checked in regularly on the phone. It's the sort of shoot where, given the risk, you want everything over and done with as quickly as can be, but that's impossible, for two reasons. Firstly, Richard could only learn to drive a car like the Vampire on the job. This meant he had to do at least several runs so that he could acclimatise and build his speed up. Secondly, we're making TV, so we need the shots. The first couple of runs, therefore, at around 200 mph, wouldn't give you the 'REALLY REALLY fast' sensation.

Around 4 o'clock, Pat rang to say all was going really well. Hammo had just done his sixth run and not only that, he'd hit 314 mph, an unofficial land speed record. They hadn't told him though, because they wanted to save breaking the news to him until he'd finished driving and then catch his natural euphoria. Pat then said they wanted to go for one more run in order to get shots of the after-burner. Would I give permission for that?

I thought about it, then said yes, which I knew I always

was going to do. It is a peer-pressure affliction amongst TV makers that, even if it may not be strictly necessary, you always go for 'one more take'. You do not want to be the one who says: 'Nah, what we've got will be good enough.'

And whatever happens as a result, it's a lesson that one never seems to learn. Years later we would do it all over again when we asked Hammo to take the Rimac for 'one more run' up the hill, just to make sure we had enough shots.

The next call from Pat was the one telling me that Richard had crashed. Then another one, more relieved, saying: 'He's conscious and talking.' Then another one, much graver, saying he was in the air ambulance on his way to Leeds.

I jumped in my car and joined the M1, heading north. Now I had time to think in the late afternoon traffic, the dread and panic were building. I got through to the hospital and asked the guy on the phone a closed question – 'Richard's okay, isn't he?' – desperate to push him into the only answer I could bear to hear. His answer was quite the opposite. Richard was in the Neurological Intensive Care unit and his condition was critical. Worse still, he then told me that 'critical' was the only information he was allowed to give out. I begged for more detail but he wouldn't budge. On the M1 the traffic was now at a rush-hour standstill and I remember screaming: fear, panic, powerlessness, futile wishes about being able to turn the clock back. Critical critical critical – what the fuck did 'critical' mean? It could be anything.

But if I thought I had it bad, Mindy had it far worse. She too was driving up to Leeds, and by now the hospital had also told reporters who'd called that Richard was critical, and the first she heard of that was from the news on the car radio. And for her too, no detail beyond 'critical'. No context, nothing your brain could work with to fabricate a crumb of comfort.

Later that night we both got to the hospital around the same time. In his bed, Richard was unconscious but looked eerily uninjured: some bruising around his eye where the soil had forced its way into his helmet, but nothing to trumpet that his life was in danger.

The doctor explained, though, that it very much was. The shock of the impact to his head – the tyre had blown out at 288 mph so we now also held the very unwanted record of the fastest crash ever – meant that brain swelling was now extremely likely, and if it swelled too much it would kill him. All we could do now was wait.

The hospital kindly gave us a private waiting room to sit in. Mindy stayed with Richard, so I went there and soon James arrived, followed by Elaine, who ran Specialist Factual at the BBC, therefore technically our boss, and also a dear friend who'd taught me my first moves in the dark art of editing. Once I'd downloaded everything I knew to the two of them we all sat quietly, swimming in our own thoughts. My brain was in full fantasy overload, imagining Richard well again and being Richard, then leaping across to Richard being dead, with Mindy widowed and his two girls having no dad.

At one point James asked, in only the way he could: 'Wilman, how's things coming along with my max speed run in the Veyron?'

'James, for fuck's sake,' I replied, knowing absolutely that he wasn't being callous, just that he was dealing with things in his own James-type way.

'Why "for fuck's sake"?'

'Well, look where we are!' I said, gesturing at our NHS surroundings. 'Do you really still want to do that, after this?'

'I trust in engineering,' he said firmly and Jamesishly. Then all three of us allowed ourselves a little laugh, the absurdity of the conversation providing a tiny pressure valve of release.

When morning finally came, we knew two things. Firstly, Richard was going to live, and secondly, our show had changed forever. We'd expected plenty of news coverage, but the press had gone nuts. Way beyond anything we could have possibly imagined. When Jeremy arrived his car was swamped like Princess Diana's at her paparazzi peak.

I spoke to the office and Rachel, our production assistant, told me two Formula One drivers had rung to ask how Richard was and send their best wishes.

'What, called in person or had someone leave messages?'

'No', she said. 'They called themselves. They were sweet.'

Blimey, I thought. That's a lovely little gesture at a time when you really need little gestures. So yes, respect to you both, Eddie Irvine and Jacques Villeneuve.

Over the next two days Richard became not only conscious, but also started to provide some extremely welcome black comedy, because he was quite clearly off his rocker.

At one point I walked past his ward door while he was with the doctor and he shouted:

'Wilman! Bloody hell! What are you doing here?'

'Well . . .'

'I've had a massive crash so they've put me in here. But what are you doing? I saw James and Jeremy earlier. Everyone's here! What're the odds?'

Everything he said was delivered with great cheer and exuberance; we would humour him about us happening to be in the area, but trying to have conversation with any sort of thread was like playing mental Whac-A-Mole.

The head nurse took me to one side and explained, in layman's terms, the science behind his current doolalliness.

'Think of your brain like a filing cabinet,' she said. 'His has been tipped over and all the files in it have spilled all over the floor. They're still there, but just in a mess, and it'll take time for them all to be picked up and put back in the right order.'

Sure enough, when I walked past again later on:

'Wilman! What the bloody hell are you doing here . . . ?'

*

162

While Hammo began the long, slow process of repair, we likewise got on with the business of righting the filing cabinet that was our show. Unlike with Freddie Flintoff's crash, nobody on the *TG* team was offered any counselling. Instead we were investigated both internally by the BBC's Health and Safety team, and the government's Health and Safety executive. Now to be clear, I am not for one second saying this as a whinge. We were, after all, a show that kept a boundary between us and everyone else so we couldn't go moaning when we didn't get full TLC. Also, the investigating was actually done very sympathetically and although there were a few findings about how communications between us and the Vampire people could have been better during the build-up, overall we received a clean bill of health. Ben the Stig and Grant Wardrop the producer had done sterling work with the safety prep pre-shoot, and Pat and the Vampire people were great on the day. Also, Hammo . . . what a legend. The telemetry showed that when the tyre blew at 288 mph, he was on it: he'd tried to steer into the skid and even managed to pull the parachute lever!

The absence of counselling aside, there was a much bigger difference regarding the aftermath of Richard's and Freddie's crashes. Freddie's completely knocked the stuffing out of the show. I absolutely get that because firstly Freddie's injuries came across as that much more drawn-out and distressing, and it felt right for the world to simply leave him be. Secondly, the *Top Gear* of Freddie's era had reverted back to being just another show that belonged to the BBC. It didn't have the surrogate parents that we had all become, protecting it as our baby, and consequently there was no will to bring it back.

By contrast the mood around Hammond – both in the office and around the country – was all about celebrating the day when he would return. For sure his injuries were titanic, but without meaning to demean the severity of them, his accident had been spectacular, movie-like. Consequently the mood was: 'He lives! We're back! Rejoice!'

Knowing this to be the case, we set about preparing the comeback show with great care. Job one was to cut together the film of Hammo's jet-car day out. Actually that was job two. Job one was protecting the footage, and knowing the unseen rushes were gold dust for any news outlet in the world, we had them locked down on their own server in the edit, far removed from all the other *Top Gear* material.

The editor, James 'Boycie' Bryce and I would make a rough cut, send it to Jeremy, then once we'd all discussed it over the phone, delete it immediately. However, whilst we were protecting anyone from sneaking in via the back door, BBC News decided to put their shoulder to the front door, demanding that since the crash was such a newsworthy event they should be the first to show it.

I said no. They said it was the right thing to do. I said if they wanted it they'd have to come down and physically take it off us, and that wasn't going to happen.

BBC News then appealed to Jana Bennett who, as Director of Television, *would* have the power to decide who got it first. Mercifully the wise and empathetic Jana came down on our side. It's their moment, she said, they're the ones who've all been through it. It stays with them.

With that battle won we continued prepping the comeback show, which now had a transmission date: 28 January 2007. Without question it would be our biggest box-office draw of a show yet.

Then, someone in the office spoke some words: 'Oh shit. Have you seen what else is on that night?'

'No. What?'

'The *Big Brother* final. Same time. Eight o'clock.'

Big Brother was one of the biggest shows on television, bigger than us. And as for the final, that was always a blockbuster. We were a sprat swimming into the mouth of a Great White. We were fucked.

2007–2015

'We're Back!'

As to whether people chose to watch us or Davina, that was out of our hands. All we could do was make Hammo's return a fitting moment.

Eventually Richard himself came back to the office to start work. Everyone was hugging him, a few made jokes about whether he'd got into any fights, had he driven himself here, etc. A few tears, some piss-taking and everything in between. We were a really tight office, we'd nearly lost him, and him walking in was kind of the counselling that nobody had had.

We then got down to business: a) how he would first appear in the studio and b) how we should talk about the crash.

On paper that looks like quite a simple job list, but there were important elements to get right, because it is an absolute golden rule of television: never, ever, put the audience in a position where they don't know how they're supposed to react.

In this case we had to respect the fact that the audience would feel incredibly emotional about Richard's return, but at the same time we were *Top Gear*, not the Kardashians, so there was no room for any mawkish weeping and hugging. This was the show that left a man behind in the field when his car broke down, so we had to try and achieve a balance whereby people could well up a little, get emotional, but also have a laugh if we were to make light of things: two disparate tones would need marrying into one.

Jeremy had brought his studio-brain A game, and suggested Richard do a big OTT razzmatazz appearance, but that since it was *Top Gear*, the whole thing should be slightly shit. You know the rest, you saw it. The crap entrance, with his descent down some budget airline stairs, hemmed in on the narrow steps by too many dancing girls, was just what the studio audience wanted. It broke the ice. People knew they had permission to laugh, and the roof came off the place.

Jeremy then asked Richard: 'Are you now a mental?' James followed this up with offering him a tissue in case he now dribbled. The following day this would cause the brain injury charity, Headway, to detonate, and eventually the complaint would be upheld against us. Did we care? No. Would we do it again? Absolutely. These two were exercising the right to talk to a mate as mates would do in a pub. Obviously our pub had millions of viewers peering through the windows, but to us that made no difference. Headway had a right to do what they do; we had a right to do what *Top Gear* does.

As for the chat about the crash itself, that began with Jeremy saying: 'Okay, the moment you've all been waiting for . . . Davina is outside the House.' This was a classy piece of self-deprecation. It now didn't matter that Big Brother would beat us in the ratings, because we'd got the joke in first.

All three of them held the audience's hand through the runs and the crash itself, which momentarily pulled the room down into a pool of grimness, but then Jeremy made the joke about Richard having to do the run twice for his 314 mph to qualify as an official record, and everyone had permission to laugh again.

The three of them, that night, were quite simply masterful.

The next day we waited like jackals for the TV overnights, desperate to see how close we'd got to beating *Big Brother*.

The figure eventually came in and we'd actually beaten them, with 8.7 million viewers. Pre the crash, five had been our magic number, our ceiling, and now a car show was heading into *EastEnders* territory.

We resumed work with no aspiration of keeping that kind of audience. A couple of million extra may have tuned in for our big comeback event, but they would soon disappear. Fortunately though we'd put together some good ones to keep the newcomers interested: the Stretch Limos film, Reliant Robin space shuttle, Race Across London and Amphibious Cars the second outing – this time all the way across the English Channel. James got to do his Bugatti Veyron top speed run which, coming straight after Hammo's return, served as a bit of an intentional statement that it was business as usual at *Top Gear*. Also, because James didn't crash, we were able to talk to him afterwards about what it felt like. What he recalled was not just the sensation of travelling at 253 mph, but of what that number did to his perceptions of any other speed. 'When I got down to 70 mph, back at the motorway speed limit, I honestly thought I could get out and walk,' he recalled.

Hammo too wanted some Bugatti action, and indeed got it with his YouTube hit, the Veyron versus Eurofighter drag race.

The outlier that year though, and a lovely surprise for it, was the Britcar 24-hour race. We'd conceived the film as a way of using up all the bio-fuel we'd made in the 'Top Gear Does Tractors' episode, and as such didn't hold out any great expectations for it. Sure we had some fun with the arse biscuits sponsorship, but beyond that, the lads would be in an old three series against some seasoned endurance racers, so we assumed we'd just run around Silverstone in the dark and get what we could. Then the film took on a life of its own. Hammo's crash in the night, putting our BMW out of action, kickstarted a full-on underdog fightback saga. And when the plucky little fella did make it to the finish line there was its pilot, Jeremy Clarkson, wiping away the tears.

Not only did these films give us a 2007 to be proud of, but more amazingly, they kept the punters from drifting back to *Call the Midwife*. We were now regularly pulling in more than 7 million, occasionally drifting back into 8 million.

At which point the BBC top floor came a-knocking, because they wanted to shift *Top Gear* over to BBC One. This process is a well-established one. *Ab Fab*, *Have I Got News*, *The Apprentice*, *Miranda* . . . plenty of BBC Two shows have made the leap across once their popularity grows, and now we were next up for promotion.

It took us about five minutes to say no, we'll stay where we are. Partly we did it out of loyalty to Roly, our BBC Two Controller. He had been so good to us; the BBC Two boss always gets a bit of a kick in the teeth when BBC One stroll across the playground and nick their ball, so we were happy standing by him. Also we were displaying – rare for us – some tactical cunning. On BBC One we'd get the same viewers, say around 7 million, and that would make us 'a hit show'. On BBC Two, however, the very same number made us 'a phenomenon'. And in truth, we rather liked being a phenomenon.

Afghanistan

Richard had thrown himself into work, but he still wasn't match fit. You just have to look at his eyes in the Polar Special to see that.

Just before Christmas 2007, however, when we'd wrapped Series 10, the four of us were invited on a trip that turned out to be just the most welcome tonic. You won't find it on any DVD extras or YouTube or indeed anywhere, because we didn't take any cameras. However, that trip remains one of my most cherished moments with those three.

The destination was Afghanistan. We'd been invited by the MOD to fly out and literally 'entertain the troops' who wouldn't be seeing their families and loved ones over the festive period. It would involve three or four days in Kandahar and Camp Bastion, with Richard, James and Jeremy meeting the soldiers, signing autographs and generally letting them know that back home, they hadn't been forgotten about.

I finished the edit for the final show of that series and drove straight from the edit to Brize Norton to meet the other three. We then boarded a military passenger jet filled with troops and took off for Afghanistan. Was I excited? Very. Was I nervous? Yes, that too. Quite a few of the seats had been removed to make space for full-on intensive-care beds, complete with drips and monitors, for bringing back the wounded, which was a reminder of the reality we were in. Then, just before we started our descent into Kandahar, the pilot told us this landing would be very different from an EasyJet landing in Malaga. In order to minimise the chances of being hit by Taliban rocket fire, which was a very real threat below 3,000 feet, the plane would be descending fast, very fast, and we would be in total darkness – all interior and exterior lights off; a pitch-black missile.

Given that you're reading this now, it's safe to assume we landed safely. Then, after a day and a night of meeting and greeting in Kandahar, we were put on a transport helicopter for the journey to Camp Bastion.

I think it's from this point on that the Afghanistan trip became forever one of my most treasured work memories. For starters, the journey began with high jinks. Jeremy and Richard, knowing full well about James's fear of heights, deliberately nabbed the two seats behind the pilots. That left the rear seats for James and me, which faced outwards, looking directly at the helicopter doors. Before take-off we got our next little adrenaline rush as the pilot told us that, again, in order to minimise the chance of a missile strike, he would be climbing as fast as fast can be to get to 3,000 feet. On hearing this, again with James's fear of heights in mind, Hammond and Clarkson asked the pilots to leave the side doors facing James and me fully open. Given that we were strapped in, the pilots were happy to oblige, and duly took off at a proper lick. For good measure they also tilted the helicopter as they rose, so that James and I were instantly on the world's highest fairground ride, rising from 500 to 1,000 to 2,000 at a bowel-emptying speed. As the late great A. A. Gill once said, some people show their fear with screams, some show it with silence. James and I never said a word as we climbed, not even when the pilots fired out precautionary chaff, which arced out like lazy, beautiful fireworks beneath us.

Eventually the helicopter levelled out and we were able to get our first look at Afghanistan. God's palette at this moment was only working with two colours: the blue of the sky, and the copper-tinted landscape of the desert and rocks below. But it was more than enough. Never have I seen such a breathtaking view; I'm not a travel writer so I won't even try, but here was another country, like Vietnam, where the most impossibly beautiful place had become bedfellows with war. A soldier we'd met earlier told us how the British soldiers had learned the hard way not to try and win the hearts and minds of the locals with innocent gestures. Out on patrol they'd given a young boy some sweets and the next time they came back that way they found him hanged, as a warning from the Taliban not to engage with the occupiers. This whole vista, completely empty for miles and totally serene, was mind-bendingly at odds with that story. You just felt like you could land anywhere and have a picnic.

We eventually landed in the town-sized Camp Bastion and set about our two days of Vera Lynn duties. Hardly anybody had a camera phone back then so it was auto-graphs all the way, which Jeremy, James and Richard signed endlessly, relentlessly and happily.

Life was delightfully simple: we had a tent, some camp beds and a mess hall for food. In fact a little too simple, because there was no booze. The whole camp was dry.

What this meant though was that instead of us having

to fret over what the next Big Race would be, our whole existence was now reduced to trying to find some beer. I'll never forget the cheer of jubilation when James walked into our tent and produced two cans of Heineken donated by some kindly soldiers. Two small cans between four of us: we sipped that lager like it was our last drink on Death Row.

Even ablutions became funny. Some wag in charge of stores had furnished us with four fluffy pink towels, and I will never forget the sight of James coming out of the shower block wrapped in one of them, tiptoeing gingerly across the duckboards, as a convoy of armoured vehicles bristling with .50 cal machine guns thundered past behind him.

Our little Afghan holiday was perfect. It had been a very long time since the four of us had managed to be together without a care in the world. Now, out here, thousands of miles from the stress of *Top Gear*, our biggest task was finding the next can of Heineken.

And that meant, as we passed it round, that we could also finally take a private moment to savour the fact that our fourth musketeer was still with us.

The Specials

And so we come to yet another seam of editorial gold that we discovered by accident, rather than through skilful prospecting. The Specials were definitely the best example of my belief that we spent a lot of our *Top Gear* career slightly behind our own curve. By this I mean we weren't smart enough to proactively think up the idea of doing something like a feature-length show, but once we accidentally did one, we were bright enough to know that we were onto a good thing.

Our unwitting journey into Specialdom began as we sat down one day to discuss an idea Jeremy had had for a film.

'When people go to Florida for a fly-drive holiday,' he began, 'they have no choice but to hire some dreary shitbox from a big hire car company and it probably costs more than a thousand dollars for the week. If you like cars, that's torture. So why don't we see what we can buy for $1,000?' He wasn't done: 'Then, you have a fly-drive holiday with a car you actually like, *and*, you sell it at the end of your trip and get some money back.'

Everyone was sold, so we got down to brass tacks. Cars: Jeremy wanted a Chevy Camaro, Richard a pickup, James a Brougham Cadillac. Next, the route: start in Miami, end in New Orleans. Then we jotted down a few ideas for mucking about along the way: 'We'll give the Stig a cousin! A big fat hick from the Deep South!' Then Richard Porter chimed in: 'How about, when you're driving through somewhere Bible Belty like Alabama, you all put slogans on your cars to wind up the locals?'

Sitting in the safety of a Notting Hill coffee shop that offered three types of milk, Porter's idea seemed like an absolute wheeze, so into the notes it went.

Once in Florida, we embarked on our road trip assuming we would get a good thirty-minute two-part film. However, as we coasted northward through the state, more and more bits of nonsense kept weaving their way in. Some were small, such as Jeremy fitting his car with a portable shower to cool him off in the immense heat. Yet this inauspicious moment featuring a shower head bought for a few dollars was the genesis of presenters modifying their cars. Then, having seen all the animal corpses lying at the side of the road, there came about the idea of dining on roadkill. This in turn led to Jeremy taking Gavin the researcher – the one the six-year-olds had kicked in the nuts – quietly to one side and delivering the rather nerve-inducing request: 'Can you get me a dead cow. Oh, and don't tell the others.'

Christ knows where Gavin began his search in the Florida *Yellow Pages*, but source a cow he did. Unfortunately, we were a day or so away from filming that sequence when Gavin closed the deal, so by the time that animal was forklifted onto the Camaro's roof in the 99.99 per cent humidity of summer, its corpse had already been fermenting for a good forty-eight hours. It was basically a bovine Hindenburg, with its vast reserve of internal gases now desperately eager to explode. However, despite Jeremy's best efforts during his handbrake turn cow-ejection manoeuvres, it held together as it hit the ground. At the time we thought of this scene as just a funny, throwaway sequence, but The Cow on The Roof would soon start to feature in loads of 'Top Ten Top Gear Moments' lists. We didn't give the 'why' of that too much thought – I suspect it wasn't actually the cow itself, more that it marked the beginning of the 'road trip' magic that the Specials would go on to deliver in spades. However, the event that unfolded a couple of days later, that one would stay in every Top Ten, forever and all time.

In truth, Alabama Petrol Station Day couldn't have got off to a more pleasant start. We covered some miles in the morning, then treated ourselves by finding a hotel with a satellite TV, where we could all take a rare couple of hours off to watch England in the World Cup. England won their game to take them through to the quarter finals, and in a pretty jubilant mood we started applying some cheeky slogans to the sides of the star cars.

In order to spice things up, the presenters had decided to decorate each other's cars, rather than doing their own. That inevitably removed a layer of cautiousness. Maybe James thought we were in Wiltshire, but whatever, he saw no problem in painting 'Man Love Rules OK' on Richard's pickup. Once all the sloganning was complete, we got back on the road and since we were merely mischievous rather than suicidal, the plan was that we wouldn't stop anywhere, but instead just keep driving along the Alabama highway whilst the cameras picked up disapproving looks from the locals. And that would be that.

Then, for a change of backdrop, we turned off the highway onto a normal road. For some reason the camera car I was driving was up front, so Ian the cameraman and I stopped so that we could get the camera on the tripod, and shoot a few drive-by shots of all three cars.

'Lads, we're pulled over at the side of the road by a petrol station,' I said over the radio. 'We'll get an up and by shot of all of you as you come past.'

'Petrol station?' replied Hammo. 'I could do with some petrol, I'll fill up.'

Now, what you need to know about a *Top Gear* film crew is that when they're on a road trip, a petrol station is like a cliff edge to a lemming. If you mention one, if you even think about one, everyone in the convoy will suddenly want to go into it. Each car will say they need petrol but truth is it's all about mooching up and down the aisles, looking at what new and unusual savoury snacks are to be found on the shelves. We're literally the David Attenboroughs of snacks.

And so the radios came to life. Jeremy: 'I may as well get some too.' James: 'My needle's looking a bit low as well.' And within a couple of minutes everyone was parked on the forecourt, so we decided to film the presenters filling up and having a chat about being looked at by scary motorists.

At this point, if you saw the episode, I'll let the show take over. Petrol station lady comes out, sees the slogans, goes mental. I think my favourite moment is still her asking them angrily: 'Y'all gay looking to get beat up in a hick town?' and Hammo replying: 'No, I live in the

Cotswolds,' as if that fact would smooth the troubled waters.

She goes in, gets on the phone, and by the time we've faffed around doing a bit more filming, the first pickup truck full of local unamused gentlemen arrives. Why we didn't read the room and leave earlier I don't know. Maybe because we were now so blissfully living in our *Top Gear* sitcom, we thought this was just a bit more sitcom.

The pickup truck men were angry. Another man arrived and started shouting even more angrily. Jeremy then decided he actually didn't need any petrol or Pringles and scooted off. Richard wanted to, but James's crap Cadillac chose this moment not to start, which initiated some panicky jump lead balletics between the two of them. Eventually James too was on the move, and another pickup full of angry locals took off after him and Jeremy. By now the rocks were starting to hit Hammo's car and the camera cars. At this point everything in Ian the camera-man's world and my world became scary *and* Laurel and Hardy all at the same time. I jumped into the camera car I'd been driving, saw it was full of crew and sped off, rocks smacking into the tailgate and sides as we left. Meanwhile, Ian, who'd bravely been filming till the last, finally called it a day, grabbed his camera and jumped into the passenger seat of our car, shouting 'Go go go!' at me as more rocks hit the van. The only problem was, I didn't hear him . . . because I wasn't there. I'd jumped into the wrong car and sped off. Ian was now staring at an empty driver's seat, with more rocks bouncing off the back. Cue running yet more redneck gauntlet as he scooted round to the driver's side, then set off after us, powered by four-star unleaded and hatred for me.

Meanwhile, a few miles up the road, James had somehow got ahead of Jeremy but the two of them were still being chased by the pickup truck stuffed to bursting with upset locals. Jeremy then overtook James, giving the angry pickup people a front-row view of James's boot, bearing the words, in Hammond's elegant handwriting: 'NASCAR sucks.' The three cars ploughed on at speed until mercifully a police cruiser lit up his lights and intervened, and the redneck express duly made off.

Soon the whole convoy was reunited, parked around James, Jeremy and the police cruiser, as all of us vigorously removed the slogans from the sides of the star cars.

The police patrolman was much more tolerant than he needed to be. For sure he was not pleased by our fuck-wittery, but he didn't press the point. Instead he gestured at the wide sweep of empty, endless countryside before us, and said gravely: 'You see all that out there, if you end up out there with the wrong people, then . . .' he spread his hands in resignation '. . . I can't do anything for you.' Nobody asked him to elaborate.

His next advice, and it was definitely more of an order than advice, was to get the hell out of Alabama right now.

Our convoy hit the highway and, with the Mississippi state line just a few dozen miles away, we all started to breathe a collective sigh of relief. However, Mother Nature clearly had relatives living near that Alabama petrol station, because she swept in to punish us. In an almost theatrical fury the skies turned black and then dumped the most intense rainstorm upon us. There's a well-worn cliché about the rain being so heavy that there's no oxygen between the drops, and that's exactly how it was. It hit so hard you thought the windscreen would break. Our windscreen wipers, thrashing back and forth at full tilt, were barely coping. Then Hammond's panicked voice came over the radio. His wipers were non-existent. He was totally blind, but nor, given what we'd just left behind, did he want to pull over and stop. Since we were right in front of him we tried to become his eyes, telling him to steer left or right whenever he veered out of his lane, and instructing him to brake whenever we did, just hoping he wouldn't crash into us and take us both out. This sequence was featured in the film but my God, the power of television, mighty as it may be, did not convey one tenth of the tension of guiding a totally blind man at the wheel of a two-ton pickup, on a highway full of other cars, through that storm.

Having made her point, Mother Nature called off the storm and so ended our most stressful filming day ever. But, every cloud and all that, when Boycie and I cut the film together back in London, we realised there wasn't a hope in hell of making this twenty-five-minute film any shorter than an hour, and the 'Top Gear Special' was born.

Not only that, the film had well and truly cemented the role of the cheap old underdog car as the main cornerstone of the Specials to come. Jeremy's love letter of a piece to camera to his bashed-up Chevy towards the end of the film, where he compares coping with the foibles of the Camaro to living with a tricky back door in an old farmhouse – of how it only opens with a certain kick that only the owner knows – remains for me his absolute best. Any casual viewer with little interest in cars who had stopped by for some Sunday night entertainment now witnessed a masterclass from all three of them in bringing four wheels and a seat to life. You didn't have to understand cars, you didn't have to own a nice example or even be any good at driving one. You would though, get pulled into caring about a beat-down dog that, in our hands, could become Rocky Balboa.

The feature-length road trips from this point on became an important *Top Gear* fixture, our poor man's version of *The Morecambe and Wise Christmas Show*. For the next one we chose Botswana, and in contrast to its American predecessor, that shoot was utterly blissful. Obviously the setting was beyond beautiful and Kubu Island, the ancient gathering of rocks and trees in the middle of the Makgadikgadi salt flats, remained the trio's favourite destination for the next twenty years. However, a huge part of that film's joy was, for us, down to the simplicity of making it. As with all things that rise in ambition on TV, the Specials would, over the years, require more props, more planning and more people, but back then the Botswana crew was tiny. We hadn't even thought – world's biggest car show – to bring a mechanic on a road trip involving three old shitters crossing the middle of Africa. Luckily, though, the minicam operators, Jonathan and Gary, were old car nerds and ended up spannering when required. I think apart from finding a local driver to play the part of the Stig's African cousin, we planned absolutely nothing. Stuffing James's car with raw meat before heading into the wild animal-filled bush – that was Jeremy having a light bulb moment as he passed a butcher's shop while hunting for bits and bobs to make his car animal-proof.

Actually I tell a fib about pre-planning. We did – but at very short notice, like an hour before – plan that Hammo should drive Oliver, his little 1963 Opel Kadett, into a deep part of the river, but God clearly prefers his *Top Gear* made properly on the fly, so punished us by making Richard forget to switch his in-car cameras on when he drove in. Loads of panic from Hammo, oodles of Meryl Streep-level shouting and drama as his car sank, and not a second of it on film. That meant we had to drag him out and do it all over again, and this in turn meant the engine now had so much water damage that we had no idea whether he could get Oliver going again.

When the show went out plucky little Oliver became a star in his own right: if we made that film today he'd have a TikTok account and be on *Love Island*. It was Jeremy's

Lancia Beta, however, that set a new standard for our now firmly established trope of old shitters battling the odds. Not one electrical wire, not one mechanical part in that car was on speaking terms with the bit next to it. Richard and James absolutely did not know, come the climax of the film, whether Jeremy would arrive at the finish line in the Beta or the Beetle. Their guess was honestly as good as yours.

Next in line for our Specials odysseys was Vietnam, a film which many fans consider to be the best, but unlike Botswana there was no honeymoon vibe to the making of this one. Vietnam, for me, was extremely fraught.

The problems hit us before we'd even left England. Keen students of our work will remember that the Vietnam Special was in the same series as the Cheap Lorry Challenge film, where each presenter bought a five-grand lorry and did lorry-driver type things. In the early parts of filming all went well, then we got to the shooting of the final sequence. This climactic moment involved each presenter testing the toughness of their lorries by driving them through a big obstacle, and Jeremy had opted for a brick wall. The team in the office hired a local brick-layer to build the wall on the track down at Dunsfold, but unfortunately none of us thought to brief him or supervise him and as a result the brickie, keen to do a sterling job for Britain's favourite car show, built us something slightly stronger than the Great Wall of China. Now obviously none of us knew this until the moment Jeremy drove through it. You'll maybe have seen it on the film: truck hits brick wall, the interior of the cab takes the impact with a volcanic massive bang, and the whole pedal box is pushed violently upwards into Jeremy's foot and shin, causing him to shriek in agony.

We got him to a doctor, who diagnosed hefty damage to the foot and the ankle, and his orders were straight-forward: total rest for at least a week. This was a bit of a problem, given that we were all due to fly to Vietnam in just over twenty-four hours to shoot the Special, and in return the doctor was aghast when told what was on the menu for Jeremy's foot. Not only did he do his nut about the prospect of a ten-day scooter ride on Vietnamese roads, he wouldn't even allow Jeremy to fly in case there were deep vein complications.

Fortunately, the *Top Gear* parallel universe we lived in didn't just give us the right to sink amphibious cars, fire Minis down ski jumps and generally live permanently as nine-year-olds. It also encompassed medical matters. And so, having listened to the doctor's orders, Jeremy rang me and said: 'Fuck it, flight's booked, crew's booked . . . let's just go.' His own, well-founded medical diagnosis was that, far from kickstarting a burst of deep vein thrombosis, a nice hefty long-haul flight was actually an opportunity to lie down, watch movies and wash down painkillers with a bucket of Minuty. I mean, he's a persuasive guy – you've read his columns – so we decided not to worry BBC

Health and Safety with any bothersome paperwork from his doctor and flew out of Heathrow as planned.

Once we started filming, however, the shoot turned gnarly quite quickly. Problem one was caused by our organisational naivety. We in the office had recced the route beforehand, and when you do that you estimate the time it will take to cover the distances according to a homemade *Top Gear* formula. So for example, if it takes a normal civilian say, eight hours to cover 320 miles, we would add another five or six hours to do the same distance in order to allow time for filming stops and breakdowns. In Vietnam we'd calculated that we'd manage an average of 20–25 mph. However, once Richard, James and Jeremy got on the roads on their bikes, with Jeremy literally having just taken his scooter test, the best we were managing was 20–25 kilometres an hour. On top of that there was simply nowhere for a film crew to stay outside of the places we'd recced. You couldn't just say: 'Oh well, it's 9 p.m., let's book in here for the night,' because there was no 'here'. We simply had to keep ploughing on until we got to wherever, and even if that was midnight there were still scenes to shoot, after which the crews would slump off for a few hours' kip, knowing we'd now be on the road the next morning even earlier than planned. Amidst all this Jeremy was pottering along unsteadily on his scooter, on dark potholed roads, with his ankle and shin sending out shooting stabs of pain because – who knew – our medical assessment hadn't been as accurate as his doctor's.

But the physical pain wasn't the worst of it. More damaging was the fact that he and I were becoming more and more disconnected. I was in my van, trying to deal with the fact that all the local drivers were about to go on strike whilst at the same time Jeremy was alone in the dark on his scooter, with a bollocksed ankle, the only one of us thinking about where the story was going and what content we needed to shoot. Unequivocally he had the worst of it, and the bigger point, because without story we were nothing. Without story, the shoot would just become an exercise in getting a film crew from A to B.

Such was the pressure, he even started to descend into his own miniature *Apocalypse Now* madness. We'd just finished filming a scene with the Stig's Communist cousin – a segment we knew immediately would end up on the floor because it was so shit – and he saw a massive storm cloud in the distance, and started shouting manically: 'Rain! Rain over there! We have to get into it! Film me in it!' and then set off at high speed towards the storm. All the camera kit was spread out all over the place on account of the scene we'd just shot, so no crew could follow him, and he'd also forgotten to turn his own little bike camera on, which meant Jeremy dived into the biblical tropical rain, shouting and emoting for all he was worth, to an audience of himself and a couple of baffled locals.

Everything came to a head late one night when he needed to shoot a scene and I refused to send enough cameramen to cover it, meaning the shooting took even longer. He completely lost it with me. It was the worst and most distressing argument we'd ever had, finishing – quite theatrically it has to be said – with the lift doors closing between us as both of us said: 'Fuck you.' 'No, fuck you.'

Whilst I'm here though, I must pick up on something an ex-fixer on the Vietnam shoot wrote recently. He too notes that it was a stressful shoot and said Jeremy spat at me. That never happened. We had a barney, as I've said above, but nobody spat at anybody. And anyway, we were far too tired to muster up phlegm.

Early next morning Jeremy and I found ourselves sitting on the steps of the hotel, both distressed about having argued so badly, both having not slept. It was clear, when we took a moment in the light of day, what the problem was. This type of film had gone up a notch in terms of scale, it had caught us out and we were now once again playing catch-up. We both talked about the respective mind monsters running around in our heads, realising in turn we hadn't seen the other's pain. I apologised for the schedule being a fuck-up and we agreed to rip it up and make a new one.

'Come on then,' he said, draining his coffee and stubbing out his cigarette. 'Fresh start. Let's get to work.'

'I'd love to,' I replied, 'but we haven't got any film kit with us. The local drivers have gone on strike.'

He thought about that for a second and then: 'Fuck it, big breakfast it is then.'

After that the shoot turned itself around. The BBC accounts department got a call telling them the filming

-days would be going up, the scenes we shot started to be funny again, the adventure was adventurous and Vietnam gave us a beautiful backdrop.

As we progressed further north, Jeremy and I even perfected our own air-to-air cigarette system that allowed him to have a smoke on the move. I'd light up a Marlboro, lean out of the van window, he'd pull alongside on the Vespa with mouth already open, I'd pop the ciggie in and he'd veer off. I don't know whether this made him cocky but shortly after, as evidenced by millions of viewers, he binned the bike whilst riding along in a straight line.

On the topic of arduous journeys I want to say, for the record – because some online jurors have questioned this point – that on those Specials Richard, Jeremy and James drove every mile of every journey. Every mile to the magnetic north pole, every mile across Iraq, Syria, Burma, Uganda, Vietnam, India, Botswana, Chile, Bolivia and so on.

Now obviously one could argue that sitting down and changing gear is hardly up there with a shift in a Siberian salt mine, but some of those roads were utterly brutal, in cars that went out of their way to double the pain and misery.

Richard's old Toyota Land Cruiser in the Bolivia Special springs instantly to mind. At one point when we'd been driving for hours in the mountains in the darkness, with many more hours still ahead of us, I jumped in with him thinking it would help to ride shotgun and keep him awake. The road was bad, for sure, but I have never, ever been in a car that banged and clanged and rattled and squeaked and shrieked so deafeningly and so relentlessly. It was a mobile Guantanamo Bay, and he'd been putting up with it for days. What I did realise quite quickly, though, was that there was no way in hell he would fall asleep in that torture chamber, so I made my excuses and popped back to the serenity of the filming car.

When we finally did call it a night on those brutal drives, we were hardly checking into the Savoy. One night in Bolivia, with no hope of reaching a camping ground, we pitched our tents on either side of a dirt track in the middle of a jungley nowhere. Pretty soon a couple of unfriendly chaps arrived and demanded, through our fixer, that we pay a tax. We looked around us: mud, leaves, insects, mud, more insects . . . I mean, a tax for what?

We did, on this Bolivian trek, finally manage to stay in a . . . you couldn't call it a hotel, it was more some planks of wood arranged in room-shape formations, set in a clearing. The electrical wiring looked like it had been done by Jeremy when he was seven, but that aside there were beds, and some of the rooms even had a bog, which was obviously a godsend after several days of crapping with a shovel. Clearly some of the staff working at the lodge valued them too, as evidenced by Clarkson, who was lying on his bed when a maintenance chap strolled into his room, uttered a cheery 'Buenos días', then sat on his lavatory and took a dump.

'It's for Charity . . .'

To the outside world Comic Relief – Red Nose Day – is a gargantuan television extravaganza. A whole night with both channels featuring contributions from the country's biggest stars.

Behind the scenes at the BBC, though, it's got the machinations of a village fete. Busy people with a lot on are pressganged – via gentle emotional blackmail – in the same way the parish council might drum up contributions for the Bring and Buy stall: 'I know you're busy . . . but we don't need you to make anything fancy, just a lemon drizzle cake.' And now *Top Gear* had become big, we too were expected to get the baking tray out.

When the call came, asking us to make a half-hour one-off show, I immediately said sorry, but no – we were far too busy with the next *TG* series. Then management unleashed the nuclear warhead: 'Understood, you're all up to your neck, completely get that, but would you mind just coming over to see Richard, just so that we can all talk it through?'

This Richard was Richard Curtis, he of *Four Weddings*, *Blackadder* and *Notting Hill* fame, and co-founder of Comic Relief.

'Oh shit,' I announced to the office. 'They're properly turning the wick up now. I've got to go and see Richard Curtis.'

I was then bombarded with a barrage of protests and

stern warnings, all along the same line of: 'Do not bend! Do not give in! We haven't got the time!'

'Jesus, relax will you. What do you take me for?' I countered as I headed for the door.

'Honestly, if you come back and say we've got to make another show . . .' warned Rowland sternly.

'Oh my God, guys. It's me! I've got your backs!'

Over at Comic Relief HQ I sat down opposite Richard Curtis, my spine stiff with firm resolve. The creator of some of the greatest comedy ever then began by congratulating me on *Top Gear*, telling me how entertaining . . . and funny . . . it was. As he spoke I distinctly felt my spine detach itself and clatter to the floor. Two minutes later I was eating out of his hand.

Back at the office I delivered the news they'd all dreaded; cue chorus of 'Judas', 'Twat', 'Judas Twat' . . . Once this had finally died down, we set to work.

Fortunately Jeremy, James and Richard were out on a shoot, which meant that that night in the hotel bar they could turn their minds to the matter, and in the morning rang back with a plan:

'We want to do *Top Gear* meets *Ground Force*,' said Jeremy. 'I mean, *Ground Force* is a great show, and everything's quite gentle and considerate about it, so just think what fun we could have fucking up some celeb's garden?'

Now, if you've never seen *Ground Force*, its schtick is that a friend of a member of the public nominates that person to have their garden spruced up and made over. When that person goes off innocently to work a team of expert gardeners move in, do up their garden with new paving and plants and flower beds, the person returns home at the end of the day, bursts into tears of surprised joy and everyone clinks a celebratory glass of champagne. Cue credits.

All of that seemed perfectly doable, except for one fly – actually make that an eagle – in the ointment. The work we intended to do would definitely *not* be an improvement. How could we find a celeb who would take it on the chin when he or she came home to find their garden completely bollocksed?

Logic said that the most likely victims would be people who were very close to Comic Relief – board members, ambassadors and such – who would have no choice but to take one for the team.

Eventually, this avenue of research whittled us down to one candidate: Sir Steve Redgrave, five-time Olympic gold medallist for rowing and the most decorated male rowing-type person in Olympic history. Much more important to us, though, was the fact that he had a garden and his wife, Lady Ann, was up for being in on the whole charade. Once Sir Steve had left the house she would let us in and the garden was ours.

On the appointed day, the Top Garden Gear Ground Force team assembled, early morning, near his house. As we watched Sir Steve drive past, heading for a day of meetings in London, we prayed he wouldn't see anything out of the ordinary about the humungous collection of diggers, flatbed lorries and concrete mixers filling up his local layby.

Once he was out of sight, action stations. Off we set, up his driveway for ten hours of horticultural anarchy.

As the day rolled on, though, it became clear that Mrs Redgrave – who had been fantastically game for the high jinks at the start of proceedings – was now getting a bit jittery about our delinquency, maybe thinking we were going a bit further than she'd envisaged.

Her worry was that Sir Steve was a very fastidious type of man, a man who liked order and everything to be just so. Then she added: 'And he really doesn't like surprises.'

I surveyed the garden. A part of his lawn was now concreted over. The new garden shed we'd built was now a smouldering ruin, after being blown up by rocks from the new rockery we'd laid. In the corner a brass band was standing in the flower bed, belting out the traditional *Ground Force* music 'as live'.

'Christ. It's a bit late now,' I replied.

I reassured her that Comic Relief would put everything back to good as new afterwards and told her that Jeremy had had a lot of experience in calming people who had got cross with him.

Ann was very understanding and left us to get on with preparing our grand finale. In essence, for this, Jeremy had installed a water feature – a regular highlight on the real

Ground Force. The plan was that when Sir Steve returned and he and the presenters were standing with their champagne, toasting the new garden, Jeremy would switch on the water feature, but, because ours came with added special effects, the cherub on the top would shoot into the air and land on the new greenhouse we'd also built him, causing a few of the glass panes to break and fall out. Cue a panto round of 'whoops, sorry about that', then end of show.

We got everything done just as Steve's car came back up the driveway. Mrs Steve had her fingers crossed as he walked round the corner, into a smiling Jeremy, Richard and James, saying: 'Ta-da!'

Sir Steve surveyed the scene in complete silence. I have never seen such contained rage. He looked at the grinning presenters with murder in his eyes, walked past them and went indoors.

Whilst Jeremy and the Comic Relief people went after him to try and calm him down, I started to ponder a bit harder: maybe as hard as I should have done two weeks earlier.

He rows for a living, I thought. In his career he must have rowed over thousands of hours, for thousands of miles. Backwards. As with all Olympians, the difference between success and failure would be measured in tiny increments: inches, tenths of seconds. If you operate at that kind of level, you don't have any space in your head whatsoever for arsing about.

We had properly bollocksed this one.

Amazingly though, when Steve eventually emerged from the house he was wearing something close to a smile. He'd calmed down, the whole 'it's all for a good cause' speech had sunk in, and he was even okay to film the final scene. And so, Sir Steve, Ann and the three presenters all took up position with their champagne glasses, ready to pop the cork and say a cheesy 'Cheers!' when the water featured was switched on.

As everyone was getting ready, I did one final check with the pyrotechnics guy who had rigged a few of the greenhouse window panes to break.

'You didn't go daft did you?' I asked. 'Just double checking.'

The face he pulled was the wrong one: 'Eh? I thought you wanted a bit of a proper finish.'

It was too late. At that second the water feature started up and the little cherub sailed into the air. Then, in one of our greatest ever unfeasible moments – and we've had a few – the tiny cherub landed on top of the greenhouse and all the glass panes exploded outwards, with the force of that helicopter explosion on top of the building in *Die Hard*. Glass fired out in all directions, carpeting what was left of the lawn with thousands of fragments. Sir Steve looked on, now too stunned to commit murder.

I turned to the Comic Relief chap: 'I think these repairs, you may as well just get him a whole new garden.'

He didn't disagree.

New World Order

Fortunately, back with our Specials hats on, it seemed the mood around the rest of the world was much more peaceful than in Sir Steve's garden.

Often the four of us are asked to choose our favourite Specials and as it's me writing this book, I'll put my top two as The Three Wise Men and Burma.

It wasn't just the fact that this brace of films was sprightly and entertaining, it was also because they represented a world which, for a brief moment, seemed to be a nicer, friendlier place. Looking back, that window of niceness was indeed brief: around five years between 2010 and 2015, but in that time the petty, small-minded thinking – be it from a Farage, a Trump or any Fundamentalist – that seeks to divide cultures and to smother curiosity had taken a back seat.

It was in this climate that Jeremy bounded into the office excitedly one morning, stole my chair without asking and declared: 'Next Special. It's going out at Christmas. There are three of us . . . We are the Three Wise Men.'

Brief flurry of high-fiving, then we got to working out a route. Obviously Bethlehem was the finish line, but where had the OG Three Wise Men started out from? All the scholarly research pointed to Iran, a country we dearly wished to visit, but although the world was indeed opening up, Iran was the one place that hadn't got the email and we knew we'd be refused. What about Iraq though? First three letters were the same as 'Iran' and it *was* in the Middle East. Off we went down to the Iraqi embassy with our Polite Trousers on, and sure enough, got permission. We were also given the thumbs up to film in Syria, which meant we now had a plausible route: start in northern Iraq, nip through the bottom of Turkey, down into Syria, over to Jordan, then bish bash bosh into Israel and Bethlehem. Obviously we knew this was unlikely to match the journey taken by the original Three Wise Men, but it was a safe bet that no theological scholar was ever going to waste brain cells watching our nonsense, and everyone else on Boxing Day would be too drunk to notice.

With the route settled, more delightful elements weaved their way in. One evening Al Renton, the series producer, said to me: 'The Baby Jesus. It has to be the new Stig. We find him in the manger in Bethlehem.' This was a genius thought. We'd recently parted ways with our existing Stig, Ben (I'll get to this in a later chapter), and the question of how to replace him in a suitably surreal Stig-like fashion had been vexing us. Now Al had cracked it. The only problem was BBC management: how would they feel about this radical re-interpretation of the New Testament? As ever, I decided the best course of action would be not to bother them.

At this point I must once again hand over the story-telling to the film you saw. We have the spectacular intro-ductory sequence with the door of the Ilyushin cargo plane opening in mid air to reveal three screaming Wise Men in their three grand roadsters, the scary arrival in Erbil Airport in Iraq (bit hammy with the flak jackets when you look back but we can't get everything right), and then onwards through the breathtakingly beautiful and friendly region of Iraqi Kurdistan.

Naturally there was a fair bit of health and safety faff around the cargo plane sequence, but from memory not quite as much as there was about eating the local salad. The medics told us to avoid this at all costs as, given it would have been washed in the local water, our W1A tummies would simply not cope.

Come day three, however, none of us had had any trouser accidents, so one evening after a beer or two and now very smitten with all things Iraq, I extended a hand of friendship to the salad on the buffet table. It went down fine, I had another beer and chatted with the crew, and then suddenly I felt a bit of jostling in the bowel department; nothing catastrophic, but enough for me to make my excuses and head back to my room. Now as it happened we were staying in the most surreal location, an abandoned theme park, with the accommodation consisting of little chalets spread out all over the place. Mine was an eight-minute walk – it's forever burned into my memory – from the restaurant. At about four minutes into the journey the commotion in my bowels had escalated from a rumble into a full-on pub fight: tables tipped over, chairs through windows, the lot. At this point, the dilemma I'm sure many of us have faced at some point kicked in: continue at a steady pace so as not to cause further unrest, but take longer to reach sanctuary, or speed up and risk the pub fight becoming a full-on tear gas and water cannon riot, but hopefully making it to the porcelain palace in time.

I opted for the latter.

And it worked.

Nearly.

I actually did make it to my front door, but then as I was fumbling with the key, my inner plumbing was in such a state of medieval warfare that my brain just said to my bottom: 'It's all good, he's made it. He's on the loo.'

I'm sorry about the next bit – blame Penguin, they did insist they wanted behind-the-scenes stories for this book – but yes, in a word, never in human history has a person shat himself so much, whilst standing outside a front door in his clothes. In fact it was still going on, and now visibly pouring over my shoes, as a chambermaid walked past. I smiled gormlessly and gave her half a thumbs up.

'Do you need anything, sir?'

'No, no, nothing. All fine, thank you.'

The only silver lining in this brown cloud was that a couple of days later Richard helped himself to a nice plate of salad, and duly took over from me in using up all the bog roll of the Middle East.

Bowel issues notwithstanding, we entered Syria and arrived in the city of Aleppo, and this is where the memories become very sad – for the presenters, for the crew, for everyone. Aleppo was one of the friendliest, warmest places you could ever wish to visit. Jeremy, Richard and James, when shopping around for stuff with which to modify their cars for the desert crossing, were showered with greetings and offers of help from every quarter. Cafés invited them in for free teas and cakes, locals into their houses for the same. Then a young chap approached James and said shyly: 'Welcome, Mr Slowly.' It was the funniest and most beautiful moment.

The following days were pretty heavenly too. In the desert the whole cast and crew camped out under the stars and Jeremy, who loves, and I mean *loves* a desert above any other setting, wandered off into the depths of it at night-time, just to soak up as much . . . desert, as possible. Then we all – the whole crew of around fifty – settled down for the night in one ginormous tent.

Even James cracking his head open when the tow rope knocked him over couldn't dampen our spirits, especially with the *Carry On*-style chaos that surrounded him when we arrived at hospital. And accordingly, the next day, we added to the *Carry On* spirit with Jeremy and Richard turning up dressed in burqas.

And to top it all, we got to drink in the splendour of the ancient city of Palmyra.

To put it simply, those days in Syria were some of our very happiest on a shoot. But just a few years later, we're watching on the news as Palmyra is used as target practice by ISIS, and as for Aleppo, one of the oldest inhabited cities in the world and remembered by us for its well of kindness, it's bombed and shelled to rubble and its inhabitants flogged, tortured and thrown off buildings by yet more ISIS. I don't have the insight or eloquence of Jeremy Bowen so I'll stop here, but Syria will always have, for *Top Gear*, the most painfully bittersweet memories.

With the Three Wise Men filming complete, myself and the editor cut the show together and then naturally the BBC execs, given that this was 'the Nativity as done by *Top Gear*', wanted to have a good look at the film before it went out. And . . . we still hadn't told them about Baby Stig.

Two of the very biggest execs came to the edit suite for the viewing and to their credit thoroughly enjoyed what they saw, stopping only to scribble the odd note when Jeremy and Richard appeared dressed as Middle Eastern women and one of the Son of God's presents turned out to be a Nintendo Game Boy.

Then came our nativity scene and the camera cutting to the manger, to reveal Baby Stig.

Silence. Then laughter. Then silence. Then: 'Have you shot an alternative ending?'

'No we haven't,' I replied. We knew from experience that once the 'alternative' exists, its very existence can give oxygen to the arguments of the doubters and worriers, so best not to go there in the first place.

The two execs were actually surprisingly relaxed about the whole thing, but a *Top Gear* Christmas Special was now quite an event in the schedules. The audience would likely be around 8 million and by now – although we were sworn to secrecy at the time – we were even sending a DVD of the Christmas show up to Sandringham, for some Royal Family viewing.

Anyway, the show was given a once-over by a BBC ecclesiastical specialist (who knew?) and finally it was decreed that were it to be transmitted, none of us would burn in Hell.

As it turned out, around 2,000 viewers thought we should though, because that was the number who complained. But . . . what if we were right, and the baby Jesus actually was a tiny anonymous racing driver? I mean, nobody knows for sure.

I shall finish (for now), my wander down the Specials memory lane by telling you a bit about my other favourite: Burma, or Myanmar if you're a BBC newsreader.

What a country of contrasting wonderment. I think it was the only time that *Top Gear* went on 'a Special' where we also felt like explorers in a lost world.

The moment we struck out into the lush countryside from Rangoon with our trio piloting their second-hand lorries, our mobile phone signals all dropped, *Hot Fuzz* style, to nothing, and stayed that way until we crossed over into Thailand ten days later, where they all erupted again as if to say: 'Where were you?'

As for the rest of that shoot, to me now, it's like one of those collages your phone puts together from your photo library, full of rich and contrasting memories.

One morning, for example, we were driving along in a lush, remote part of the sticks, when a man staggered drunkenly into the middle of the road. We slowed down so as not to hit him, and when he came up to my window, clearly distressed, his hands out, begging, I grabbed a bottle of water and some snacks. 'Don't put your window down!' barked our fixer urgently over the radio. 'He has rabies! Move on!'

Feeling utterly helpless we complied, all our vehicles skirting round the poor soul as he wandered about hopelessly on the hot tarmac. The fixer told us that since there was no medical way of treating him out here, the villagers would have cast him out and left him to die.

Then, in complete emotional contrast, presenters and crew all slept that night on the floor of a Buddhist temple. It was the perfect temperature, the mattresses were spot on, the temple itself serene and beautiful and at 5 a.m. we were woken by the world's classiest alarm clock: the sound of the monks, from little kids up to adults, filing in for morning prayers. Outside we had a hot water urn, a catering tin of Nescafé and another tin of powdered milk. At this point another observation from the wonderful writer A. A. Gill. He once said that good coffee is not about the quality of the beans, or the water, or the barista. Good coffee, he wrote, is all about context: where you drink it, who with, under what circumstances. And that morning, as we stood outside next to our big Nescafé tin, with the sun coming up over the temple, I finally knew what he meant.

Then there was the saga of the horses. If you remember the film, the three of them, short of fuel, had procured horses to go into town to find more and Richard drew the short straw. His horse was a stallion, young – therefore stupid – and with its gentleman bits fully intact. It was prancing around, testosterone spilling out of its ears, like a four-legged version of Jay from *The Inbetweeners*. To make matters worse its nose was about five feet from the back of James's mare. We were looking at an equine perfect storm and sure enough, when he tried to mount James's ride, Hammond hit the tarmac hard, with his arm taking the full force of the landing.

An hour later Richard, the fixer and I were at the local hospital, where Richard's wrist and forearm were X-rayed. Obviously I felt his pain – well actually I didn't because my arms were fine, but as I looked at my pal, sitting there in his eggy lorry driver's vest, his face wincing as he cradled his arm, it was pretty obvious he wouldn't be able to drive a knackered old lorry and I knew, in my role as the exec producer, where my responsibilities lay.

'Just going to talk to the doctor for a minute,' I said to Hammo softly. 'See if there's any news. You stay here.'

'Yeah, thanks, mate,' he said through his teeth.

Outside I found our medical man. 'Could you ask the doctor,' I said to the fixer, 'that if Richard's arm *has* got a fracture, then he could maybe tell him that it's not a fracture, but just a nasty sprain.'

As the doctor listened to the fixer his face became a mixture of frowning and bafflement.

'Obviously if it's a big fracture then yes, tell him it's a fracture,' I continued. 'But if it's a sort of smaller one, then can we say just a sprain? Richard doesn't like to make a fuss.' I then added that obviously for the doctor's troubles, I'd be happy to make a donation to the hospital. And of course, him.

As they were talking Richard came out to join us, asking what news there was. The fixer, completely unaware that there was Dick Dastardly shit going on, immediately said to him: 'We are just asking the doctor, if the fracture is not too big, to say it's a sprain.'

Hammond stared at me with resigned contempt: 'Wilman, you twat! Jesus God! Can you stoop any lower?' As it happened, I could. Since Plan A – lying – had failed, I then guilt tripped Hammond, saying how a whole huge film shoot would now grind to a halt, primarily because he couldn't stay on a horse. 'You live in Wiltshire. You're the one who's the horse rider!'

'For the last fucking time, I don't live in Wiltshire!'

'Whatever. You live where they ride horses!'

And so this bizarre argument continued until the X-rays arrived, which showed that there was, mercifully, no fracture and to the bafflement of the doctor and the fixer, our argument just switched off like a tap, and it was back to camp for beer.

Our Burmese road trip then took us into the most exotic area of this exotic country: Shan State. When I say exotic, I mean it in a Graham Greene thrillerish way. For decades this vast area in the east of the country had been a battleground for countless warlords fighting for control of the state itself and its richest natural resource, because Shan State is Burma's biggest opium producer.

The Burmese government, however, had recently persuaded several different Shan warlords to sign ceasefire agreements, peace had broken out and as a result we were the first BBC people to be allowed into the area in donkey's years. In all honesty when they heard 'BBC' they probably thought they were getting Jeremy Bowen, rather than Jeremy Clarkson, but *Top Gear* was what was on offer.

To give you one small example of how isolated Shan State was, when we camped up at the village where we were staying for the night, a group of girls soon started to appear, all carrying little cameras. 'Crikey,' we thought for a surprised moment, 'looks like we're known even out here.' The girls, however, walked straight past Jeremy, Richard and James and made a beeline for Hannah, one of our producers. What they all wanted was to be photographed with Hannah, because she was the first girl with blonde hair that they had ever seen in the flesh.

If you recall the film, this is also the place where we were invited, as honoured BBC guests, to the big evening gathering between two former rival factions.

Come the evening, the members of those two factions started arriving at the village and although there'd been a ceasefire, clearly nobody had said 'and can you also hand in your weapons.' There were rifles stacked everywhere. Then out came the beers and the local whisky, the gloriously named Hankey Bannister. This was the point at which Hammond got stuck in with some officers, and thanks to a cocktail of Hankey Bannister and painkillers, he was soon in la la land.

The rest of us were getting trashed cos ... just cos, and I remember at one point our security guy coming over, pointing at a pissed soldier and saying: 'I wish that twat would stop messing around with that grenade.' It was that kind of evening.

Come the wee small hours we all headed off to our beds, which was when we got the nightcap of all night-caps. As I was settling down our chief fixer came hurtling in in a complete panic and shouted at me to come with him immediately. Outside, at the edge of the clearing, there was a proper commotion going on: lots of shouting, lots of panicking. He told me that a local villager had been sitting near Hannah and, fired up by the hooch, had made a pass at her. He hadn't touched her, he'd just said some pissed-up words in his own language and Hannah wasn't even aware. The other villagers though, *were* aware, and outraged at him insulting a girl and distinguished BBC guest in this way, had dragged the chap into the bushes where – and now I understood the fixer's panic – he was going to get macheted. Besides me, Chris the Specials producer was there, and the pair of us, now stone-cold sober, started rapid firing our pleas into the heads of the villagers: 'Hannah didn't even know he'd made a pass so there was no way she could be insulted.'

'In our crappy country where we come from, girls get ten times worse than this in the pub on a normal Friday night.'

'If you do this, it won't give her any honour or make her feel better or anything like that. Instead she'll be scarred for life.'

On and on we pleaded, all the while against a backdrop of shouting and howling coming from the bushes. In the end, I guess, nobody wanted to actually hack this guy apart. It was a matter of saving face, and thankfully the logic behind our pleading gave them the excuse to back down. The desperate young man in his baggy red T-shirt was hauled out of the bushes and sent on his way. The rest of us milled about, fearful of re-inflaming any passions with our nervous presence, but not wanting to just go to bed either, because this wasn't like telling your neighbour to keep the music down. Finally though, we all crashed, and next morning the only real evidence of our Colonel Kurtz evening was Hammond's DEFCON 1 hangover.

So yeah. Shan State. If you ever go there and you're in Duty Free, my advice: leave the Hankey Bannister on the shelf and go for the Toblerone.

The *Top Gear* That Never Was

I'm aware I jumped around with the timeline when I was writing about the Specials, so let's return to 2008. We've shot three more series since Hammo's triumphant return, and the show is selling very well around the world. The only trouble is, we haven't really cracked America. Yes, we have a decent and extremely loyal cult following, but we're only shown on BBC America, and there's no money in that for anybody.

By contrast, *Strictly Come Dancing* has been rebadged and reformatted as *Dancing With The Stars* and is now being shown in America on one of the major networks, ABC, and making tons of cash for everyone involved. However – stick with me on this one – *Strictly* is attractive to big networks because it's easily formattable. You take the main components of the show, put local presenters and talent in, and bosh, you're away: American *Strictly*, Italian *Strictly*, North Korean *Strictly*, and so on.

Our problem, though, was the popularity of the trio. Viewers in other countries only wanted to watch Jeremy, Richard and James. So, if we were going to make some serious dollar money in America there was only one option: make an American version of *Top Gear*, starring our three, for a big American network.

It was decided therefore that a *Top Gear* deputation should go to the States to try and sell our sorry arses. The sales team consisted of:

- Wayne Garvie: a huge cheese at the BBC's commercial arm, BBC Worldwide
- Andy Wilman: supermarket shelf logistics executive, Sainsbury's

- Jeremy Clarkson: former Paddington Bear travelling salesman

Once we got to Los Angeles we began slogging round all the American networks – CBS, NBC, ABC – showing the execs a sexy sizzle tape of our past shows, then we'd sit back, wallets open, ready to discuss how much we'd like to be put in them.

Annoyingly though, the big networks were either not interested or lukewarm. One criticism was that Jeremy, Richard and James were too English, which then generated some quite random discussions:

TG Sales Force: 'Well, how much are we too English?'
Random American TV Exec: 'It's hard to say. But there's definitely something that's too English. You're all really English.'
*TG*SF: 'Gordon Ramsay's English. Everyone likes him. And he's really English.'
RATVE: 'Oh sure, Gordon's great. But there's something that works about him being English. Not sure with you guys.'
*TG*SF: 'Would it help if our three had a bit of a nip and tuck done? We admit they're a bit tatty round the edges. Maybe Jeremy gets his teeth done.'
Jeremy: 'What's wrong with my teeth?'
Wayne and Andy: 'Are you fucking joking?'

And so it went on. Meeting after meeting, in daft offices full of signed baseball gloves, all of them ending with: 'Let's pick this up another time.'

Admittedly a bit crestfallen, because we were used to being adored, we would go back to our nice hotel and bathe our bruised egos in wine. It had a cracking bar, we had a drink with Eric Bana and Jeremy even had one with Russell Crowe, but the difference here was that the Antipodeans were all in town because they'd got work, whereas we were too English.

Come day two or three we still had a few networks to visit but we were getting so frustrated that we decided to liven up the meetings by picking a band and trying to slip in the names of as many of their songs as possible without the network exec noticing. (I understand that the England cricket team also did this, but for the record, we were first. Just sayin').

First meeting of the day we went for the songs of 10cc, and if I may say so, we did pretty damn well slipping them past the goalie.

Random American TV Exec: 'So, how's your trip been so far?'

TG Sales Force: 'Up and down, but you know the old saying: life is a minestrone.'

RATVE: 'No, I've not heard that.'

*TG*SF: 'Nevertheless, we're very proud of our show. The things we do for love, eh? Dodging all the rubber bullets.'

So far, quite a high hit rate, but Sales Force member Clarkson then became fixated with getting the obscure 10cc song 'Donna' in. However, since we were talking to a bloke he couldn't exactly ask: 'Sorry, did you say your name was Donna?' So instead he took another route:

*TG*SF (Clarkson division): 'The way I see it, cars are, in a sense, like **doner** kebabs.'
RATVE: 'That's an odd one. How so?'
*TG*SF (Clarkson division): 'Well, you get a flatbread, and that's wrapped round a filling, but you can have different fillings, like lamb, or chicken, and you can have different sauces, but at the end of the day they're all still **doner** kebabs.'

And then, cos he doesn't have an off button:

*TG*SF (Clarkson division): 'I like chilli sauce myself, but if you get a big bit of chilli, you're like: 'Owww! **Doner** und blitzen!'

A text pinged up on my phone from Wayne: 'Fucking kill me.'

Come the next meeting though, we felt we'd got our eye in and were confident we'd have more success with our next batch of songs, which we'd chosen from the back catalogue of the Police.

> Random American TV Exec: 'We do a lot of work with Jane Root. Do you guys know Jane Root?'
>
> *TG* Sales Force: 'Jane! Do we ever! I tell you, every little thing she does is magic.'
>
> RATVE: 'So, how can we help?'
>
> *TG*SF: 'Well, we want to talk to you about making a US version of our show, and honestly, if we can get this right, we'll all be walking on the moon.'

The chat was actually pleasant but we were definitely rumbled when we got too cocky and tried to slip in 'The Bed's Too Big Without You'. At that point the penny dropped and we were on a countdown to 'Anyway, thanks for coming by. Let's think about this and talk again . . .'

For our final meeting we thought we'd raise the stakes and go for Culture Club.

Having sat down with the network exec, we set to work.

> Random American TV Exec: 'So you are talking to other networks. When would you be looking for an answer from us?'
>
> *TG* Sales Force: 'I mean we don't want to rush anybody but, you know, time is like a clock in my heart.'

She looked at us in a way that seemed suspicious. Maybe paranoia on our part, or maybe we'd sat down with LA's one Culture Club fan. Then we suddenly realised that Culture Club hadn't been thinking of us when they'd written their silly fucking esoteric song titles. There wasn't a single song in their back catalogue with a name like: 'We Want to Make a Car Show With You'. Nevertheless we had to persevere.

> RATVE: 'If you're filming your *Top Gear* and that's a big commitment . . .'
> *TGS*F: 'Tell us about it, sometimes it's a miracle that we get it done at all.'
> RATVE: '. . . so if it is a big commitment, how would you shoot a US version as well?'
> *TGS*F: 'I guess we'd just have to get it done. I mean, I'm sure some mornings we'll be like, blimey, do you really want to hurt me, but you know, those sort of thoughts are, you know, not productive.'
> Sales Force Wayne: 'Yes, like the sort of Church of the Poison Mind thoughts.'

At this point she'd had enough. Jeremy was still determined to land the golden prize, but as he started talking about how in the end it came down to karma, and that we could adapt because we were all chameleons, she gathered up her stuff and thanked us for our time.

Back at our nice hotel we sat in the bar, looking to

Steve the angry Aussie cameraman (right) and Ellis,
unit photographer, having his first go with a camera.

emy's early attempts at
ving his picture taken.

'So we bought this tent, and now I have to make
my clothes out of leftover bits of cloth.'

Early K-p
band in Bur

Camera Car C Pilates class.

'Apparently Mr Wilman
says it's only a sprain.'

're back!

Oh shit. That's a
BBC lawyer.

BBC lawyer aerial
reconnaissance.

Switzerland. Eight lives and counting.

A caveman discovering fire.

'Scandi Flick'. Seven Lives and counting.

John suffers in silence.

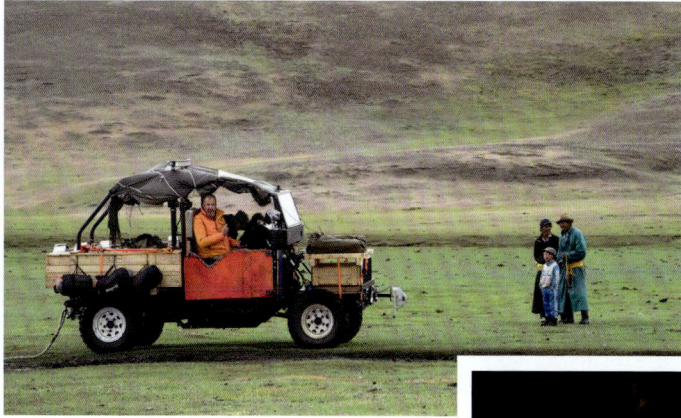
Our whole viewing audience in Mongolia
turn up for a meet and greet.

GT board meeting: Max, Joey,
Chenoa, Jeremy.

Chenoa. Employee
No.1 at *The Grand Tour*.

TV stars relaxing in
their luxury Winnebago.

Roger Moore
on the set of *Octopussy*.

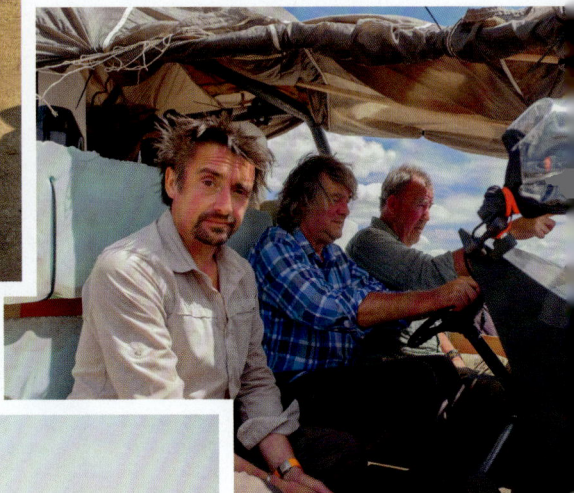

Three men and a steering wh

Director Phil Churchward and his
camera boys, Casper, Steve and Be

Russ, Nico and Marc. Extremely sound men.

per, Andy, Joey, Marc: Camera Car C.

Zimbabwe. Bus fare.

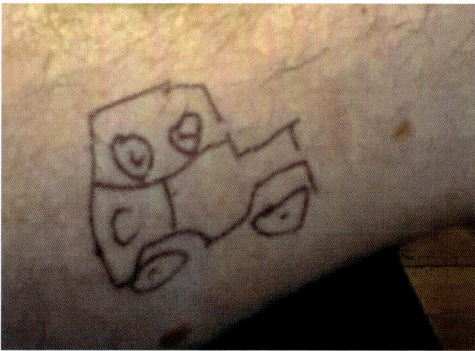

Advanced Prototype for
Camera Car C Tattoo.

e very surreal and final moment.

Camera Car C. The final drive.

Bedder Six concludes its motoring escapades.

see whether Cate Blanchett or Geoffrey Rush might be joining us, and when neither happened we got merry, then flew home.

Formula One Stars in a Reasonably Priced Car

If you ask me for my top five favourite studio moments, top of the list without question would be the moment Michael Schumacher revealed himself as the Stig. Close behind though would be Sebastian Vettel doing his impression of Nigel Mansell's Brummie accent.

All of this was made possible by virtue of our 'Formula One Star in a Reasonably Priced Car' segment, which gave F1 fans the chance to see the world's best drivers –including six world champions – as they always wished they could: on a level playing field in a 1.6 litre Liana.

Yet again, as with most of our successful moments, its creation came about not by planning but by accident.

In this case, thanks to my Lucky Pants.

Because I hated studio day so much – too much to go wrong, too far out of my skill set – I tried to turn the wheel of Fortune a bit more in my favour by always wearing the same underpants, as a sort of Marks and Spencer lucky charm. Before your thoughts go any further, yes, they got washed between shows, but also yes, I only wore those pants on record day.

Naturally the presenters and the whole *Top Gear* team got to know about them and, given everyone in the nervous telly world will take every bit of backup they can, the Lucky Pants became a Real Thing. If we had a good show, it was down to the pants. Accordingly, I was forbidden to turn up on Wednesdays without them.

Fast forward to another studio record and the Star in a Car that week is Davina McCall. At home I'm getting ready to drive down to the studio and I ask Amanda: 'Have you seen my lucky pants?' 'Oh bugger, I didn't put them in the wash,' comes the reply. 'And here's a tip: you could do your own washing now and again.'

Brushing aside this *Handmaid's Tale* rebellion, I thought about the pants situation and said, 'Nah, lucky or not, I'm not wearing dirty shreddies for a whole day. I'll just put some normal pants on and not tell anyone. It'll be fine.'

Then, and may God strike me down . . . just as I'm leaving the house the phone goes (landline, for our younger readers). It's Davina. And Davina can barely speak. She has lost her voice on account of being struck down with some sort of flu plague. She's desperately sorry but she has to pull out of today's guest slot. I put the phone down and stand there in stunned silence. Amanda has her hands over her mouth and can only whisper: 'The pants!'

It was now 8 a.m. That gave us four hours to find a replacement guest – not such a big problem if you're recording your TV show in London, but finding a celeb who is a) free for the whole day b) happy to schlepp down to Dunsfold right now and c) drive round a track in a manner they hadn't thought about doing – that is a tall order.

I phoned Jeremy. Neither of us had to spell out the gravity of the issue. The guest slot filled up around ten to twelve minutes of screen time, the films had already been edited to a precise length, and there was no way in hell that you could pad out the news section or the studio links to close a gap that big. We had to find another guest.

After a few minutes of the pair of us pointlessly naming famous people, we realised there was only one option: Damon Hill. We knew him, we had his phone number, he's incredibly amenable, he would be too Zen to worry about the fact he was being called in as a last-minute sub, he'd learn the track in a jiffy and . . . the 1996 World Champion lived down the road from Dunsfold.

There was, however, just one objection pushing back in our heads: we had made it a policy not to have motorsport stars as guests. Once we'd realised the show was attracting a broad audience, we didn't want to risk alienating that audience by being too geeky. Also, no shit Sherlock, the drivers would immediately populate the top of the leaderboard and Jennifer Saunders would see no point in coming down.

Right now though, our editorial principles had slammed face first into an unsolvable twelve-minute airtime gap, so . . .

'We have to call him,' I said.

'We do,' Jeremy agreed.

As Jeremy was about to ring off he suddenly asked: 'You've got your lucky pants on, right?'

'Course I have. Jesus. What do you take me for?'

Damon Hill, mercifully, was free and said he'd make his way over. We were back on track.

Down at the studio Jeremy's newspaper-deadline brain was now focused on finding a way of protecting our existing Star in a Car slot.

'We can't put Damon on the normal lap board,' he said, standing in the middle of the Portakabin, talking to no one in particular. 'We need to make a new lap board, an F1 lap board. We need a board!' etc., etc.

New lap board was duly cobbled together, Damon arrived and did his lap, then at 3 p.m. came the moment of truth, as Jeremy addressed the studio crowd:

'Time now to put a star in our reasonably priced car . . .'

Here goes nothing. How would our broad audience react?

I remember Jeremy saying: 'Damon Hill!' and then an absolute tumult of cheering and applause blowing the roof off the hangar.

Hammond, standing next to me off to the side, observed sagely: 'Honestly, we are fucking thick at times.'

Obviously Damon's time couldn't just sit there on its lonesome, so we went on the hunt for more F1 drivers. And, *Field of Dreams* style, with the lap board now built, they duly came.

Thinking back, it was actually quite gracious of them given that, although the spot was a bit of fun, they all must have had a gnawing worry about being compared to their peers in the same machinery. Everyone, that is, except for Räikkönen.

Kimi came along in 2012 when he'd returned to F1, driving for Lotus. If you've watched the interview, you'll have seen how his star power consumed the room. The love for him, for his curmudgeonly reticence and honesty, was so great, he only had to say 'Erm' and the crowd would break into applause.

Backstage, doing his lap, he also gave good Kimi.

Annoyingly it was a rainy day so we wouldn't be seeing him challenge for the top slot, but nevertheless we were expecting some Iceman magic. After he'd done several laps I went over to Nick, who was doing the timing. 'How's he doing?' I asked eagerly.

'Erm, well, not great,' said Nick, showing me the times. 'It's almost like he . . .' we both said '. . . can't be bothered' in unison. And sure enough, a few laps later, Kimi declared he'd had enough and headed off to his motorhome. Clearly people like Nick and I were more bothered about this than Kimi. My feeling of disappointment grew, and then duly propelled me into his motorhome. Inside it was warm and cosy, and Kimi had made himself at home in one of those La-Z-Boy chairs as used by Joey in *Friends*.

'Kimi,' I began, 'I can't tell you your lap time obviously, but how are you feeling about your laps?'

'They were fine,' he replied.

I pressed on: 'Well, if you went out again – and we have time – you could go faster. The thing is, the rain has eased off and if you look you can see the track is getting dryer...'

Kimi slowly eased himself up by the minimum distance required to be able to stare out of the window, surveyed what was clearly a drying track, then said, in the way only he could: 'No it isn't,' and settled back into the depths of his chair. No rudeness in his voice, no arrogance, merely a man saying: 'It's nice in here, and not nice out there.'

'Okay, well, that's a shame, right, I'll leave it,' I said, turning to go. Then – and I've never done this before or since – I thought, 'No.'

'Kimi,' I began again, this time more firmly. 'There's a lot of us on this show who are really excited about you coming back to F1 and it'll be the same with the audience; you must know that. If you don't go back out and try for a faster time, give it your best, then we – and you – will have to live with whatever time you've got now, knowing that Kimi could have been faster. And I think that will be a shame.'

Propelled on by my own nerves I was now sounding like Henry the Fifth the night before Agincourt, and the situation clearly didn't warrant that much melodrama. I finished speaking. Silence.

I felt like Road Runner in that moment when he runs

off the cliff and stares at the camera for a second, before plummeting.

Kimi stared at me impassively for a moment, then cracked into a smile and started to haul himself out of the chair. 'Okay, okay,' he said, heading for the door. 'Jesus, this is worse than Formula 1.'

Honestly, when his lap time went on the board – still not epic but better – I felt like a proud dad.

So that's Kimi at the laid-back end of the scale. Up at the other end of it was, I'd say, Jenson Button. Jenson came down twice and was as affable and charming as you'd imagine but boy did he sweat the details.

Jenson, bless him, had lots of racing-driver type questions. The only problem was, we didn't know the answer to any of them.

'What was the track temperature when Webber was here?' he asked.

'Don't know, I'm afraid.'

'Are the tyre pressures always the same for every driver?'

'Can't say. Probably, but you know, don't hold us to it.'

'What about fuel load? Is that always the same?'

'Erm, again, that's outside our information database parameters.'

When he asked to see our timing device and Nick, standing on the start/finish line, cheerfully waved his iPhone 3 in the air, Jenson knew at this point that the McLaren engineers would not be coming to save him, and that it was time to relax. We also didn't bother telling him that the front axle had collapsed at high speed twice, once with Lionel at the wheel, the other time with Trevor Eve. No point in overloading him with technical information; F1 drivers don't like that.

What else do I remember? Ah yes. Racing drivers know things that mere mortals don't. As you're aware, the identity of the Stig was always a closely guarded secret, but when he arrived, in full Stig gear, to show Mark Webber around, Webber immediately said: 'Oh that's Ben Collins.' He could just tell from his stance.

As for Vettel – if you haven't seen Vettel, go watch it. Easily one of the funniest interviews by *any* Star in a Car with, as I said, the highlight being his uncanny Nigel Mansell impersonation, a party trick he'd been taught to do by Adrian Newey.

Then there was Lewis. His star, as we know, is stratospheric these days, but I think we got him at the best time, at the beginning and end of his McLaren days. By 'best' I mean before the whole industry of superstardom had gathered him up in its arms. I'm sure he's a nice enough fella still today, but back then it was like having a fan on the show. His first visit was in 2007 at the end of his stunning rookie season, when he'd missed the championship by just one point. McLaren was more of an uptight team back then and religiously overthought any proposition, e.g. us asking if he'd come on the show. 'His main sponsor is Mercedes, he can't be seen in a Suzuki', etc. I mean, really. But it was

Lewis who cut through the McLaren nonsense, telling them firmly he wanted to be at the helm of the Liana.

Sadly for him that first outing was on a wet track, but even then he was sublime – particularly around the tricky second-to-last corner (effectively a motorway funnelling itself sharply into a narrow country lane) – posting a time in the wet only a tenth slower than Mansell in the dry.

After Lewis's guest spot was over, Rowland the *Max Power* kid and I went round the back of the hangar for a cigarette break. For some reason Lewis was with us and I remember he and Rowland, two young kids, animatedly comparing notes on spinners they were planning on buying for their wheels. Like I say, we had him at the best time.

The wet lap time remained an itch that he needed to scratch badly, and again he took control of his McLaren diary to come down a couple of years later, this time on a dry day, and became the first driver to post a lap time in the 1.42s. What I remember is that both times he was genuinely excited to be there. I'm no mind guru but for my ten penn'orth, Lewis has always led a life of discipline and control, be it either just him and his dad scraping together every penny to succeed in karting, or when he was at McLaren under the iron rule of Ron Dennis. *Top Gear* for him, then, was a treat, a grand day out.

I cannot bring this Formula 1 section to a close, though, without mentioning my F1 hero, Michael Schumacher. If you've seen his spot on the show you'll remember his famous Stig reveal in the studio, and also that he didn't drive the Suzuki Liana. We pushed for it, but that was never going to happen. The deal was that he'd happily do the Stig spoof reveal and do a Stig lap in something from the Ferrari stable, but no Liana. With the Stig reveal being the priority, we shook hands.

Now, one of the perks of having our *Top Gear* base at Dunsfold airfield was that, once the show hit the big time, 'A' list guests could fly in, rather than having to suffer the horror of a chauffeured limo with onboard TVs, rare cowhide upholstery, climate control and triple-filtered vodka.

Such was the case with the seven-time World Champion, who would be flying in from Europe on his big jet. Michael's pilot, a man one must assume to be more efficient than the atomic clock, had filed all the appropriate paperwork with the CAA and the Dunsfold flight control people and sure enough, come record day, Schumacher's Dassault Falcon started its descent approach on the precise bearings, at the allotted time.

Jeremy, Richard and I, on hearing the noise of the jet engines, went outside to have a look. It was, after all, always quite exciting to watch a plane land on our runway, especially one with Michael Schumacher in it.

As we stood watching, the jet engine noise suddenly changed from a 'we're about to land' whine to a much more urgent 'actually we've changed our mind and suddenly need to climb again' howl. All of us stared at the Falcon thundering back up into the ether, wondering what the hell had happened.

Then, overhead, the majestic roar of Michael's jet engines was replaced by the irritating lawnmower whine of a prop plane, specifically a Second World War Polish spotter plane owned by a Mr James May, and everything started to make sense. As it turned out, Schumacher's pilot – and the person on ground control – were quite surprised when, just as clearance for landing had been given, the voice of Mr May came over the airwaves announcing: 'This is Alfa Beta Peppa Pig . . .' and that he'd arrived for work and was coming in to land.

Once we'd eventually got Michael on the ground, he came over to sample the delights of our Portakabin office which, after eight years of service was, like our office, bursting at the seams with crap from past films that we couldn't be bothered to throw away.

Michael's manager, Sabine, indicated with a quizzical eye at something behind me on the floor. I turned to look at the humungous pile of porn mags that had spilled out in a heap. I tried to explain that these were a leftover prop from our lorry-driver film, where one of the challenge prizes was a year's supply of jazz mags, but try saying that convincingly to a powerful German woman who had not seen that particular film. Yes, it's as hard as you think it might be.

Meanwhile, Schumacher was sitting in the presenters' room, presumably wondering why we'd amassed such a gargantuan dead fly collection in the window bay, whilst his athlete's body gamely dealt with the fug of cigarette smoke generated by Jeremy and James.

Like many people, I'm extremely sad about what happened to Michael. It's the sort of moment that makes you think Fate is a complete prick.

I'll digress away from *Top Gear* for a minute because writing about Michael's Stig visit has brought back memories of another time Jeremy and I met him, that I'd like to share.

It happened back in 2000 when Jeremy and I were making our *Science of Speed* series for BBC One. We flew out to Mugello where he was testing for Ferrari, and it was the week before he flew out to Japan to try and claim Ferrari's first world title in twenty-one years. Basically all of Italy's eyes were on him to bring back the Holy Grail, so he had an awful lot on his plate. Nevertheless he'd agreed to our interview and asked us to meet him at his hotel after testing.

It was a four-star businessman's hotel, nothing fancy but the best in the area, and it had a bar. Not wanting to film Michael in a dreary hotel room, we asked the hotel manager if we could close his bar for us, and naturally the answer was no.

Then we told him it was so that we could shoot an interview with Michael.

The manager stared at us, then said: 'A moment!' and with fantastic Basil Fawlty theatrics, shooed every customer out of the bar.

We filmed our interview with Michael, who was charming, gave us more time than allocated, said he thought Hakkinen was easily as fast as him, and talked candidly about his dastardly bumping off of Jacques Villeneuve in the 1997 finale. He even, as a demonstration of his hand/ eye superiority, played slapsies with Jeremy.

Sabine the manager eventually signalled that time was up and we started packing away our film equipment. The only thing was, Michael didn't go. Eventually he asked: 'Does this bar stay closed until you leave?'

'Yes it does.'

'Oh in that case I'll stay and have a drink then.'

He then spent another half hour chatting with all of us, signing everything, and explained that since there was no way he could go out in Italy without being mobbed, being able to have a simple drink in a simple bar was quite the treat.

I'm nearly done with the fangirling. Fast forward a year, we have edited his interview for the *Speed* show and all we needed now was the relevant F1 footage to illustrate it. I put the requests in to Bernie Ecclestone's office, but Bernie wouldn't release the sequence of Schumacher walloping Villeneuve.

'That's ancient history, son,' he said on the phone, 'nobody wants to be looking at that anymore.' I pleaded with him, but Bernie was not for turning. Without that footage we were screwed.

Then, half an hour later, Bernie rang back. 'I've changed my mind,' he said. 'You can have the footage.'

As I gushed out the thank-yous he stopped me in my tracks. 'There's just one condition. All I need is Michael's blessing, in writing, that he's okay with me releasing it.' Down went the phone.

Jesus. Thanks, Bernie. Not holding out much hope, I contacted Michael's manager once more. This time Willi Weber, his other manager. Willi made it clear he was in the Bernie camp and would be advising Michael to say no, but did promise at least to put the question to him.

An hour or so later he rang back. 'Well, Michael isn't over the moon about it either,' (heart starts sinking) 'but, he also said he did agree to talk about it in the interview, so fair is fair, it would be wrong to refuse. Wait by your fax machine (google it) and I'll send something over.' Sure enough, a letter signed by Michael duly chuntered out of the machine shortly afterwards.

I'll stop now, but in my little saga of motoring adventures, that man will always be to me a 100 per cent purebred gentleman.

Where Were We?

Apologies, dear reader. My stroll down F1 memory lane has taken us well out of the timeline, so let's pick up around 2008 and 2009.

In this period we rediscovered our Big Race mojo. After the overblown Veyron v Plane affair, the purity of the GTR versus Bullet Train reinjected all the drama and excitement that had gone AWOL. The finish was almost as close as the Verbier race, but in the beginning had not looked to be that way, because when both teams set off from the west coast of Japan, it was a shoo-in that Jeremy's race would come undone once he hit the legendary Tokyo traffic. This in turn would most likely give Richard and James their first victory – or to put it more accurately, public transport its first victory. And if the car was to be beaten by anything, there was no shame in it being the mighty bullet train.

However, for a reason we still don't know, the Tokyo roads were zombie-apocalypse quiet that day, and the GTR sailed through the capital, bringing Jeremy back into contention, and yet another victory.

The most notable new string to our bow though was 'The Mr Needham Test'.

The context behind this was quite simple: as series after series had rolled by and the cocking about count had risen – £1,000 Police Cars, Railway Crossing Public Information film, British Leyland bangers, Rolls-Royce into a Swimming Pool, the list goes on – there'd been a marked increase in the number of frustrated viewers in cardigans, writing in (they always wrote, never emailed) to complain that we no longer did sensible road tests with useful consumer information.

Thus Mr Needham was invented: a fictional viewer writing the typical complaint letter, asking Jeremy to test a sensible car in a sensible manner. For Jeremy this was a gift. We actually could now tell the viewers about a sensible car, but construct the films so that the test starts completely straight and then escalates into complete *Top Gear* nonsense.

The first Mr Needham Test was on the Ford Fiesta, which began with an extremely straight *Top Gear* from the 70s drive about, whilst Jeremy drily delivered some facts and figures.

As a by the by, Mark Thompson, the then BBC Director of Television, later told us that when watching the car being driven boringly round a track, he turned to his wife and said: 'I knew it. I knew it. They keep spending money like there's no tomorrow, and now they've blown their budget and this is all they can afford to do.'

Mark, and 8 million others, then watched as the test grew into a full-on chase around a shopping centre against the Stig, before climaxing with the seminal *Top Gear* moment of the Fiesta spearheading a Royal Marines beach landing.

The Mr Needham Test was also a good example of why, I believe, twelve series down the road, we were still holding our huge audience. A lot of big shows are big because careful planning goes into their creation. Global blockbusters such as *The Apprentice*, *Survivor*, *Strictly* and *X Factor* have all their format points mapped and stress-tested to the last detail before they even see the light of day, which in turn means they hit the screen as fully formed shows. When that approach works, the shows are indeed hits. The one downside of a tightly for-matted show, though, is that eventually people tire of its predictability. New candidates and contestants only get you so far.

Our show, however: we'd been making it up as we went along. Some elements had been born out of a crisis moment – the Stig, the F1 stars; some by accident – the Specials; and as with Mr Needham, a clever response to a growing complaints bag. These organic developments not only kept the show fresh, but also helped make the loyal viewers think the show 'belonged' to them, because they were seeing it mutate as the years rolled by. Under that umbrella logic they would also see the presenters make jokes about ageing or getting fatter, and even apologising in the studio if we'd put out a boring film the week before. It wasn't a plan – by definition you can't plan organic growth – but it worked well for us.

Where absolutely none of this was working well was at home. As the films grew in size and ambition, life in the edit became brutal. We were now shooting at a ratio of something like 500 to 1, meaning for every one hour of TV we broadcast, we were shooting 500 hours of rushes. All of these had to be watched and assessed. The team had grown for sure, and we had fantastic new directors such as Phil Churchward, superb producers and researchers and very talented editors such as Jim Hart and Dan James and

Chris Denton, but it hadn't grown enough. The time-table also remained the timetable: ten shows a series, and we were now trying to cut huge cinematic films to the same schedule we'd had when putting together simple road tests in Series 2.

Worst of all, Jeremy and I were absolutely incapable of delegating. He would still write the treatments for all the films and the scripts for his own tests on top of all the brainstorming and studio and actual filming.

Likewise I remained resolutely hands on helming the office and at the coal face of the edit. We were basic-ally Ronnie Barker and David Jason in *Open All Hours*. Between us we could run a fruit and veg shop no problem, but *Top Gear* had now grown from a corner shop into Sel-fridges. For sure we took on more people, brilliant people, but neither of us handed our own stuff over, instead just taking on more. He was running Menswear, Household Goods and Perfumes, I was in charge of Womenswear, the Food Hall and the Toy Department.

On my side, the result was I'd be in the edit till 2 a.m. Then in again at weekends.

At home Amanda was sitting at home eating dinners for one every night, having put two young ones to bed, and neither of us were able to enjoy one second of this huge . . . noise, this success.

I had become an absent father and a thoughtless husband who refused to see any point of view other than my own. I was chasing financial security to a manic degree, and on top of that work was how I measured my self-worth, to a tragic degree.

Any offers of comfort or pleas for a saner working life from Amanda, I would reject in the most insensitive manner, because in my head if I dropped the *Top Gear* ball for one second, everything would be over. Only doing good work would save the day.

Around 2010 I started to believe that every ache, every cough, every little twinge the body offers up in a normal day was terminal cancer. I went to my doctor and tested his patience to the limit, pleading to see lung cancer specialists, throat cancer specialists, bowel cancer specialists. He'd refer me, the specialists would say nothing was wrong, and I'd walk out thinking: 'They must be shit, because they've missed it.'

It came to a head when I was back out in Los Angeles on *Top Gear* USA business, and I got up more than once in the night to go for a pee. Looking for a reason why, I got straight on the internet and fell straight down the worst kind of rabbit hole: peeing in the night can be a sign of diabetes type 2, and diabetes type 2 can be a sign of pancreatic cancer. There it was. Proof. I'd found the cancer that would kill me. I stayed up all night until my doctor started work at 9 a.m. UK time and rang him immediately. This time he'd had enough. He ordered me to go and see a psychiatrist.

The shrink, a very calm and sage old chap, listened to me pour everything out and was the one who pointed out to me that I was definitely being ruled by the demons of my early years. The way it manifested itself was that I now, unconsciously, believed life to be an endless series of traps, waiting to catch you out. No reward was ever actually going to materialise, because it was never deserved. On top of that, mentally beyond exhausted.

The work rate, I told him, would not change. However, knowing what was fuelling this death fixation, plus the antidepressants he put me on, did start to calm me down. On the minus side though, all they effectively did was bandage my mind up, so that I could carry on as before.

Megastars in a Reasonably Priced Car

One question I'm often asked is 'Who were the worst guests?' I've definitely got one candidate for that, whose name I'll not type out, but that one aside there were no unpleasant ones. The point is, being a *Top Gear* guest was like water finding its own level. If you commit to giving up a day of your time for a tiny fee and you also accept before-hand that you might make a tit of yourself on the track, then logic suggests you're up for it.

I can't possibly go chapter and verse on every star visitor so I'll run through some snapshots of my most memorable ones

Steve Tyler

The Aerosmith singer's assistant had a very persuasive way of encouraging her charge to speed up. Every time he approached the second-to-last corner, she would stand near the finish line and lift her top up, giving him full view of her upper lady area.

Ryan Reynolds

Not the fastest on the track but, alongside Hugh Grant, easily the fastest wit. Also extremely obliging. Just after he'd completed his laps, the soundman told me that the sound equipment had packed up and we didn't have a single in-car word that Reynolds had said. He immediately jumped back in, drove the laps again and rerecorded all his quips.

Sienna Miller

Easily the most obliging and charming. Most guests go home after they've done their stint, but she stuck around for our post-record drink, snarfed a ton of our reduced-to-clear Sainsbury's mini pork pies and nicked everyone's fags. Then a few months later she dropped by the office to lend us her head for the Skoda Roomster's glovebox test.

Usain Bolt

Never felt so much charisma emanate from a guest. At first we were worried that he'd be monosyllabic because in the motorhome he didn't move. He just lay in the La-Z-Boy chair, literally like a panther preserving its energy. He was a Jamaican Kimi. Then he stepped up onto the stage and whatever he has, it just swept across the enraptured audience.

Daniel Craig

Right now you're probably going: 'Hang on, did I miss that show?' You can relax. Daniel Craig for sure did all the guest things: went round our track on repeat, with the Stig next to him giving instruction, and he was in and out of our Portakabin office, but he never came on as a guest. Instead Craig came down when we weren't there so that Ben, who was also his stunt double in *Quantum of Solace*, could teach him the art of spirited driving. During driving breaks Ben would take him into our abysmal office so that Bond was safe from prying eyes, and over instant coffee Ben would try and persuade Daniel to come on the show. It was always a 'no' though, because whoever was playing Bond was always intertwined, in the public's eyes, with Bond himself. Nobody expected Harrison Ford to split a radish in two with a whip whilst he was in his local supermarket, but woe betide any Bond actor who came anywhere lower than the top on our Liana leaderboard. It was a shame though, because in truth, Ben genuinely believed that had he done the lap, the top is where Craig would have gone.

Brian Johnson

The audience went batshit for Brian, so much so that it took him about half an hour to get from the hangar door to our Portakabin because he was swamped by so many autograph- and selfie-hunters. We've met him in his local pub in London a few times since and what I love, besides his raconteur wit, is that he never takes anything for granted. He doesn't seem to stop pinching himself about the fact that one day he's putting vinyl roofs on Ladas, the next he's the singer for one of the greatest rock bands of all time.

Brian brings us neatly onto musicians, around whom I suffer from an affliction. The problem is that because I love music so much and always wished I'd sung in a band that lasted longer than three weeks, I get starstruck around anybody who actually is a musician. The way this nervousness manifests itself is that when I'm near one I can't help starting to sing one of their songs. Worse still, I don't realise I'm doing it. Jeremy thinks it's hilarious and if we had a music guest on he'd always hang around, waiting for me to start up.

It happens without exception. One time I was interviewing Bryan Ferry. There was a bit of a silence because he'd just finished a long answer to a question, we were looking out over some lovely summery fields, and off I went with a burst of 'Slave to Love'. It's never loud, more like I'm doing it just for myself, but absolutely loud enough. Bryan was extremely polite, looking at me like I was odd in the head, but not saying anything.

So when *Top Gear* gets going and we've got the music guests coming on, I'm in purgatory.

Mick Fleetwood has to listen to my version of 'You Can Go Your Own Way'. Lionel in his terrible motorhome gets to hear 'Three Times a Lady', Steve Tyler likewise is in for 'I Don't Want to Miss a Thing' (I'm fond of a ballad), and so on. The vast majority reacted in the same way Bryan Ferry did: bemused stare but not saying anything. Except for Roger Daltrey.

When Roger came to do his laps he was extremely affable and up for the whole day but he is, nevertheless, a no-nonsense chap. Inevitably, during a break in filming his laps, I found myself standing next to him. Why did I say 'found myself'? I went and deliberately stood next to him cos he's Roger Daltrey. It was a sunny Surrey day, we were looking out over the huge, flat expanse of Dunsfold and sure enough, off I launched into 'I Can See For Miles'. Before I could get to the third line, Roger broke in: 'What are you doing?' he said, looking at me like I belonged in a care home.

Immediately I got all flustered: 'I've got this thing where I can't help singing the songs of whoever I'm next to.'

'Well maybe don't,' he said politely but firmly.

Then added: 'They're not even the right words.'

This made my neck even hotter and I slunk off, hoping to God we'd never book one of the Stones.

Ronnie Wood

That moment, though, eventually did arrive. One day we got a call from a book publisher, informing us that Ronnie Wood was releasing his autobiography and would we like to have him on as a guest?

I was shellshocked. I don't have the word skills to convey here how much I love the Stones. I've seen them almost ten times and been obsessed with them since I was fourteen. 'Gimme Shelter' has never budged from being my number one Desert Island Disc. Now, here I was with the chance to actually meet an actual Rolling Stone. I thought about it, then finally said to Jeremy and Justine, our guest booker, 'We should say no.'

Jeremy was properly baffled: 'You'd turn down a Stone?' My worry was that I'd seen lots of Stones interviews and none of them had been much good. They're a cossetted band (well they seemed to be at that time) surrounded by tough publicists who lay down strict guidelines for press questions. 'Net result,' I said to Jeremy, 'because they've never had to try in an interview, I can't see how Ronnie will be any good.'

Jeremy was much more pragmatic: 'Yes, but I'll be able to say, "Ladies and gentlemen . . . from the Rolling Stones . . ." then a bit of chat, then the lap, bish bash bosh.'

He had a point. The Rolling Stones, after all, are huge. They have, in fact, been seen in the flesh by more people than any other human beings in history.

Nevertheless I rang the book publisher and voiced my concern that Ronnie might be a bit of a lame interviewee. She then said: 'I think you're wrong, but why don't you go and meet him at his house? Have a good chat, brief him properly, make sure he gives you what you need.'

So there I am, a few days later, driving up a Rolling Stone's driveway to a Rolling Stone's house. I am however still determined to stay focused on the order of business: put your fangirling to one side, see if he'll be any good as a guest, protect the show.

Ronnie was waiting on the doorstep with a big smile, and as soon as he said hello every single scrap of my principled resolve went out of the window.

Back then he was still with his wife Jo and she was there with the kids, all friendly chatty and sitting round a big table in a homely kitchen area. 'Ronnie, get Andy a coffee,' she said cheerily. I was beside myself: a Rolling Stone was making *me* a coffee and I'd just become a close member of the Wood family.

Ronnie fiddled with an espresso machine, telling me

that he was completely off the booze, but as a result was now getting his hits from coffee. 'I have about twelve of these a day.' Then adding: 'You want yours strong? I have mine really strong.'

'Yeah. Strong. Yeah, whatever you're having,' I blathered.

'So, *Top Gear* then, eh?' he said as he handed me my coffee.

'Have you seen the show? I bet you haven't cos you're all away touring, but it doesn't matter if you haven't,' I gabbled.

'Oh yeah, course I know it. Who doesn't?' replied Ronnie. I suddenly had this image of Mick, Keith, Ronnie and Charlie together on a big sofa in a dressing room, backstage at some vast stadium, all watching the British Leyland Cheap Car Challenge. I was now literally losing my mind.

Then Jo, Ronnie's wife, asked: 'How's your Richard these days? Is he alright?'

'Oh he's much much better now,' I said. 'You know, with injuries like that there may always be a bit of residue of something, but yeah, he's fine.'

Ronnie's *Top Gear* viewing credentials then started to look a bit shaky as he asked: 'What happened with Richard?'

'He had a brain injury like Keith did,' Jo told him.

'What? He fell out of a tree?'

'Oh, Dad!' moaned his daughter.

Ronnie was referring to the time when Keith had taken a tumble from a palm tree, landed on his head and ended up in hospital.

'No!' said Jo. 'Richard had a massive crash in a really fast car.'

'Oh, right, sorry,' said Ronnie.

By now I was on my second espresso but, not being a big coffee drinker, the caffeine was definitely stoking my already nervy nerves, so I jumped in way too loudly:

'Ronnie, it doesn't matter,' I protested a bit manically. 'You're a Rolling Stone! You don't have to know about ordinary stuff like our show!'

As we talked about his cars and the Stones, Ronnie kept offering me more coffees and I just said 'yes' every time, because he was making it. Eventually I was off my tits on caffeine and the poor bloke could now barely get a word in as I gabbled on about how good the Stones were live, which presumably, being in the band, he already knew.

In between I'd treated him and the family to snatches of 'Can't Always Get What You Want' and 'Miss You'.

Nevertheless, Ronnie and his family remained charming and delightful throughout, and then it was time for me to go. As I was packing my stuff up I said to him: 'So we'll make sure all the details get sent to your office for how to get to the track and so on.'

'No need,' he replied, opening his laptop. 'I've already got them all here. Dunsfold Park . . .' It was an innocent and perfectly logical response but by now I was at least six espressos in.

'You shouldn't have those details!' I shouted. He looked at me, quite baffled. 'You're a Rolling Stone! The Stones shouldn't have to bother with addresses and all things like that! That's mere mortal stuff!'

In truth I'd probably been trying to make a joke about me being a fan and my view of Stone status, but because of the caffeine I just came across as completely certifiable.

Ronnie saw me to my car, then a few weeks later came on the show, and was delightful. I drank tea.

Tom and Cameron

'I'll believe it when I see him stepping out of his helicopter, not till then.'

So said Jeremy on the morning that the biggest film star in the world was due to step into the Reasonably Priced Car.

It was July 2010. We were fifteen series in and our long-standing joke of writing Tom's name in the guest box on the office whiteboard and then rubbing it out with a sigh had served us well over the years; mainly because we knew it would never happen. Now, today, we might be able to put that joke to rest.

'He will be here,' I said. 'There's too much faff gone on from his side. They mean it.'

And faff there had been aplenty. He and Cameron Diaz were coming on together to promote their new film

Knight and Day, and because we were talking about two of Hollywood's most A-grade A-listers, the film company had gone overboard with the schedule for the day.

Standing outside our Portakabin Jeremy and I read through the printout:

12.00: Tom lands in helicopter.

12.05: Tom and Jeremy introduced.

12.10: Tom goes to his motorhome for helmet fitting.

12.17: Tom leaves motorhome to do laps.

And so on and so on.

'Fucking Norah,' we both said, 'this is going to be a relaxed day.'

Still, it was what it was. Then we heard the distinct sound of a helicopter approaching. It landed and a beaming Tom jumped out. Jeremy and I looked at each other, then back at the Schedule of Immense Preciseness, then at the time. It was only 11ish. 'Eh?'

Tom strode towards us, his thousand-yard grin on full beam, and we all shook hands.

'Hang on, you're not supposed to be shaking Jeremy's hand until 12.05,' I joked lamely, showing him the schedule.

'Oh yeah, those,' he said with a knowing sigh, bless him. 'But I was in my hotel and I just thought, it's a great morning, let's get down there.'

From that moment on the schedule was never spoken of again. He hardly went into his motorhome, but instead just stood around chatting with crew, our office team, whoever. Then we filmed his laps, and although it was a July day, a heavy rain shower dropped by as he was setting his times. That was a shame because he was clearly quick, and in the dry he would have had a shout at the top of the board.

Cameron Diaz then arrived and she was as delightful and funny as you'd hope Cameron Diaz would be. When I saw the vast display of exotic fruit on the table in her motorhome, I said: 'Oh my god, you Hollywood stars are so lucky. We've never had fruit in England.'

'Oh I can imagine,' she replied with mock concern, then went and got all her fruit display and started handing it round to the crew: 'Come on, try this, it's called a strawberry.'

I then ran through her interview questions, one of which was about her nose. 'It's like God's doing favour- itism stuff with you,' I said, 'because you've broken your nose at least three times and it's still perfect.'

'My nose is shit,' she replied.

'No it isn't, it's perfect.'

'Give me your finger.'

She took my finger and ran it up and down her nose: 'See? Bumps everywhere, it's shit.'

As I was getting a guided tour of Cameron's nose I looked across at Jeremy and grinned, who mouthed back: 'Oh you fucking bastard.'

Cameron set about doing her laps, which by now was on a dry track. I was standing next to Tom as he watched her going round, then he turned to me and asked if, now it was dry, he could do his laps again.

'We'd love it,' I replied. 'But is there time? You and Cameron are on a really tight schedule cos you've got to get back to London for your premiere.'

At this point a couple of the people from the film company came over, and Tom told them he'd love to do his laps again. 'That would be great,' they replied, their smiles saying the exact opposite. As soon as Tom wandered off, the film company people started up. I had to talk him out of it. There was no way he had time to reshoot his laps; the schedule was to the minute; red carpet in Leicester Square, etc.

Fortunately Tom returned, having seen the vigour of our chat. 'Tom, they don't want you to do it, there's just no time apparently,' I told him. He could have then said: 'No, I'm doing it,' but instead he asked, with a huge, respectful 'please' attached, whether they would let him.

'But when we get back to London you've got to go to the hotel to get changed for the premiere,' they replied.

'I'll change in the car, don't worry,' and so on. The man's manners, the complete absence of weight throwing, was impressive. He did his laps, he nearly – as the nation saw – rolled the car, and went top of the board. The pair of them were utterly charming, and as we were saying our goodbyes Tom said, 'We must meet up again.'

'Well that's a lovely thought, Tom, but best will in the world . . .' I said.

'No!' he shot back. 'We'll meet up again.'

I thought nothing more of it, then a year later, one day

when I was working in the edit, an email pinged up. It was from Tom's sister Cass, inviting me and the family to come and see Tom up at Leavesden, where he was shooting *Edge of Tomorrow*. He was fantastically hospitable with Amanda and the kids, even when Noah, who was now seven, told Tom that nobody knew who he was.

'Well William's never heard of you, Zac's never heard of you . . .' – basically he was listing everyone in his class at school who was also seven. Tom, who had asked Noah to help him pick up the bullet casings from his sci fi gun, was kneeling on the floor almost doubled up with laughter.

'Jesus,' he said through the laughter, 'it's a while since I've heard that.'

Indulging gobby seven-year-olds aside, Tom's work ethic was also extraordinary. I thought we were the gold-medal holders in this department, but having visited him on set a couple of times more and watched him put a shift in, I had to concede we might have to drop to a silver. It wasn't just the hours and attention to detail, it was his team-player element that impressed. On one bitterly freezing cold February night on the set of *Edge of Tomorrow*, they were shooting an outdoor scene on a set mocked up to look like a flooded and derelict Paris. The temperature was so bitingly low that us bystanders had been issued with thermal boots, even though we were on dry land. In the manmade lake of water the actors were wading through, the temperature was even lower.

Naturally the actors also had thermal protection under their clothes. The director shot takes with them for an hour and then when Tom finally came out of the water he limped to the coffee tent and collapsed in agony because he couldn't feel his leg. It turned out his thermal suit had a tear in it, but he'd stood in the water the whole time, not saying a word, so as not to break the scene.

On top of that, he can talk as knowledgeably about lights and lenses as any director of photography. There isn't a detail he's not across. I'm going to bastardise a quote from the musician Jack White, who said something like: 'If you want to create art you've got to punch the clock and put the hours in.' He's right. The creativity comes through the grind, not from the Heavens. That is Tom. As for me, I guess I loved the irony of how, back in 2002, we'd started our running joke of writing his name on our board and then erasing it with a 'yeah, as if . . .' sigh, and ended up having more fun with him than any other guest.

All Rise!

Ben Collins was over the moon that he'd got to do his Stig duties with Tom and Cameron, and a few months later it all made sense why, because he asked me how I might feel about him writing a book about his time in the white suit.

Well obviously that's a big fat no, I replied, because . . . you know why. The Stig is the Stig.

It turned out that Ben, being a bloke and not wanting a confrontation, had left out the bit about him already having signed a deal with HarperCollins, and the other bit about him already having written the book.

Once these facts became clear it was out of his hands and mine and so, a short while later, we all found ourselves sitting on wooden benches that made church pews feel like water beds, in the Royal Courts of Justice.

The BBC lawyers wanted to prevent Ben from being able to reveal his identity as the Stig. HarperCollins argued that if you went online you could find Ben's name as Stig, which meant that horse had already bolted.

HarperCollins's barrister launched their plea to the judge with some theatrical outrage about *Top Gear*'s arrogant conduct: 'A Mr Wilman has publicly called my clients HarperCollins "a bunch of chancers", he said sternly.

'I did. They are!' I said to Liz Grace, our lawyer. 'Shhh, shut up!' she hissed. 'You're in court.'

After hearing both arguments the judge went off to do some judge thinking. The BBC barristers suggested that it would be a good idea if I met with Ben and the HarperCollins team in a quiet room, to see whether we couldn't thrash something out before he came back with his decision.

We duly met in such a room. I'd been told to keep calm and use my head. No drama queen stuff. I genuinely tried my best, but my best wasn't very good. As I sat opposite the HarperCollins team, looking at their assembled faces, I just thought to myself, we've all worked so hard for so long to build up the Stig, make him what he is, and now you lot think you can come along and trash it. Drama queen time:

'Ben, what are you doing with these bottom feeders?'

Nobody said anything.

'They're just using you. You'll get a book deal, sure, and a load of promises about I don't know . . . *I'm a Celebrity*, but they actually don't give a toss.'

Ben then retorted that at least HarperCollins were paying him his worth, which was more than we'd ever done at the BBC.

This . . . was a good point. BBC Worldwide were doing extremely well out of the Stig: Stig soap on a rope, Stig T-shirts, Stig duvets . . . At one point Stig birthday cakes – those ones you get in the supermarket with a shelf life of 400 years – had outsold Spider-Man cakes.

But all the while Ben had remained on his daily fee for turning up to drive.

'You're right,' I finally admitted, 'you're absolutely right. So get rid of these pricks, come back and we'll sit down and work out a new deal.'

Despite my sincerity, my words now sounded rather hollow, with 'too little too late' written all over them. I knew it and everyone else in the room knew it.

And, despite my insults, the HarperCollins people said nothing. Truth was, they didn't need to because I was doing their work for them. Every desperate protest I made was driving Ben further into their arms.

Sure enough Ben declined my offer, we all went back to court, the judge ruled in HarperCollins's favour, and after seven superb years, *Top Gear* and Ben had to go their separate ways.

Now on telly we were indignant and angry. We bitched about him being a splitter and used his face as a target in a drive-by shooting range sequence. Our anger was definitely genuine, because the point still stood that he'd undone a lot of hard work, but inside we were so so sad, because we really missed him. Ben had been such a brilliant Stig, not just as a driver and a comrade at the track but also in fleshing out the character. When we shot the Race Across London film with Stig on public transport, I'd directed his segments and he was unnervingly smart about 'being' the Stig.

'Hang on, I'm supposed to be frightened of stairs,' he would whisper as we got to the top of an escalator, and duly strike the perfect reluctant Stig pose, his body rigid and his head staring in fear at the moving steps.

On the matter of his replacement, we made it a priority to find a driver who had no interest in writing a book or going on *Love Island*. Phil Keen definitely hit the spot. Never had we met a man so utterly content to just be in cars and doing driving. The world of celebrity, to him, meant nothing. The names meant nothing.

'Simon Pegg's the guest this week, Phil.'

'What's he do then?'

'It's Benedict Cumberbatch this week, Phil.'

'You've got me there. Say a bit more.'

If he ever does write a book, I promise you it'll be a comparison of all the differentials in the cars he's lapped.

Record Breakers

There are glass half-empty people, and then there are, as a great but curmudgeonly director friend of mine and Jeremy's – Richard Pearson – says, people who moan: 'Not only is this glass half empty, it's not even what I ordered.'

That's me. And as our *Top Gear* plane flew ever higher into ever bluer skies, I would just think: 'Fine, but now we get a bird strike.'

However, as we worked our way through Series 15, 16, 17, right through to number 20, there were no bird strikes. The quality of our work stayed up, along with the viewing figures. Jeremy wrote and did one of his best *Top Gear* films ever, the Reliant Robin drive across Sheffield, which was a sublimely scripted piece of nonsense.

Hammo and I also shot a film following some war veterans who'd lost limbs, as they set about doing their first motorsport race. Eager to help, we thought we should find them a good racing instructor. Then, cue chorus of light bulbs and celestial choirs in my head: 'Ben!' I cried. 'Let's get Ben back.' This made complete sense because

Book-writing Stig had done a lot of work for Help for Heroes, so it was an easy and lovely call to make.

When we met him at the location on race day, well over a year since we'd seen him, it was a joyous moment. Obviously on camera we all played our panto parts, with Richard mock warning the soldiers not to say anything in case Ben put it in a book, and Ben duly returning the pissed-off looks. But off camera all us *Top Gear* team exchanged massive hugs with him. Some say . . . that we were all happy again.

Elsewhere around that time, the Mr Needham tests also peaked with the Kia Cee'd review. Our luck and clout was now such that we could get Eric Clapton to test the stereo with his guitar, and Bruce Willis to review the car horn. Bruce was filming *Die Hard 5* out in Eastern Europe. The director, John Moore, had a word with Bruce and bob's yer uncle there we were watching him in his tatty John McClane vest, climbing into the Cee'd. 'What do you want me to say?'

'Nothing, Bruce, just toot the horn.'

'That's it?'

'That's it.'

Then, just as we thought our good fortune had maxed out, Twickenham Stadium called and said: 'We're tearing up the rugby pitch next week. You can do what you want with it before then.' Cue car rugby.

Elsewhere James drove a Hilux up an erupting Icelandic volcano, our Senna tribute film landed beautifully and we built some motorhomes and took them down to Cornwall. This, you may remember, is the film where Richard and James accidentally push Jeremy's extremely tall Citroën motorhome off a cliff. I remember telephoning the man who owned the cliffs to ask for his permission to do the said pushing over. He was quite old, also old-school landed gentry, and to the point. I began with my stock tactic: anticipate that whoever you're asking will roll their eyes and want to say no, so confront their reticence head on:

'You'll probably roll your eyes when I ask,' I began, 'because it's more of the usual nonsense we get up to on our show, and you know what *Top Gear*'s like.'

'No, sorry, never heard of it,' he replied.

'Oh. Right, erm, right. Well, we'll be holidaying in these motorhomes we've built, and we wondered if we could drive one of them over one of your cliffs.'

Bit of a silence, then: 'Yes, can't see a problem with that,' he replied matter-of-factly. Then he added, 'Actually, it does make a nice change to be asked.' I put the phone down thinking, just how often are people driving off his cliffs?

This run of series, 15–20, was a triumph. We'd all thought we'd be out of steam after five. Then the *Guinness Book of Records* got in touch and told us we were going to be in their next edition: Most Watched (factual) TV Show in the World, with 350 million viewers.

Back in 2002 our ambition had been to get 3 million,

refresh a car show, and in doing so keep our *Top Gear* plane at a nice respectable altitude.

Now, it was kissing the stratosphere.

Fuck.

What Goes Up . . .

The BBC's Naughty Boys

Looking back, it was actually quite a slow death. The process of us going from being the Corporation's cheeky rascals to unacceptable villains took its own sweet time.

Our fall was also from quite a considerable height, because for a long time our position as the BBC's naughty children had actually been a very pleasant one.

For starters our cheekiness was useful to the BBC, especially when we poked fun at the BBC. The Peel P50 film was a perfect example. If you remember, this is the one where Jeremy spent the day at work driving round the offices in the tiny Isle of Man-built Peel. At one point he had to attend 'a typical BBC meeting' and we were definitely *not* subtle. I wrote up a ludicrously PC title for the meeting: 'How to reduce the carbon footprint of our disability access policy for single parent mothers', then we made sure the attendees were a ludicrously OTT cross-section of BBC diversity hiring in action. We had a man in a wheelchair, a vertically challenged person, a Sikh, an Asian lady, a Greenham Common hippy and so on, then at the end of the row, next to a stack of *Guardian* newspapers, Jeremy.

Come Monday morning I was expecting a phone call from the top floor of the 'Can we have a word?' variety. But no. They were cool with it because our kind of pisstake of its political correctness, as opposed to, say, the *Daily Mail*'s bile over the same issue, was charming. We'd provided a bit of a release valve for the viewers, who could laugh at what they knew to be the case in the BBC, but overall no harm was done.

Then there was the time when we recorded *Top Gear of the Pops*, a one-off for Comic Relief. Such evenings always attract a gaggle of BBC execs, who were present as Jeremy took to the stage to welcome the crowd. With his voice in full Red Nose earnest mode, he said: 'Okay, we all know why we're here this evening.' Approving nods from the execs.

'It's so we can raise money to buy S Classes for dictators.' Audience collapses, but again it's all okay. He's just poking fun at BBC earnestness.

We also discovered that, rather surprisingly for a show so often in the papers for the wrong reasons, our antics were actually of great assistance to the Editorial Standards department.

In layman's terms, Ed Pol are the Content Police, telling programme makers what's transmittable and what's not. The main players here – I have to name check them because they are the most delightful people – are David Jordan, the big Ed Pol boss, Su Pennington, Natalie Christian and Harry Dean.

One of the main jobs of this team was to teach programme makers the difference between 'getting complaints' and 'breaching editorial standards' and the point they were constantly trying to get across to nervy programme makers was: 'It's okay to get complaints. You've just got to make sure that when you do, you can defend against them. But yes, it's fine to get complaints.' When programme makers do confuse the two, the danger is their output can become timid, which is exactly what Ed Pol do *not* want.

And now here we were, sparking fury in the *Mail* and the *Mirror* every other week, but very rarely having a complaint to Ofcom upheld against us. Jeremy's 'lorry drivers murder prostitutes' riff? Defensible cos the internet is bursting with stories of murderous lorry drivers.

Likewise building train carriages out of caravans and calling the cheapest carriage 'scum class': that generated a hefty letters bag and plenty of anger petrol for the papers, but our actual point was that train companies talk a lot about offering a wonderful service, but in reality treat you like shit. Result, no upheld complaint.

Basically we were providing technicolour examples of line crossing/not line crossing that could be used as teaching tools.

But, as good as we were at walking the line, sometimes entitlement creeps in, you get giddy, and you plain just fuck up: Mexico.

The Mexico debacle came about when we reviewed a Mexican sports car in the news, stating that there was no way the car could be any good because everyone involved would be lazy and feckless. As our sternest critic Steve Coogan put it, we punched down. We then wondered whether the Mexican ambassador would complain about what we'd said and got in another punch by concluding that no he wouldn't, because he'd be asleep.

As it happened the BBC editorial policy team had given us the go-ahead to include this 1970s kicking, but that's by the by. We were responsible for the words. The next day our post bag and email detonated as outraged complaints and death threats poured in from Mexico. The ambassador, Eduardo Medina-Mora, who had indeed been awake and watching, protested strongly. Battle lines were drawn, with Mexico boiling up on one side and the BBC defending us on the other.

As for us, we started to realise that what we'd said was unkind, unfunny and crap but didn't apologise and stayed hidden behind the BBC's defence of us.

Ambassador Medina-Mora, however, and his wonderful Head of Communications, were very much the bigger men. One morning an email popped into my inbox, inviting the four of us to their embassy to celebrate the country's Independence Day. This invitation was both daunting and intriguing, but thankfully intrigue won out, and on the appointed day Jeremy, James and I (Hammo was filming) got suited up and headed over to the embassy.

Nerves were high as we walked in, resolutely huddled together. The Head of Communications chap then greeted us so warmly that we felt like we'd personally led the fight for independence against Spain. There was also a huge table bearing rows and rows of freshly made margaritas, so we started to help ourselves. The ambassador then joined us and was equally gracious, telling us how he'd personally found the part about him being asleep very funny.

'But of course when you insulted my country, that wasn't,' he added, with firm parental kindness. Ironically he had got the apology that he didn't need, whereas the one he'd demanded for his country hadn't been forthcoming.

By now Jeremy, James and I felt about two inches tall. Here we were having slagged off this man and his people, and yet here we also were, invited into his home to drink and eat. Jeremy vowed there and then to write his next column as an apology.

That concluded the fence mending, and not before time. The three of us don't really drink spirits, but we'd now got a taste for the margaritas, without having a clue how strong they were. We kept going back to the table to get some more, and then some more, and then wobbled round the room trying to make conversation with distinguished diplomats and academics. By mid afternoon we were at the 'Eh! You're me best fucking pal' Eight Ace stage, and left utterly shitfaced. James woke up the next morning still in his suit.

I think my point here is that, even when we screwed up as badly as Mexico, everything ended up getting resolved in such a charming way – thanks, obviously, to the good people of the Mexican embassy, not us – that we didn't really learn any lessons. Everything would work out okay and our responsibility was to be irresponsible. Our *Top Gear* parallel universe was now like a *Tom and Jerry* cartoon where, if your head is squashed by an anvil, it simply pops back to its normal shape five seconds later.

Which is why, I guess, we thought it was okay to do the Slope joke.

This happened during the Burma Special – if you've seen that moment you'll know it but there's no point in shying from it here so I'll lay it out. A local Thai person walked across our finished bridge and the exchange between Jeremy and Richard went along the lines of 'That's a magnificent bridge, but there's a slope on it.'

In our minds the term was not taboo. It was the sort of slang you heard in Vietnam war films, similar to the 'kraut' or 'sausage heads' or 'eyeties' phrase prevalent in Second World War *Commando* comics, which were still very much on sale, very much part of our boomer upbringing, and so parochial that you couldn't really take the contents seriously.

And so, having consulted the imaginary editorial policy department we'd recently set up in our own heads, we judged it to be the right side of naughty and decided to go ahead. We also reasoned, with even more entitlement, that the BBC was so woke that they wouldn't even notice a *Commando* mag reference. And we were right. The show went out and nobody internally said a word.

I should explain at this point that the BBC Ed Pol system works on a referral basis. Their department can't possibly watch all the output, so instead the onus is on the programme maker to 'refer' an issue in one of their upcoming shows if they think it might cause problems.

That's exactly what we hadn't done on this occasion. Then, when a grizzled *Daily Star* hack watched the show and worked out what we were up to, I knew we'd been rumbled and went over to tell David Jordan. He was utterly furious with me, not just because of what we'd done, but because we'd taken the piss out of him and his team. So many times they'd backed us on marginal calls, and here we were deliberately sliding offensive stuff past him under cover of woke darkness.

David's fury stung hard. It was an absolute parental wake-up call.

However, a much larger shark fin was surfacing over at Broadcasting House, because our Director of Television – the head honcho – was now a chap called Danny Cohen and he and Jeremy, politically and philosophically, were about as far apart as Jeremy Corbyn and Jacob Rees-Mogg.

Up to now we'd managed to rub along okay with the Islington liberals that ran the BBC because the vast majority of them recognised that we were helping fulfil the remit of the BBC needing to 'speak' to everyone, and the Lord Sugar element over at Worldwide liked that we were making them a fuck ton of money in global sales.

Danny Cohen, though, clearly had much less tolerance for us, and what made things worse was that he was exactly the sort of TV executive that we liked to wind up.

Following the slope incident, Jeremy, Richard and I were summoned to see Danny Cohen. The meeting had been organised by David Jordan, who could see the storm clouds gathering between Cohen and *Top Gear* and thought that getting us in the same room might be useful.

We sat down for lunch and salmon salad was served to all of us except Danny Cohen, who had hummus instead of salmon. Jeremy looked at this Islington no.1 food group and asked him why he was eating that shit. David stared at the ceiling. The lunch continued in that vein and by the end zero bridges had been built. I guess we were on a rotation of Entitlement, Contrition and Obstinance and that day we gave Obstinance.

In our defence though, there was also Indignation, because we felt we were being tarred with a Bernard Manning brush, and you only had to look at the sheer mass of our foreign Specials to see just how much we loved being absorbed in the cultures of and surroundings of different places across the world.

Clearly, though, the conflict wasn't over, because one day a deputation of Cohen's execs came to our office and told us the *Top Gear* office would be subject to an internal investigation, looking at the work culture and practices therein. This would involve confidential interviews with every member of the team to ask them what the work environment was like, whether they felt threatened or uncomfortable, etc.

What we had going here, in my opinion, was a witch hunt. The fact is, offices traditionally only get investigated in this manner when rumours swirl around of toxic behaviour on the production itself, behind closed doors, e.g. *MasterChef*. But with *Top Gear* there was no smoke that indicated any such fire. All our transgressions, all our hot-water moments, were visible and outward-facing, and nothing to do with life in the office.

As angry as I was about the investigation, I wasn't concerned about it, because everyone in the team was their own person and we had nothing to hide. Our office was without doubt noisy, hectic and demanding, and yes, series producer Al's bald head made for a good drum kit, and for sure we wanted failure to be something that hurt, but nobody was persecuted for it happening.

The only people who were victimised were ones who used apostrophes incorrectly, but I think you'll agree that's allowed.

Our office was also a lot of fun, with excellent highs when we pulled off a good film. On top of that we'd grown our own: many of the producers had started out as runners, and turnover was low. To steal a phrase from our main cameraman Ben Joiner, 'We may be a dysfunctional family but it's our dysfunctional family.'

Fortunately, the exec conducting the interview had been chosen by David Jordan who, fair-minded as ever, was doing his best to make sure his irritating children would be scrutinised impartially. Sure enough this exec was a man of absolute integrity who, despite the hopes of others around, had no axe to grind and wrote up the facts as he heard and saw them.

After speaking to everyone on *Top Gear*, he published his report. Its findings were that we were a brilliant team, we were a strong united office that had each other's backs, but that our relationship with the BBC was totally and utterly broken.

And 'broken' didn't refer to the fact that Jeremy and I had done a bad thing behind Ed Pol's back, because that was a one-off transgression. 'Broken', in the context of this report, was more about how our office felt in relation to the Corporation. As an example, the exec in charge of the report cited his chat with Nick, one of the producers, who had overseen the shoot where we'd closed the mall and filled it with all the cars and automotive products made in Britain. This show-stopping event had been reported in the papers, had got rave reviews from the fans and had also been a proper BBC 'moment', the sort they would put in one of their trailers to showcase the brilliance of the Corporation. But as Nick pointed out, he'd been inundated with congratulations and back slaps from everyone . . . except the BBC. 'I told him if you're on *Top Gear* you just feel invisible in this place,' Nick said to me later.

Anyway, the management tribe who didn't care for us had gambled heavily with this report and lost, because once you drill down hoping to find one problem, but instead find another, then you still have to accept the findings.

However, as to that main finding – namely the gulf between us and the BBC – management did fuck all.

In fact, just to drive the wedge in a bit deeper, the top floor decreed that another exec producer at my level must come and sit in the edit whilst we were putting the show together on a Thursday night – literally to be their watchdog, making sure we didn't play silly buggers with the content.

The Thursday night edit was when we stitched the whole show together, having recorded the studio the day before. It was usually a past-midnight shift, but it was invariably a fun evening of banter and over-ordering Chinese takeaways, involving myself, Al the series producer, Brian the studio director and Joe the online editor. Only now it would no longer be fun, because we had a stranger in the room, with a remit to watch our behaviour.

Looking back now I feel sorry for the guy. He didn't want to be there any more than we wanted him there.

Unfortunately, I had no such measured feelings back then. Every time he made a comment that I felt was beyond his remit I snarled back. But to be honest I was so angry I just saw him as collateral damage. I felt that once the office investigation had given us a clean bill of health then the whole business should be done. But for certain elements of that management, it clearly wasn't done. Elsewhere in this book you'll see that where we screw up, I put my hand up, so I feel justified in saying: that whole investigation affair – what a fucking joke.

Luckily though, the time had come to shoot another Special, and that was just what the doctor ordered. All of us – the presenters and the whole *Top Gear* team – could get away from this shitty politics, go somewhere lovely and shoot a nice, fun film. Somewhere like . . . Argentina.

Argentina

Argentina. We'll get to the 'did they or didn't they' in a moment but let's go right back to basics.

The genesis of the Argentina Special was the cars. Jeremy, Richard and James had a hankering to take some lovable V8s of senior citizen status on a long and arduous road trip. Argentina and Chile fitted the bill perfectly. Amazing scenery, roads in both the punishing and the beautiful category, and on top of that we had a superlative finish point: Ushuaia, at the southern tip of South

America, a town nicknamed 'The End of the World'. Then, for the finale, we would play a game of car football, in honour of the infamous 1986 World Cup final between England and Argentina when Maradona scored his Hand of God goal. As a cherry of all cherries on top, Gary Lineker had agreed to fly out and take part in the game. Sorted.

As for the V8 cars themselves, Roger Moore May wanted a Lotus Esprit, Bullitt Hammond fancied a Mach 1 Mustang, and Risky Business Clarkson was set on a Porsche 928 GT with a manual gearbox.

Now, before we go any further, let's get the elephant shooed out of the room. We didn't frig the number plate. Richard Porter's excellent book, *And On That Bombshell*, available in all classical Greek literature bookshops, lays out succinctly and accurately as to why we couldn't have done such a thing, and I'll reiterate the same points here. Let's say the sceptics are right. Let's say we did frig the number plate. To do that, we wouldn't have been able to start the construction of the film with actual cars, we'd have had to base the whole Special around a comedy number plate. As was proven, remember, the number plates were genuine; they'd been on that Porsche for donkey's years. So we would have needed a car with a genuine number plate with a particular arrangement of comedy numbers and letters. First off we'd have to go to the DVLA and bribe them to break the law by telling us who has number plates of this nature, and where they live. Then, assuming we'd got away with that, we'd have to hope that the number plate wasn't on a Fiesta diesel or a bus, but on something tasty, as befits a *Top Gear* Special. The chances of that happening: that it's not just a sporty V8, but also one that happened to play a special personal moment in Jeremy's life as it sped him towards his dying father, are a trillion to one.

I've got better things to do than try and appease the Twitter warriors, but I tell you what, I'll happily give the fee for this book to anyone who can present credible evidence that we deliberately chose those number plates.

The office eventually found and bought the cars, with Jeremy's Porsche being a particularly tough search, because less than ten manual versions of the 928 GT were ever sold in the UK.

We also welcomed a new member to our support team, Max Hurst. Max was a specialist in keeping old Lotuses going – busy man – and given what lay ahead for James's Esprit, we thought it prudent to recruit a Max. As for Max himself, he was a lovely, soft-spoken genial chap. Max clearly didn't have a second career as a fortune teller though, with him gushing about how much he was looking forward to travelling through some of the world's most beautiful scenery with only one car to look after. 'What a treat!' he exclaimed. 'It's going to be like a holiday!'

Max would team up with Bob Ives, the 4x4 and offroad genius we'd first recruited for the Bolivia Special and had been saving our sorry incompetent arses in many corners of the world ever since.

The cars were shipped to the start point in Bariloche, a beautiful town in the Patagonia region. Bariloche is famous for its chocolate, its Swiss alpine style architecture, and for being a haven for Nazis who fled Germany after the Second World War.

Those first days of filming were sublime. As we travelled south we mucked about at the ranch where Butch Cassidy and the Sundance Kid had hidden out, then one evening we stayed in a small, cosy hotel with a bar straight out of an English pub. Since we had booked out the place, I took over behind the bar, on landlord duties. As I stood there pulling pints badly, Jeremy was scrolling through Twitter.

Checking in on Twitter had become part of our daily norm, because fans who saw us out and about could now post updates about what we'd been up to. We'd huff and puff if there was a spoiler in there, but were resigned to it. Suddenly Jeremy looked up: 'Hey, have you seen what these guys have written?' He showed us all a photo taken by some fans a day or so earlier and one of them had written how the number plate on the Porsche – H982 FKL – was clearly a cheeky reference to the Falklands War.

We thought about it for a minute, but didn't take it too seriously since we hadn't put it there deliberately. Al Renton, our series producer, was the man on point for dealing with all the arrangements down south in Ushuaia – the heartland of Falklands war veterans. Taking a swig from his half foam, half lager pint he said he'd let the authorities in Ushuaia know about the Twitter post and assure them the plate was most definitely not a prank.

We thought no more of it and our journey south trundled forth.

James fell off a horse and busted his ribs, but given he could still change gear we strapped him up and onwards we went.

The drive down the Chilean coastline was a life moment as we watched the tiny icebergs bobbing about in the aquamarine sea, then we'd pull up at what looked like a warehouse and find inside the funkiest, coolest hotel.

After that, a section of Argentina that was like a Lost World. But instead of dinosaurs its secret was a plethora of incredible driving roads, completely open to the horizon, with wisps of snow kissing them, and so so empty.

Because this was a 1,600-mile trip, our longest to date, we decided to do something we'd never done before, and insert into the schedule . . . a day off. That meant in the hotel bar the night before the day off, we could get shit-faced beyond words, giving one of our soundmen, Rob, an early stag night before he flew home to get married. The next morning Rob the soundman woke up in the ball pit in the hotel's kiddies' playroom. With the added new invention of 'a day off' in the mix, this was turning out to be a truly memorable trip.

As we got closer to Ushuaia we monitored the Twitter traffic more carefully and inevitably the number plate reference had been picked up by our fans, with the comments being the usual haphazard, disconnected journey across Logic Town:

'Lol Falklands War. What are they up to this time?'

'Just looking at those 928s. Not many manuals around'

'What's the Falklands War?'

'Lol I bet they've put a James Bond gadget on James's Esprit'

'They always like to wind up the locals. My favourite was Alabama petrol station.'

'Shit. Just googled and there was a real war between England and Argentina!!!'

'Alabama was insane. They were lucky to get out of there alive. I come from Louisiana and they don't fuck about down here.'

'Methinks they might piss off a few people in Argentina, but lol what's new'

'Not sure Richard's car will make it. My dad had a Mach 1 and the transmission was always playing up.'

And so on and so on. It was fun to read but crucially there wasn't a sinister undertone in the air. Al, our series producer, was now down in Ushuaia, overseeing the build of our car football pitch in the shipping container yard down by the docks. He was in constant touch with the local authorities, who were happy with his assurance that the number plate was a coincidence. They warned Al that the local Falklands veterans might get unhappy and need a bit of reassurance too. Other than that, all was calm.

Back in the convoy we'd thought briefly about swapping the plates out for something innocuous, but decided against it because it would ruin the continuity on camera.

Not far north of Ushuaia we took a freight ship across the Strait of Magellan then spent the night camped on a stony beach, under a canopy of the most blindingly brilliant stars we'd ever seen.

We were now on the Isla Grande de Tierra del Fuego, the largest island in South America, with its 18,000 square mile mass split between Chile and Argentina, and we were firmly in the Argentinian half as we drove south through the town of Rio Grande, before finally arriving at our last stop, Ushuaia, with our hotel overlooking the town from a hilltop.

Shoot-wise we were now just a couple of days from wrapping. The cars were carrying a few mechanical wounds but only had to endure two further harebrained sequences: the car football finale, and before that, a race down the ski slopes of the local ski resort. (If your brain has now just shot ahead to the *Grand Tour* Jaaaaaag film in Colorado then yes, we don't like to throw away a good idea.)

So there we were the following morning, all up bright and early, cars in position at the top of the ski slopes, cameras ready to roll on some snowy, mental-age-of-nine nonsense.

We managed to shoot a couple of runs before the resort owner arrived in haste on a snowmobile. He explained that there was a deputation of Falklands veterans at the bottom of the resort, who had demanded we stop filming.

We said we'd meet the veterans just as soon as we'd finished filming, but the owner's face said different. It said spooked. Up to this point he'd been a helpful and accommodating man but now he insisted we stop filming, permission to be on the slopes was withdrawn, and we must go down immediately to meet the veterans.

On the way down on the back of a snowmobile I was thinking: 'I can sort this. I'm Mr Wilman.' That's not meant in an arrogant way, more that I had a legendary reputation for negotiating to get things we needed from car firms, governments, aircraft carrier captains, whatever.

At the bottom of the slopes, our fixer, some of our team and I sat down with the deputation of veterans in a café. There were about four of them, in their fifties, which would have put them at about twenty-odd during the Falklands War.

Their faces were the definition of stern. Through our fixer I explained all the logic as to why we could not have possibly fabricated the plates and put them on as a cheap joke. At the end of this long and protracted translation process, their faces had surely broken some world record for not changing expressions. Then back came their response. They didn't believe us, they didn't care what we had to say and we were to pack up and leave town right now.

We countered with a plea to at least finish our filming. We'd shot a whole film that needed an ending and we'd be gone in twenty-four hours.

No. Right now meant right now. In fact, the veterans added, we had until just 6 p.m. to be out of town. If we weren't on the move by then, a mob would be coming up the hill to our hotel and whatever happened next would be on us. We were stunned – stunned by the certainty with which they appeared to be able to rustle up a mob and make this happen. They were, after all, just town citizens, not the law, but clearly the authorities did not matter to them. Alongside stunned, I was also now starting to panic. Normally a film crew of our size – this one numbered almost fifty – takes a full day and a fair chunk of the night to break down all the film kit and prep it for travel, then pack all personal equipment and turn our 4x4s from filming vehicles back into travelling vehicles. Let's say a good twenty hours. But as it stood now, with it already being 11 a.m., we'd have to do the same job in just seven.

Still processing this terrifying turn of events, the crew, along with Jeremy, James and Richard, piled into their vehicles and set off back to the hotel.

I still couldn't quite believe what was happening and so, along with my Chilean interpreter, stayed behind and had one more go at persuading the veterans of our innocence.

Fifteen minutes later, having failed comprehensively, he and I headed back to the hotel. When we arrived at the bottom of the hill leading up to the hotel itself, another group of veterans was already waiting, blocking our path. Their leader looked old enough to have been in the Falklands War, but his sidekicks were in their twenties and thirties, way too young to have fought, but nevertheless clearly spoiling for some combat right now. The veteran leader came up to the window and told us to turn round and leave. We explained we were all quitting town as requested, but in order to do so I had to actually get to the crew hotel to help organise our departure. By way of response the veteran and the younger guys started shouting and banging on the bonnet of our 4x4, pushing it backwards by force. Now a bit panicked, I reversed back and then felt a jolt and heard a crunch as my rear end biffed into the side of a parked car. Two police officers standing by, watching the scene unfold, approached the window and spoke rapidly to my interpreter. At least, I was hoping, they could sort this mess out and persuade the group to let us through. Their response, though, was rather different.

'They're going to breathalyse you for dangerous driving,' he said.

'What the fuck?! Did they not just see what happened?'

'I think they saw whatever they wanted to see.'

As we sat there, waiting for the breathalyser to arrive, one of the veteran's supporters stuck his head through my window. He was stocky and tough, like a dock worker, and this being Ushuaia he most likely was a dock worker. He smiled at us and said something in Spanish. I smiled and nodded and offered him a cigarette, which he took. The fixer looked at me: 'Jesus, you don't scare easy.'

'Are you joking? I'm crapping myself. I just didn't understand what he said.'

'He said that they were going to have a lot of fun with us tonight.'

The fixer knew also that he wouldn't be spared from any of the fun either, on account of him being Chilean – all our fixers were Chilean – and in this part of the world the Argentinians and the Chileans do not get on one bit.

Looking at the veterans and their heavies, I realised I'd made a huge mistake. I'd assumed that if veterans in this area were to take issue with us, the maximum grief we'd face would be a deputation of their equivalent of the Chelsea Pensioners – some slightly offended, finger-wagging old blokes, whom we'd be able to calm down with some good old British apologising once they'd turned their hearing aids up. What I absolutely hadn't expected was a well-organised, anger-fuelled group with long memories, backed up by hardnosed younger dockers and also, it was clear, the local plod.

And now here we were, all alone, with zero Jason Statham skills, thousands of miles from any help. From where we were sitting in our car, I could even see the docks where our football pitch had been built – the boundaries marked out by shipping containers, now waiting for us and Gary Lineker.

FUCK! Lineker! Lineker would be at Heathrow, maybe already having taken off for Buenos Aires. I rang Al immediately, who'd just experienced the same penny drop. He'd called our guys at the *TG* office and told them to go action stations in trying to head off Gary. About ten minutes later he called back. British Airways had managed to intercept him as he was preparing to board and now, obviously not quite sure why, he was heading back into London, having had a nice day out at Heathrow.

A few moments later the breathalyser kit arrived and fortunately, unlike its operator, the machine itself didn't take sides and pinged up a zero reading. After that we were allowed up the hill to the hotel where, in the lobby, a full-scale *Top Gear* evacuation was under way, with kit boxes strewn and luggage all over the floor.

In one of the hotel meeting rooms another producer and I sat down with a local town official, some more police and two of the veterans who'd been at the ski resort, to discuss our next moves.

Given that the veterans would now have seen from the activity in the lobby that we were doing our very best to pack up as quickly as possible, I once again asked for more time – for another night – so that we could wrap up in an orderly manner and drive in daylight. Once again the veterans refused: be on the road by 6 p.m. or a mob would be coming up the hill. The policemen and the local official confirmed that there'd be no extension. Yet again we'd just been reminded who was in charge.

We were then given our route. Once on the road our convoy would drive roughly 250 kilometres back the way we'd come, heading north up through the town of Rio Grande, then over the border into Chile, with instructions never to return. To make sure we did as instructed we'd be accompanied by the official currently in the meeting, plus a police car carrying two policemen.

It was now around 2 p.m.: four hours until the pitchfork squad arrived. We'd all been on the go since 5 a.m. and I was struggling to get my thoughts in order. Logically we would be safe once we were out of town, under the charge of our police escort and having complied.

The second irrefutable piece of logic was that Jeremy, Richard and James would be the main target of any mob hate, which meant they had to be removed from harm's way ASAP. Also, with them gone, the film crew would hopefully be in less danger. I asked one of our local fixers to look for flights out of Ushuaia and he found one leaving in a couple of hours for Buenos Aires. It was a no-brainer. Naturally the three of them protested in an 'all for one . . .' way, but they couldn't refute the argument that their scalps were the prize, as shit-looking as those scalps may have been.

So, in two nondescript cars, they departed for the airport with Al the series producer, Hannah, our one female producer, plus one of our security guys. Fortunately the drive to the airport was trouble-free, the local airport was all but deserted, and a while later we got news that they were all safely onboard.

This now left just Team *TG* to undertake our own evac. Fifty-odd cameramen, soundmen, fixers, researchers, producers and mechanics, all rapidly breaking down lenses, wrapping cable wires, stowing tripods, etc. Film kit is not the sort of stuff that can be lobbed into duffle bags, so the hurrying element had to be done at a frustratingly precise pace.

Meanwhile outside, the two Falklands veterans who had been in the meeting were now openly photographing all the number plates on our vehicles. Why did they need this information? They wouldn't say. What were they doing with it? They wouldn't say.

I then realised I hadn't told anyone at the BBC that life for us had absolutely gone to shit. I called one of the execs in our orbit and explained about the veterans and the danger from the impending mob invasion. Having processed all this, the BBC exec then asked the one question that seemed to be the most vital to a BBC exec in London: 'So are the number plates real or did you fake them?'

'No, we didn't fake them. But how about – radical thought – we worry about all that when, or if, we get back?' Exec conceded the point, then said that calls would start being made.

What precisely the BBC could do I wasn't sure, because it's not like they have BBC SWAT teams at TV Centre. For sure there'd be a British embassy in Buenos Aires but the Argentinian capital city was further away from us than London is from Athens. And anyway, the last people some

Falklands War veterans would likely listen to would be the British government.

Whilst I was still smarting at the BBC's Pavlovian reaction, it became clear that some of the film crew were now starting to think the same way.

A couple of the senior ones confronted me, demanding to know whether they were now in peril because of yet another of our pranks. I once more explained exactly why it couldn't logically be the case and eventually they believed me. This was an important moment of air clearing because whatever was coming our way, we all knew we'd have a better chance of dealing with it if our dysfunctional family was standing firmly together.

6 p.m.

Spurred on by the Falklands veterans' incentive scheme of all stick and zero carrot, our convoy actually trundled down the hill and out of town a good few minutes before the angry mob deadline, leaving behind a very relieved hotel manager.

Taking the lead up front were the two policemen from the hotel, in some ageing little French car. Behind them, in his car, was the town official from the meeting. Then came our filming convoy – roughly fifteen 4x4s, plus a couple of spares and baggage trucks driven by local helpers. Then finally, at the back, like Jehovah's Witnesses leaning on your doorbell, a couple of carloads of veterans, who we assumed were tagging along to make sure we actually did leave the country.

Just outside town we pulled over at the ski resort. Earlier in the day the owner had been very apologetic about what had happened and we knew he had a pizza place where we could grab some food to see us right for the journey. He also had a petrol pump and offered to let the convoy refuel. The local official said there was no need because we'd be passing through the village of Tolhuin, which itself had a petrol station. In the end we decided that since we were here we may as well take the ski resort owner up on his offer. On such tiny spins of a coin does Fate rest, because later on we would shudder to think what might have happened, had we not.

Back on the move we hunkered down for our night drive. The remote roads – think of the most desolate parts of Scotland or Wales – were empty save for our convoy. Mobile phone signal was also zero, so save for our sat phone, patchy at best, we were cut off. The progress through darkness, though, felt safely welcoming, because every revolution of our tyres took us further away from the dangers of Ushuaia. In a few hours we'd be waving our passports at Chilean Customs people.

Around halfway into our journey, between 8 and 9 p.m., the fixer who was riding with our police escort came over the walkie talkie and told the convoy to halt. We were now on the outskirts of the small town of Tolhuin – famous for its local bakery apparently – and the police wanted to check it out before we continued on. We sat in the darkness in silence. A few minutes later the police car returned and the fixer's voice once more came over the radio. She did her very best to speak calmly and factually, but over the airwaves her fear was palpable. Basically the main street that we'd be using to go through Tolhuin was now lined with locals. They were waiting on either side with piles of rocks and stones at their feet.

Everyone knew our options were zero. We couldn't go back towards Ushuaia, nor were there any turnoffs on the road, and out here in the middle of Buttfuck County, we'd now learned that nobody was coming to help. The only option was to run the gauntlet.

Suddenly, at the back of the convoy, headlight beams swished around in the air as the two veterans' cars did a 180 and headed back towards Ushuaia. The photographing of the number plates now immediately made sense: any angry mob along the route had the details of exactly who to attack.

The fixer came over the radio once more, passing on police instructions that we should cover our car windows as best we could with coats and jackets. This activity provided a brief moment of distraction but throughout the convoy, fear had set up shop in every vehicle. You could hear it in the silence on the walkie talkies. Also the penny had dropped that if the police were telling us to cover the windows as best we could, then the presence of those same police would count for nothing in the village.

With our makeshift protection in place we sat there on the remote unlit country road, knowing exactly what we had to do, but with nobody wanting to fire the starting gun. Eventually though, we slowly rolled forward into the village. I was at the wheel of one of the camera cars, about five or six cars from the front.

A few hundred metres up ahead on the left-hand side, we saw the petrol station we'd been advised to fill up at. The biggest concentration of crowd was gathered under the station lights, all of them ready with their stones. There was no way in a living hell that we'd ever have been able to use it, and if we hadn't dropped in at the ski resort, we'd never have had enough fuel to reach the border.

Given that none of us had ever run the gauntlet of an angry mob, we didn't know what speed to go at: too slow and we and our cars would be battered to pieces; too fast and it would be chaos of a different kind.

Then suddenly we all saw something that made the decision for us. Up at the top of the village, a hundred metres or so beyond the mob on either side, a local at the wheel of a flatbed truck was trying to manoeuvre so that it would end up parked lengthways across the road. If he succeeded in getting his roadblock into place we would be rats in a barrel. Nobody needed telling that and everything got very frantic very quickly. Every vehicle accelerated towards him and within seconds stones and rocks started to slam into the sides of our cars, bouncing off the bodywork and smashing windows. As the hail of missiles kept coming there was obviously no time to think – every car just had the same objective of getting round the truck, which luckily was still not yet where he wanted it to be, but getting closer.

At this moment our dysfunctional family became the machine it needed to be. Like a ragged school of fish the convoy zoomed forwards, every driver keeping their foot down as they aimed for the shrinking gaps either side of the roadblock truck. We could also now see that at the back end of the truck a ditch ran alongside the road, and the driver was clearly relying on that to help him hem us in. As we all aimed for an exit the crashes and bangs coming from the rocks was incessant. At the wheel, I braced for the moment a stone would star the windscreen, whilst in the passenger seat Boycie the director was calmly acting as a spotter. 'Man in road, go left.' 'Two more on that side, go right.' His logic was spot on because there was no way any of us could run over a local, even if that local was letting fly with half a rockery. CLATTER BANG CLATTER BANG. Silhouettes of locals leaping out to let fly. There were now too many of us heading for the gap at the front of the truck and to my right I saw James's Lotus, with Max the mechanic at the wheel, veer into the ditch on the other side. As I swept round the front side of the truck, I saw him powering out of the ditch, which mercifully had been shallower than it looked. In the back seat of my car Nick the camera assistant – legend for life – was filming everything on his phone.

Vehicle after vehicle swerved round the truck – in the

end he just couldn't make himself long enough – and the thud of stones lessened as the village receded. Then the walkie talkies burst to life, a tsunami of messages tumbling over each other: 'Anyone not get through?' 'Everyone get through?' 'Anyone hurt?' 'Who's hurt?'

We charged on at speed for another ten minutes or so, then pulled over to take stock.

A lot of the vehicles, including the police car, had suffered smashed and starred windows. Immediately, and in a most welcome way, the sight of the battered plod-mobile put paid to any conspiracy theory that they had led us into the trap. Likewise the Ushuaia official, whose car had also been in the wars. It was plainly the veterans who'd fired up our reception committee.

Amazingly only one person – Max – had been injured, with a cut to the head. So much for his expectations of a pleasant fortnight away, nattering about camshafts with James. As Max stood in the beams of an SUV, with the medic staunching the blood running from his temple, it was clear what the next decision had to be: ditch the star cars. Judging from the amount of hits they'd taken, they were literally catnip for any Argentinian who could throw a rock.

Whilst crew members were taping up broken windows the star cars were pushed off the road into a clearing amongst the roadside trees.

I told the guys who operate the in-car cameras they had twenty minutes to get all their equipment out. Again, given the complexity of the installation, this is usually a full day's work.

Now it's a fact of life that a film crew is, in essence, a collection of neurodiversities dressed in North Face fleeces. Being OCD or similar is part of the job. And as it also happens amongst any crew, it's the in-car camera operators who win the Rain Man Award every time. It was of little surprise then that one of the in-car camera guys delicately opened up a tiny screwdriver on his Leatherman and started to painstakingly unscrew the first of 10,000 screws.

'Oh my God what are you doing?' I asked.

'De-rigging,' he replied, as if we were in Basingstoke at a classic car show.

Luckily the camera nerd's assistant – clearly yet to develop his neurodiversion – pushed us both out of the way then, using bolt cutters he'd borrowed from the mechanics, cut through all the main cables that plumbed the camera equipment into the cars.

This exchange had actually been just the sort of tiny moment of black comedy relief that I needed, but I'd now had another thought so I went and sought out our security guy.

Our one was ex Special Forces and had worked with us a long time. I'm not allowed to say his real name, so let's call him Tarquin (my book, my rules).

'Tarquin,' I said, 'we got lucky back there, didn't we? None of us stopped, all of us through the roadblock . . .'

'We did, we did, fucking lucky there, pal,' replied Tarquin.

'Right, but if it does go pear-shaped and we all end up trapped, and we're out of the cars and we're surrounded, what do we do? How do we protect ourselves? I mean, we're not fighters.'

At this point I suppose I expected Tarquin to suggest we all grab camera tripod poles, stand back to back and shoulder to shoulder, and form one of those fighting formations, like Russell Crowe does in *Gladiator*, when all the baddies in chariots come piling into the arena.

But no. Instead Tarquin said: 'Well, when you've got a mob coming at you, like, a proper big mob that's out of control, there's not much you can do. I mean, truth is, you're as well getting the dressing-up box out and pulling a frock on and a lady's wig, something like that.' With his combat assessment dispensed, he pulled on his cigarette and said no more.

Now I know many of our critics often accuse our show of descending into panto, but oddly enough we never travel around with a dressing-up box full of frocks. Nevertheless, Tarquin's advice that wasn't advice did afford me another little black humour chuckle, and suddenly things didn't seem so bad. We'd got through the attack in one piece, the veterans had turned round and were following their slime trail back home, and although we were scared and the night was still young, we were holding it together.

Then the policemen and the local Ushuaia official approached alongside two of our fixers, and you just knew from their faces that the light relief moment was over.

The fixer explained that the police had managed to get through, using our sat phone, to their counterparts in the next town we'd be going through – Rio Grande, which was about 60 miles away. They'd told him it wasn't just a village mob waiting for us, but a crowd in their hundreds – dozens and dozens of car loads. It didn't need saying, but we'd got through the village relatively unscathed because it was one way in and one way out. In Rio Grande, however, there would be turns and side streets – a whole warren to trap us in. On top of that the village attack had served as the starting gun for every other angry local: 'Don't worry, amigos, we'll finish what you started.' We asked our police if there was any way the mob could be controlled, but they just shook their heads.

Mathematically, there was no way we would get through Rio Grande without someone getting injured, badly injured, or worse.

Everyone in the crew gathered together and took in the news. You could almost see the fear spreading amongst us like a fog.

Then we all got back in our vehicles and instead of moving off, we just sat there, as if staying still would keep us safe. The fact was though, we had no choice but to try and get through Rio Grande, because this was the only road to the border.

Then up ahead, from the direction of Rio Grande, we saw approaching headlights. Eventually the headlights became two motorbikes, which slowly ambled up and down the length of our convoy, taking stock of our numbers, before opening their throttles and gunning it back towards Rio Grande. The power dynamic on display, the way that they'd taken their own sweet time, was absolute. That was my most scared moment, the time I briefly said goodbye to my family.

Suddenly, the radio came to life. It was Bob, our 4x4 wizard. 'I think I might have something here.'

Nobody needed a second invite. We all legged it over to Bob's car where, whilst we'd been saying prayers, he'd been quietly deploying the skills that back in the day had made him a Camel Trophy winner. Bob pointed at the sat nav map he'd been studying. 'About 20 miles up there,' he said, pointing in the direction of Rio Grande, 'there's a dirt track off to the left. That should go all the way down to this river . . .' his finger traced the track to what was clearly a river, 'and that river is the border with Chile. If we can get there and cross that, then we're out of here.'

Oh my God the relief. Just to have hope, to have an option.

Obviously it was imperative to get to that turnoff as quickly as possible. After all, who knew, following the visit from the scouting bikers, whether the mob might tire of waiting and come looking for us?

One of our fixers took the coordinates of where the track would meet the river, and set about calling his office in Chile. Meanwhile our other fixer told the police about our new plan. At first they tried to forbid it. I guess in his head he'd been given a job to do – get us to a specified border crossing – and orders were orders. We told them sorry, this is the new plan, and eventually they backed down. A few minutes later the other fixer returned. His office had spoken to a senior figure in the Chilean border police and a group of them would be waiting by the river on the Chilean side, to meet us once we'd crossed. They would have to arrest us for illegal entry, then they'd escort us to a formal border crossing point where we'd be 'unarrested' and welcomed to Chile. Now, all we had to do was get to that river.

Engines fired up, headlamp beams ignited and our convoy was on the move once more. We covered the 20 miles to the turnoff without any trouble and then, one by one, turned off the tarmac onto the dirt track. The two policemen in their little battered car parked up and then declared, in what was a bit of a lump-in-the-throat moment, that they would wait at the turn and if any of the mob came driving down from Rio Grande, they would try and stop them. We thanked our tiny rear guard profusely and trundled into the darkness.

It was about a 40-mile drive along that dirt road, to the border. Along the way, tension returned anew. All the time we were looking in our rear-view mirrors for any sign of alien headlights approaching; nerves were also on extra high alert in case one of our convoy got stuck on the sandy track and held us up. This indeed happened a couple of times with the local Argentinian mechanic's truck.

In the early hours of the morning we finally reached the river, having been on the go for nearly twenty-four hours, with over half of them spent taut as piano wire. We decided to sit and wait for daybreak before trying to cross the river and then took it in turns to sit on top of the 4x4s, using the height as a sort of crow's nest, on the lookout for an approaching Rio Grande mob. If that were to happen we would just jump into the river and swim across, as substantial as the distance was.

However, when dawn broke no baddies had appeared and over on the Chilean side we could now see the deputation of border police, ready to greet us in an arresting sort of way.

Off-road Bob took charge and through a combination of his bottomless well of skills, us following his orders to the letter and every tow rope in our possession, we eventually hauled, slogged and churned our cars through the water, up the river bank and into the safety of Chile.

Once there the border guards carried out the most gentlemanly arrest in history and after that it was a case of just trying to stay awake, with the exhaustion now coming in waves as we drove to the official border point to be un-arrested. But . . . our dysfunctional little family had made it.

The Final Series

Our perilous adventure may have been over, but its aftershock followed us across the Atlantic. Back in Blighty, the front pages of the tabloids were splashed with photos of our abandoned star cars, which had been found by the police where we'd ditched them and impounded.

In London the Argentinian ambassador bayed for our blood, claiming we had insulted her country and deliberately gone down south to provoke trouble. Arrest warrants were in force for Jeremy, James, Richard and I back in Tierra del Fuego, on the charge of incitement to riot. Meanwhile the British press were trying – and failing – to prove that we'd frigged the number plates.

Naturally – and understandably – the BBC management microscopes went once more up our editorial bottoms, but their investigation found no evidence of prankish behaviour and with that fact established, they robustly refused the Argentinian ambassador's demands for the Patagonia Special not to be shown, and out the show went.

And so, with the planets temporarily in harmony, we set about shooting Series 22, completely unaware that it would be our last.

When I look back at the films we made for that series, I'm actually pretty shocked, in a good way, because clearly we still had what it took. The Australian road trip in the Northern Territories, which climaxes with the three of them herding a giant herd of cattle in luxury Grand Tourers, provided so much prime-grade material that it was almost the length of a Special.

Then, back in England, we made what I confidently claim is possibly our funniest 'Build' film, where we attempted to show the NHS what's what by creating our own ambulances. The final shot of Hammond pressing the quick-release catapult delivery system and launching his patient through the window of the makeshift hospital nearly made my son sick with laughter. It was a complete fluke, and I guess we just thought well, luck seems to be on our side at the moment.

Then off we went to St Petersburg for a Russian version of our race across London. This time Richard, who was championing two-wheeled power on a very expensive carbon fibre, ultra sleek, state-of-the-art bicycle, ran out of luck as, fifteen minutes into the race, he put the front wheel into a tram line and turned it into the sort of wheel that Dali would paint. But then it turned out 'luck' had just popped out to the shops for a moment, because it returned with a passing cyclist-cum-fan of the show who donated his own transport and enabled us to continue.

Elsewhere Jeremy was shouting his way along the canal system in a hovercraft, James was bumbling around in a Renault Twizy, and I, with a film crew, was in charge of the Stig's journey on public transport. Now, I can proudly boast that all the main components of our races were run fairly and squarely, but in these crosstown contests the Stig was never going to win. He was merely there to provide comic relief. As I said earlier, Ben Collins relished this aspect of the Stig, giving us proper theatre. Phil Keen, however, had no time for this part of the job and man alive did he hate that day in St Petersburg. For mile after mile in his Nomex suit, he ambled around the pavements and parks of St Petersburg, following my instructions to be baffled by posters of cats on the Metro, or stand in apparent mourning looking at a dead pigeon on the pavement. His gloom aside though, we came away with a tremendous Russian film.

As for life at the track, the A-listers were still turning up. A very witty and charming Will Smith one week, accompanied by the rising star that is Margot Robbie, then on another we had the company of the world's biggest pop star: Ed Sheeran. Ed was, like Johnny Vegas, one of our Stars in a Car who had yet to take his driving test. But after the customary explanation to Phil who Ed Sheeran was, he and Ed set about their *Karate Kid* tuition patiently and diligently, and in the end Sheeran set a worthy lap time.

So yes, Series 22: top-quality content. There was only one problem. Behind the scenes the wheels of the giant *Top Gear* machine were slowly, but inexorably, starting to come off.

The biggest problem was the timetable. Right from the get-go back in the early 2000s our schedule had always been tight, and as I said earlier, that problem only ever grew as over successive series the films became more ambitious and the number of months in the calendar, annoyingly, remained firmly at twelve.

In order to counteract the effects of this ever more pressured schedule, the main goal of our timetable – and we'd learned this the hard way from the early years – was to get all the films shot before we went into the weekly cycle of recording the studios. Because once that studio cycle began, Monday to Wednesday was then off the table for shooting films, which meant a knackered squad having to do their best, shooting what still needed to be shot, from Thursday to Sunday.

Having managed to achieve this for a good few years, we were now starting to slip back into the clutches of timetable hell. You finish Series 21 that little bit later, which means you start working on Series 22 that little bit later still.

Once you're in a rush to get the films shot before the studio window opens, the knock-on is that you lose the time – very important, not a luxury – to sit around brainstorming decent ideas. One option to counteract this would obviously be to shoot simpler films, but with the level of expectation now upon us a new film couldn't just be a simple road test à la Series 2. In our panicked heads, the fans now demanded à la carte dining every episode. In truth they probably would have forgiven us a few meh episodes, on account of the sizable editorial credit we'd banked with them, but we were way too insecure to see it that way.

So, once you're in this vicious circle of no time to brainstorm/no allowing yourself a drop in quality, the quickest fix is actually to go big: go abroad, shoot big films. It's somehow easier when you've got the world as your playground, as opposed to, say, Basingstoke, to think up new stories.

Series 22 was a classic example of this tactic in action. Off we went to Australia to herd cattle; off we went to St Petersburg to race across the city; off we went to Canada so that Jeremy and James could take their own sweet time rescuing Richard from a snowy mountain. All these films duly provided great material but we went too far with the 'go big, go abroad' solution and as a consequence chewed through too many weeks.

Sure enough, by the time we finally did start the studio records we'd only shot enough films for seven episodes, leaving us three short. And at that point the insanity of the workload spiralled as the timetable collapsed in on itself.

Monday: voice over the films and review rough cuts. Tuesday: write the studio. Wednesday: film the studio. Thursday to Sunday: get back out filming. By mid run I wasn't even going down to the studio records anymore, so behind were we with cutting the films in the edit.

Now I know all this may sound like I'm actually just going for gold at the First World Problem Olympics, but I'm afraid we'll have to agree to differ. With immovable deadlines marching towards us every week, keeping all the vast myriad of components that made the *Top Gear* machine run in harmony was becoming impossible. Gaskets were blowing, fuses tripping, bits falling off.

And so it was in this environment that on Wednesday 11 March, we recorded what would be our last ever studio. This was one of the days when I wasn't down there because there was too much to do in the edit and looking back I kick myself, because this record was always going to be stressy. Trapped in the collapsing timetable, we were now due to shoot another film the following day, and as soon as they'd completed their studio record, the presenters would have to hightail it up to North Yorkshire to be on set early the following morning.

We had a good guest booked: Nicholas Hoult, promoting *Mad Max: Fury Road*, but from what I was hearing during the day the overall studio record was indeed fraught, with stuff going wrong and, because we were trying to set up a film at the same time, only half the team were there to put those wrong things right. Nevertheless Jeremy, Richard and James and the skeleton crew gave it their all and then after a killer day our three were packed off up North.

Back in London I did a late shift in the edit and once the record was over, kept my phone off so as not to be disturbed. Then, when I switched it on the next morning, it had literally doubled in weight from the amount of text messages, voicemails and missed calls it was carrying. All the messages were saying the same thing: there'd been a bust-up. I had a voicemail from Jeremy too but it literally didn't make any sense. I tried calling him back but his phone was off.

Meanwhile Jeremy phoned Danny Cohen and turned himself in. He was suspended pending an investigation, and all the cogs and wheels and pistons that made up the whole *Top Gear* machine suddenly fell silent.

Spluttering Engines

A few days later, from the window of Jeremy's West London flat, I could see countless photographers down below, all waiting to get a picture of him. That wasn't going to happen though, because he'd confined himself to his quarters.

I looked at him reading a text message as he stubbed out yet another cigarette. If it could have talked, the overflowing ashtray would now have said: 'Are you having a laugh?'

The text was from the country's most famous PR guru, a man so skilled in the art of persuasion that he could probably convince Pride of Britain to let Rose West present an award. Now he was on the phone offering Jeremy some help.

'What did you say back?' I asked.

'I said no thanks, you're alright.'

This wasn't the first media mover and shaker who'd offered a helping hand. That one had been declined too.

I looked at my oldest and closest friend, sitting at the table staring into space.

Over at W1A the BBC were taking statements and discussing his fate, but as of yet no smoke had appeared from the chimney atop the Broadcasting House Vatican. Our plane was now losing height, with engines stalled, in fog.

But inside I knew our time on *Top Gear* was up, because there were now just too many factors conspiring to seal his fate.

For starters there was the outside pressure on BBC management. The petition by loyal *Top Gear* fans to save Jeremy was now approaching a million signatures. This level of support for a TV personality was unprecedented but sadly, every signature going onto that petition was also just as likely to be one more nail in the coffin. The simple fact was the BBC could never give in to that kind of pressure, not in a case like this. It would send out a message that popularity gives stars immunity and the bigger the appeal, the more firm their resolve would have to be.

One possible route to salvation would be him giving an actual visible demonstration of his remorse – checking in for therapy or anger management – concrete evidence that remedial action was being taken. It's a tried and tested method in the media world. The famous person negotiates the penance, does the penance and the TV channel can say: 'They've done the penance.'

In truth I don't know whether that sort of route was a possibility, because I wasn't privy to the top floor debates at the Beeb and so have no idea how strong the 'sack him' / 'keep him' factions were. All I can tell you is what I believe, and I believe that even if it were offered, Jeremy would not have gone for the visible penance option. These are my reasons.

Firstly, despite his media surroundings and his metropolitan and Cotswolds lifestyle, his DNA is still shot through with a lot of Yorkshireness. He genuinely doesn't understand the notion of therapy or the idea of paying to sit opposite someone who says, 'Tell me about your childhood.'

The BBC telling him to go and get help for anger management therefore would just be like oil and water. His logic was always 'If you have a bust-up you go to the pub and sort it out over a drink,' but this situation was way beyond pub remedy.

I believe he also thought it would be cynical to 'be seen' to get help. There is always an element of machinations around this sort of negotiated path, and for all his visible faults, he hasn't got a politically manipulative bone in his body. You know those times when you're out in other company with a friend and they say something in innocence that they shouldn't and you kick them discreetly under the table to shush them? Jeremy is without doubt the sort of person who would say: 'Why did you just kick me?'

But although he may be binary in this way, and yes the guy you see on TV may use a hammer to put a stamp on an envelope, that's only part of the picture. He's one of the smartest people you'll ever meet and his emotions run deep – really deep. He was aware of what rested on his shoulders, what he'd built and now had put in jeopardy, and a big part of what was in jeopardy was a whole tight team that he loved being part of. Because make no mistake, although he sat at the top of the tree, he was a proper team player. If things went to shit on a shoot, he may have kicked the cat for a moment, but then he was always one of the first to man the pumps, to find a way out. You saw it in smaller ways too – the post-studio brown food and beer sit down was very important to him. I've talked to many of the old team about this since, and they all agree that, as antsy as he could get at times, there was no malice to it. He cared about what he did, and what he was doing was in a team.

Could he be demanding? Absolutely. So was I, so was any good director. But his 'demanding-ness' was always based around improving a shoot. 'We need some horses, and we need them quickly.' He often thought of new story elements on the fly and expected everyone to pull out all the stops to get them, but so would I. That's just a newspaper room in action. A good example of him raising the bar on the hoof was the time his motorhome went over the cliff in Cornwall. We had the cliff, we had the permission. Then Jeremy suddenly said: 'Hang on, what if I'm sitting having an ice cream and the cliff is behind me, and as I do a piece to camera about what a lovely day it is, the car goes off the cliff behind me in the distance.' That sounds simple, but it's a fucker to coordinate, and obviously a one-shot deal. There would have been gnashing of teeth had it failed, but it's a level of demand worth bothering about.

But although as the figurehead he had plenty of power, the truth is he could never really wield the tough axe. He has, for example, never fired anyone in his life. And never could.

Sometimes he would moan to me about a director or researcher not being up to the job and often I would say, 'Okay then, I'll get rid of them,' even though a lot of the time I had no intention of doing so. Instead I just enjoyed watching his allergic reaction whenever I said a head would go on the chopping block. 'Oh, no, hang on a minute, let's not be hasty. Maybe just, you know, a firm word...'

Finally, if you part the robes of his mantle as King of the Outspoken Opinions, Jeremy is, behind all that, just a worker bee. For sure he generates his own ideas but if the BBC or a newspaper tell him to do some work by a certain time, he will just get on and do as asked. Back in 2002 when Jane Root gave us the *Top Gear* gig she had stipulated that the show must go from being a half hour to a full hour. I kicked off, certain that we could never make a show that would sustain for an hour. Jeremy had his concerns too but one day I remember him saying: 'Look, we've been tasked with making the show an hour, that's the job we've been given to do, so how about we stop moaning and we get on with it.'

So, yes, given that he knew he'd done wrong – and believe me he punished himself more than any newspaper or public outrage ever could – and given that he, at the end of the day, sees himself as another cog in the team, maybe he didn't take up any of the normal TV lifelines because he felt he didn't deserve them. I'm sure you all have your views on his BBC downfall, because Jeremy is as much a generator of opinions as he is a giver of them. I'll leave you with yours, but from being there at the time, the ones listed above are mine.

For sure that day in his kitchen I was certain I was looking at a man who had accepted he was going to be fired and was now just waiting for the moment.

'May Day . . .'

We – Richard and James and everyone working in the office – waited as the days went by for the outcome of Jeremy's suspension. I spoke occasionally to the late Alan Yentob, the Gandalf of the BBC top floor, who liked Jeremy and who you knew wanted a good outcome but could not tell me which way the wind was blowing.

Then out of nowhere, on the morning of 25 March, the end came. Some of the papers had even been briefed the night before, but as for the *Top Gear* team itself, there was no warning that Jeremy was to be fired.

In a complete fury, I called the person in the BBC press office involved in orchestrating the release and let fly about all of us having to find out in this way. I remember at one point calling him a heartless cunt but he didn't take the bait, mainly because he was following orders and more likely, he didn't really care what I thought. Later on I'd get it: a broadcaster has to control the release of information of this magnitude, and we were the collateral damage, but back then I was all over the place.

An hour or so later I got a call from the office of the Director-General, Tony Hall, asking me to go up and see him over at Broadcasting House.

As befits the Director-General of the British Broadcasting Corporation, it was a proper office with a proper Bond villain meeting table and some proper chairs. I sat in one of them, Tony sat in the big one at the head of the table and told me how sorry he was that it had all come to this. They were, in truth, heartfelt, considerate words.

I guess Tony knew how close Jeremy and I were, how far back we went, and he wanted to offer a moment of human contact.

However, with all my shredded nerves being as they were, at DEFCON 1, I wasn't ready for this kind of moment. I remember telling him what a massive waste the whole affair was and how the sacking need never have happened, and then I guess my brain had had enough of being on a war footing, the magnitude of what we'd lost suddenly hit me, and I just cracked up. I started sobbing, at his big Bond villain desk. Now Tony Hall may be a considerate man but he's also British, and the Director-General, and it was pretty clear that he wasn't ready for this either. Maybe the Bond villain desk had some sort of panic button next to the shark tank button, but pretty quickly his assistant entered, with tissues, and I gathered myself together and we said our goodbyes. Well done me. Really smooth.

Back over at White City the BBC Two Controller came over to see me to talk about how we might get the show up and running again. In truth I sat there thinking: 'I know you're just doing your job, and I know the BBC technically "owns" a show called *Top Gear*, but for the last thirteen years it's not been your show, and the show it is now is definitely nothing you created. And . . . you have no fucking idea what you've just thrown away.'

Like I say, I thought all this but I didn't say it, because with nothing left to fight for, I was done with throwing toys out of the pram. So instead I gave my notice shortly afterwards. However, although I may have been done with toy throwing, I certainly wasn't above a bit of pettiness. At the BBC there's a rule that if a show wins an award, the actual physical award belongs to the BBC, to be displayed in its trophy cabinets. Over the thirteen years we'd been on air we'd won a load of them and, after a board meeting at which only I was present, the decision was taken – unanimously – that those trophies belonged to us. So, one quiet Sunday morning I took my son, Noah, into the building and together we heisted the lot. Okay, it wouldn't make up for all the Sports Days and Nativity plays I'd missed but at least this eleven-year-old could partake in his own little *Ocean's Eleven*.

As for the day I actually left the BBC, I'll never forget it, mainly because of what a nothing event it was. The *Top Gear* office was empty on account of the show being on ice, so there was nobody to say goodbye to. Then, at the moment my notice expired some noughts and ones in the BBC system talked to some other noughts and ones, my pass stopped working and there I was, standing outside the building, no longer a BBC man.

For a moment, looking up at the revolving door I'd entered and exited for so long, I felt a bit like Sybil Fawlty. Some of you may have to google that reference but for those of a more bus-pass disposition, it's specifically the episode when she mistakenly thinks Basil is carrying on with one of the female guests. She stands there with hands on her hips and, reminding him of their marriage, says with maximum disappointment and disdain: 'Fifteen years, Basil!'

That's how I felt right then: 'Fifteen years, Basil!' Only Basil was the BBC and fifteen years was actually twenty-two years – the time Jeremy and I had been making stuff together for the Corporation.

In truth my indignation didn't last long, because at the end of the day we'd laid out our working conditions

– 'leave us alone!'; 'stop shouting at us!' – conditions which in turn meant we'd made our own nettle-strewn bed. And on top of that there had been some wonderful people – Jane, Roly, David and his team, Tara, Liz the lawyer – who'd all had our backs.

But once the indignation waned, immense sadness soon took its place, because after thirteen years, the wreckage of our *Top Gear* plane was now strewn all over the runway. And what an immense and beautiful thing it had been.

The Grand Tour

Avengers Re-assemble

About a week after Jeremy's sacking, Jeremy, Richard, James and I found ourselves round the kitchen table in Jeremy's flat.

The meeting agenda was quite succinct:

AGENDA

1. What the fuck do we do now?

In the 'plus' column, the four of us knew we still had ability: Series 22 had shown that. Also, we were used to being in control of our own destiny, and therefore capable of finding a way forward.

In the 'minus' column, there was the nagging worry that we no longer had an audience. Would people, despite the million-strong petition, decide they'd had enough of us now that the initial drama had died away? Also, to the same point, would any broadcaster want to employ us? Finally, shuffling around in the room as a little elephant – but not acknowledged by any of us – did we still want to work together anymore?

That last point would soon be forcibly raised anyway, but for the present we remained British, sat on our emotions and concentrated on the employment options. Of the UK broadcasters, Channel 4 weren't interested. Sky were absolutely 'do not darken our doors'. ITV had made enthusiastic noises but we probably wouldn't get the budget we needed and nor were we in a position to demand that they don't sell car-related advertising around us.

Once we'd crunched this thin amount of data I then made the observation – quite a smart one I like to think – that our only logical chance of finding an employer would be in America.

What names did we know? Netflix. Hmmm, the big streaming people with no schedule, loads of money too. Interesting.

HBO? I thought back to our 'Try and slip in the song title' meeting of many years back. Okay, not HBO.

That left the big networks – ABC, CBS, NBC – but we couldn't see how we and they would fit editorially, and anyway Jeremy and I had already been on a fishing trip to hook one of them and come back empty-handed.

What about AMC? They'd made *Breaking Bad* and we all loved *Breaking Bad*. And *Walking Dead*?! Fuck me that was another good one. Soon though we realised we were just naming American TV shows we liked, but one useful thought we did have was that if America it was, then we'd most likely need an American agent.

Luckily, over the next few days, the American agents came looking for us. They'd presumably read of our demise in *Variety* and *Hollywood Reporter*, and soon we were in discussions with two of the biggest agencies, CAA and WME, with both of them offering a similar pitch: come with us and we'll help find you a new home and do the deal for you.

All the time we were having these discussions, I gave hardly any thought as to what the BBC might be doing. I mean, why bother when to me it was already obvious what they would do? Management pride at W1A would go into overdrive as they sought to prove to the licence payers that, sad as it had been to fire Jeremy, *Top Gear* would continue and remain as popular as ever. The internal mantra would be: we own the name, we own the brand, we own the show. The four of us had merely been temporary caretakers and now it was time to install new and even better tenants.

The other reason I didn't think about what they were up to was because I was pretty sure they would fuck up. Nobody senior would realise that the only chance of success was a proper top-down reinvention, in order to exorcise the ghosts of Clarkson, Hammond and May. Instead, propelled by the urge to prove as quickly as possible that it was business as usual, *Top Gear* would carry on with the same ingredients, only with a new line-up. On top of that, very few execs at the BBC had bothered to really look hard at why our show worked. They had seen three guys mucking about with cars, they had seen irreverence, they'd seen beautiful and exotic locations, and as long as those headline boxes got ticked, the show would be back on the road.

What they wouldn't have seen was all the nuance that had actually gone into three grown men falling over, that there was a massive difference between what Jeremy, Richard and James were doing and some lads having a stag night laugh.

Then there was the dynamic between Richard, James and Jeremy, which indeed the BBC themselves had smartly allowed to develop organically over time.

Now though, with the priority being to get the show back on air quickly, they would have to recruit fast and try and manufacture an onscreen chemistry sharpish, and the second you put the word 'manufacture' alongside 'chemistry', you're flogging a dead horse.

So yes, with all this logic running around my head, I definitely paid little attention to whatever the BBC might be up to.

The only problem was, so busy was I being chuffed with my logic that I didn't see the real and present danger that genuinely was heading our way.

The fact is, the BBC was actually being very cunning. Unbeknown to Jeremy and I, they were quietly making a play for Richard and James to split off and come back to *Top Gear*.

This was a damn fine move, because pulling this off would kill two birds with one stone. With two of the old show's stars in their new iteration of *TG*, there was a much better chance of some of the old magic reappearing on screen to make the fans happy. Secondly, with our quartet shattered, whatever rival show Jeremy and I might have in mind would be wiped from the battlefield, because no new employer would likely be interested in just me and him.

To make matters worse, there were some decent psychological buttons that the Beeb could press with Richard and James. Firstly, as recently proven, Jeremy, talented as he is, was a total liability. Why hitch the horse that is your own careers to a wagon as unstable as that one?

Secondly, the four of us had just lost a guaranteed handsomely paid deal to make another three years of *Top Gear*. And here now was the BBC offering to make that problem go away for RH and JM, with the promise of some huge cheques.

Third, Richard and James could now run the show editorially, and of all the buttons the BBC could press, this was probably the canniest. The fact is there had always been a sense in our dynamic that, as vital as Richard and James were to the success of the show, the editorial strings were always being pulled by Jeremy and me. There was some truth in that because I was fairly dictatorial in the edit, I was the one there all the time looking at the options, and given the speed we were working at, a benign dictatorship was the only way. Likewise at the point of conceiving and indeed shooting films, Jeremy was overwhelmingly the best out of all of us when it came to editorial ideas and execution.

Maybe as a producer I should have paid more attention to this imbalance along the way, but the truth is I saw Richard and James to be so valuable and indispensable that I guess I assumed they thought the same way about themselves.

Be that as it may, this power imbalance was a crafty little scab for the BBC to pick at, because it absolutely did resonate. In particular, and I don't think he'll mind me saying this, it resonated more with James because he didn't always see eye to eye with Jeremy on editorial, and on top of that he loved making his solo shows. As proud and aware as he was of *TG*'s achievements, I expect it was always a blessed relief for him to be away making his *Toy Stories* and the like.

So, a big cheque, security from Jeremy instability and the keys to the editorial cupboard: a formidably tempting offer.

As I say, for a while Jeremy and I didn't know that James and Richard were being courted but when we did get wind of it none of us – completely in line with our bloke-based friendship – actually talked about it. Instead there would be this slightly tragic male panto, with all of us discussing what bike Richard was thinking of buying, or James's plans for doing up his house; anything but the woolly mammoth, its head swaying in the corner of the room.

The BBC however was keen to turn up the wick on their Richard and James campaign by sending out a public signal that the natural home for the two of them was back at W1A. And so, pretty soon, carefully orchestrated 'accidentally captured' paparazzi pics started appearing in the papers showing James and Richard walking along outside BBC HQ with chief talent schmoozer, the late Alan Yentob, a man who missed Jeremy, but loved the Corporation more.

With the courtship now no longer a secret, the four of us had to have a man-to-man chat, and once we'd got through the customary prevarication about James's new floor tiles we finally said hello to the elephant. Bottom line, they were both interested in the BBC offer for all the reasons mentioned, but were obviously also keen to find out whether there was a real chance of the band staying together. So for now they would ride two horses. Neither Jeremy nor I argued with that. It was a position they were absolutely entitled to take.

However, with the lie of the land now clear, the endeavour to keep the band together pushed forward at a super-charged pace. Very quickly we chose an agent: Lance, from WME. To us Lance was almost a parody of Ari Gold from *Entourage* (Lance's boss at WME, Ari Emanuel, actually is the real-life inspiration for Ari Gold) and we loved him for it. We had this picture of Lance constantly pacing up

and down in his Hollywood office, with one of those telephone mouthpiece things attached, barking instructions
to an army of assistants as he fielded hundreds of calls per
day. Lance also had absolutely ZERO time for small talk,
which in turn meant we would delight, on our conference
calls, in trying to force him into actual small talk.

CONFERENCE CALL BEGINS...
LANCE: 'Hi.'
US FOUR: 'Hi, Lance.'
LANCE: 'So, I've heard back from Netfli—'
US FOUR: 'How was your weekend, Lance?'
LANCE: 'It was great thank you. So Netflix has come
    back—'
US FOUR: 'Wasn't it Labour Day or something?
    Did you take the kids anywhere nice?'
LANCE: 'Yes we had a great time. So, Netflix...'

Once we'd done the 'annoying Lance' ritual, he would
then give us the lie of the land. And the way the land was
lying was actually starting to look good, because we had
serious offers from both Netflix and also ... Amazon.

We hadn't really thought of Amazon because back
in 2015 Netflix had even more supremacy in the streaming market than it does now. However, the Amazon
offer wouldn't leave our minds. Admittedly Amazon
were offering more money than Netflix, but what also
intrigued us was the very fact that Amazon was still a bit

of a minnow in the streaming world. We reasoned that at Netflix we would just be 'another big show' in their huge slate of output, whereas on the Amazon platform, with its smaller list of contents, we would be a really big deal: basically the same thinking whereby we'd chosen to stay at BBC Two rather than go to BBC One.

Likewise we potentially had more value to Amazon than just providing them with a good show. They wanted to grow their streaming service fast, launch Prime globally, and our – sorry about this – oven-ready trio, with their *Guiness Book of Records* following, could be just the ticket.

By summer 2015 a contract was on the table, and within it sat the two main components we required. Clause 1: guaranteed editorial freedom. The Amazon execs, even if they disliked an episode intensely, would not be able to make us change anything. They couldn't tell us what films to shoot, we wouldn't have to wear Stetsons and Jeremy wouldn't have to inject his face with Botox.

On top of that, enough money to make a good global show, with hopefully enough left over to pay ourselves well.

We then had to leave Richard and James to deliberate. Hammo crossed the floor first because the deal was good and, as irritating as Jeremy and I could be, he valued our editorial. Eventually James came too. Despite the prick-liness that could test our relationship, in the end there was enough Stockholm Syndrome in there to save the day. And boom: we all signed with Amazon.

Rebuilding the Plane

The deal was eventually closed in August. Once the ink had dried the enormity of the task that lay ahead hit us with the same force you see in the footage from one of those crash-test films.

Yes Amazon had paid well, yes they'd given us creative control, but in return they wanted a huge pound of flesh. Firstly, the timetable. Our new employers required our new show to be ready to transmit in twelve months' time. Now I know to a layman twelve months sounds like a year – obviously because it is – but in TV terms, twelve months is a quick nip to the loo. To conceive, research, shoot and edit twelve shows' worth of material in that length of time would be an enormous enough task for a show that already existed, with an existing infrastructure: offices, researchers, producers, directors, etc. But at the time of signing the number of staff employed on our new show numbered just four. Us four.

The other issue was that our show would have to have a new name, a new look and . . . this was the kicker . . . be as close in spirit to our old show as possible BUT . . . not so close that the BBC lawyers could shut it down. We had to skim the orbit of *Top Gear* without a barrister noticing.

The editorial challenge – creating a new show and shooting it – was already a bowel-emptying prospect all on its own, but having to pass every idea we thought of through legal hands, that would put the timetable in very real danger.

At least we couldn't afford to waste any time moaning about our lot, so we rolled up our Battle of Britain sleeves and got going. Top of the to-do list was an office and some staff. Here we were thrown a lifeline by the wonderful Eric Fellner, one half of the British film company Working Title. Eric lent us some space at their offices and, whilst trying not to eavesdrop on the third *Bridget Jones* film being developed next door, I set about hiring. Employee no.1 was an old *Top Gear* stalwart, Chenoa Finlayson-Pugh. Then we hired Zoe Brewer, a formidable production executive we'd once worked with, to be our new money queen. However we really did need more, because there were only so many times we could send Hammo down to Ryman and watch him come back with the wrong packets of everything.

Over at *Top Gear* a lot of the team were already tied up working on the new iteration, but we did manage to entice away the most vital person, Phil Churchward, who had been our main director for the last several years. With Phil and his extraordinary aesthetic powers on board, we knew we could deliver the epic, (legally safe) films Amazon were expecting.

Next was a call to our old script editor Richard Porter, who was quite surprised to be hearing from us because he'd fairly laid into Jeremy in his excellent chronicle of the *Top Gear* years: *And on That Bombshell*, available in all eighteenth-century French Literature bookshops. However, once we'd explained that that was all water under the bridge and that far more challenging waters now needed to be navigated, Porter, possibly to stop having to listen to any more water analogies, dived in with us and started swimming. Also, we desperately needed his wit and his astonishing levels of car geekiness.

Whilst all this practical legwork was going on, we simultaneously had to burn brain cells trying to crack the important editorial conundrums, such as what the show should look like and what it should be called.

Spinal Tap

With the legal instruction front of mind that our new creation had to be *Top Gear* without being *Top Gear*, we decided we wanted to keep some sort of studio element to break up the films. Enter, stage left, our lawyer, Mark Devereux. Mark is a legend in media law circles, and I guess I'd say that if you've seen *Clarkson's Farm* he's the legal equivalent of Charlie. His word is – literally and figuratively – law, and anything coming out of Jeremy's mouth that's Jeremy nonsense, goes into a mincer.

Mark explained that the BBC couldn't stop us having a car show with films punctuated by a studio. If you're interested in law it's quite illuminating stuff because the point is you can't copyright an 'idea', only the details of the idea. To put it another way, a designer can copyright his or her specific design for a chair, but you can't copyright the concept of a seating device with four legs.

So yes, we could have a studio, but it couldn't be like the *Top Gear* hangar.

All four of us went our separate ways to ponder the studio problem, and naturally it was Jeremy who pondered it the most. Sure enough the next time we met up, he'd had a brainwave, one that had come about whilst watching the hot box set series of the moment, *True Detective*, starring Woody Harrelson and Matthew McConaughey.

'Chaps, I was watching *True Detective* the other night,' he began, 'and in this one episode there's this religious Bible Belt meeting, and it's held in a big tent sort of thing.'

'A tent?'

'Yeah. It's not like a Big Top Tent you get at the circus, nowhere near as fancy as that. It's a really simple struc-ture – a big piece of canvas over the top, and some poles holding it up.'

Jeremy's thought was that we could have a tent like this as our studio, put it up wherever we liked and film the studio bits in different locations. 'We can travel around the country, we can even go abroad,' he exclaimed excitedly.

Now that . . . was a very, very good idea. The only problem was, it had come out of Jeremy's brain, which meant that it had materialised with absolutely fuck all considerations about any practical issues attached to it.

How much would it cost to build? How much would it cost to move around? How big would it need to be?

By way of response Jeremy's brain got out its Dustpan and Brush of Impatience and swept all the questions into the Dustbin of Annoyances.

The tent idea required a second meeting with Mark the lawyer and Brian the studio director, who had also defected from *Top Gear* to come with us. Well when I say 'defected', he was earning double bubble by doing the new *Top Gear* as well, but to be fair we only needed 50 per cent of his loyalty.

'I was watching *True Detective* the other night . . .' Jeremy began once we'd got them sat down, and once again delivered his tent spiel.

Afterwards Brian and I watched the *True Detective* episode with the tent, and Brian's director brain went into overdrive with worryingly pertinent studio director questions. 'What about the noise from wind and rain? How do we light it? What about the flooring? How do we get cars in there . . . ?'

Once again Jeremy's Dustpan of Impatience appeared. 'Don't worry about all that! We're just talking! Crowds gather in tents all the time! My God how do circuses get by? How hard can it be?'

Now as it happened some big shot Amazon execs – our new bosses – were flying into London in the coming week and they wanted to meet the four of us to say hello but, more importantly, to discuss what progress we'd made with developing the new show.

In truth we had bugger all to offer except Jeremy's tent idea, but at the mention of this, Mark the lawyer, bless him, shut him down firmly.

'Do not, under any circumstances, mention the travelling tent at this meeting,' he warned. 'It's not costed out and you don't know what you're getting into with it.'

At this point I should probably put some context onto Mark's concern. The fact is our deal with Amazon was structured very simply. They give us a chunk of money and in return we give them a show – I think the legal phrase was 'of first-class quality'. And then what we didn't spend was ours to keep. The leftover was our pay.

You don't have to be Lord Sugar to see where Mark was going: yes, by all means, deliver the goods with your show and make it 'first class', but don't commit to something you don't know the cost of, something where the bill could be fucking mental. Three of us understood this implicitly, whilst the fourth member was doing his best to get his head round it.

Anyway, the day arrived for our first face-to-face meeting with the big Amazon cheeses from America. The four of us, plus Lawyer Mark, went over to Amazon's London offices and as we rode up in the lift, Mark sternly reiterated the main point:

'Do not mention the tent.'

We exited the lift with Jeremy clearly having taken Mark's words to heart. The look of concentration on his face was like a four-year-old in a school Nativity play trying to remember his lines.

In we went to a big meeting room, and this being our first time on Amazon property, we didn't really know what to expect. From memory there were four Amazon execs, but what struck me first was the hospitality that had been laid on, because spread out on a table was a vast selection of quiches. Maybe somebody on the Amazon side thought the five of us might be ravenous after our four-mile taxi ride across London and the polite thing to do would be to lay some snacks on. As to why quiches, and so many of them, I'll never know. But here we all now were, nine grown men, standing around a table bearing a Northern wedding amount of egg flans in various flavours.

The meeting kicked off with a bit of an awkward silence. One of the Amazon execs gestured at the table, asked if we were hungry and, maybe it was nerves, but suddenly I became fixated about us making inroads into the quiches. 'You start on the mushroom one, I'll hit up the salmon and spinach,' I whispered to James. Then to Richard: 'Hammo, you get going on the Lorraine.'

'I've had lunch, I'm not hungry,' Hammo whispered back.

'Oh for Christ's sake, just start eating.'

The three of us duly began munching away, but I couldn't get to Jeremy, who was on the other side of the table, making small talk.

Then, inevitably, one of the American execs asked the question we'd been dreading: 'So, what thoughts have you guys been having about how the new show would look?'

There then followed a pretty awkward silence, but in my head, that was okay. As long as we kept eating the quiches we could just stay quiet, then maybe after a moment or two of quiche-eating, waffle our way out of the question.

Unfortunately, the only thing on the planet that abhors a vacuum more than nature is the person who wasn't eating any quiche. I could just tell, looking across at him, that he couldn't hold it in anymore. Sure enough, Jeremy's mouth opened and, like a piñata exploding, out came the words: 'I was watching *True Detective* the other night . . .'

Now, as I said, on paper the tent was a great idea; add in the fact that in Amazon's eyes it was kind of no longer their money and there was absolutely no reason for the execs not to like it. I think Mark tried to utter some lawyerly caveat about the tent needing to be costed, but the damage was done. The Americans simply loved the idea too damn much.

And so, in that quiche-filled room, our Spinal Tap Stonehenge was born.

Growing Pains

On the bright side of tent world – and make no mistake I am scrabbling here – the tent's existence did help us settle on our new name. It would enable us to travel around *Grand Tour*-ing.

The registering of *The Grand Tour* was actually quite a straightforward, if expensive procedure. However, we also had to slog our way through much more baffling legal obstacle courses in order to head off any BBC infringement challenges. All the work was in the nuance. For example, we were allowed to have another tame racing driver, but as a point of difference to the Stig, he couldn't be anonymous and he would have to speak. Likewise we could have a scoreboard for lap times, but Jeremy would not be allowed to hand write the times on magnetic strips and stick them on a board. Yes we could have a studio audience, but none of them would be allowed to stand around or behind the presenters. Then it got worse. I give you, for example, the discussion about whether James could still say 'Oh cock'. Was this, the lawyers ruminated, a saying of James's that he could claim as everyday use, or . . . part of his *Top Gear* persona? The four of us were sitting there thinking: 'are we being filmed for one of those Ant and Dec pranks?' If James can't say 'Oh cock!' will Jeremy have to start saying things like 'Actually you may have a point' or 'To be fair . . .' Whilst Richard says: 'I'll have the fish.'

The low point – or high point – depending on how much comedy there was to be found in all this, came when a legal person raised the issue of stopping to admire the view. The concern here was – I kid you not – that on road trips to exotic foreign climes, Richard, James and Jeremy often spent a moment or two taking in and comment- ing on whatever breathtaking surroundings they found themselves in. Basically . . . admiring the view. Again, we asked in ever more distressed tones: what are we supposed to do here? Stand in front of the Atlas Mountains at sunset or the Namibian Skeleton Coast bathed in morning mist and go: 'Well that looks shit.'

On the brighter front, back in London we'd now hired a team of producers and researchers and found ourselves an office in West London, which meant we could start brainstorming some stuff to shoot. In this area we were still match fit and over a couple of days worked up most of the films for Series 1. Just so you don't have to go look on IMDb, let me remind you of a few: Grand Touring in Italy with Hammond being a yob; Holy Trinity of hyper-cars in Portugal; our version of the Tom Cruise film *Edge of Tomorrow* in an army base in Jordan; road trip to Morocco; second-hand Maseratis in France and a Beach Buggy Special in Namibia.

Now, everything we'd written down made sense – to me, to the presenters, to Porter. We'd done this before. However, even though our contract gave us editorial control, the Amazon execs in America still wanted updates on our filming plans so they could see how their money was being spent, and accordingly weekly calls were set up between myself and LA.

That sounds like a simple job for an exec producer. The problem was that for the last thirteen years I'd never been required to pitch, sell or explain any film idea we had. The BBC had left us alone and like spies dropping off messages at park benches, we'd just handed the goods over when they were ready.

Obviously, I knew that in the end the *Grand Tour* films would be okay, but having to outline them as flat facts – not yet real and therefore not yet entertaining – was torture.

'So yes, in Morocco the guys will get into an argument about which car is the heaviest, and then, erm, build some scales to weigh them on . . .'

'So yes, in Italy, whilst Jeremy and James are in an art gallery, you'll hear the sound of Richard driving noisily somewhere in the distance. BUT . . . when they get to a track later on, James won't want to drive around the track so he'll do some painting.'

'So yes, at the race track in Portugal, James won't be able to drive his Ferrari back to the hotel so he'll have to get a lift from the delivery driver.'

And so on, and so on, one tragic explanation after another.

As for the reaction from the Amazon execs, think of those capsules that get sent into space containing a Blur song and the works of Shakespeare – everyone hopes that one day another life form will find them and make contact, but in reality we all know they'll just drift around in space, unfound, forever. That was my weekly phone call. My words – the contents of the capsule, just floating around the Amazon solar system, not registering with any other life forms.

I mean to be fair, put yourself in their shoes. On

YouTube they've watched a Reliant Robin space shuttle exploding, Minis going down ski jumps, caravan airships emerging from hangars, amphibious cars sinking in the sea, cars playing football and rugby, a pickup truck survive a building demolition, a pickup arriving at the magnetic north pole – they've seen all that, they've got the cheque book out, and now I'm telling them the highlight of the luxury SUVs film in Germany involves driving past some funny road signs.

On one call I finished off by saying that we were at least ready to shoot our first film, which would involve a road trip to the Continent in Maseratis. Now for a brief moment the Amazon execs had hope in their hearts. In their minds they were clearly already filling in the blanks and seeing exotic Italian cars sweeping through a breathtaking Alpine backdrop, maybe set to the soundtrack of *The Italian Job*. I then immediately shattered all that by saying that the cars would be cheap second-hand ones – the unloved models – and that we'd be filming in northern France in November, where the scenery would be a cocktail of industrial ports, grey skies and drizzle. 'It's counterintuitive,' I said eagerly. 'You've got the whole imaginary dream of life with an affordable Maserati, and then the reality, which is shit. Imagine that? It'll be funny.' Silence. My capsule continued floating out into the Milky Way.

Clearly, the only way we could calm the nerves of our new employers was to get filming and deliver the goods for real.

As it turned out, we couldn't even get that right. The whole film crew shipped out to France for the Maserati shoot, cars were transported over, everything in place, and then, the night before the presenters were due to depart for French shores, I got a call from James. He'd slipped on the pavement coming out of his local Indian restaurant, a bit pissed, and fractured his arm.

Naturally I had to inform our paymasters in Los Angeles. I got on the phone and, changing 'a bit pissed' to 'wet pavement', told them that one of their star signings was heading off to our first shoot, an arm down.

By now I just knew they must be thinking: 'why did we get involved with these clowns?' but I was ready for that.

'Now, what you all need to do is not worry,' I added optimistically, 'because these sort of moments are precisely where we come good. The thing is, James has fractured his right arm but . . . his car is an automatic!'

Massive uncomprehending silence.

'He can still drive it!' I explained. All this did was send everyone into a different kind of tailspin, because in the American TV world 'talent' and 'injuries' usually very quickly becomes a holy trinity involving 'lawyers'.

So whilst James, Richard and Jeremy were messaging each other saying things like: 'Oh this is fucking brilliant. James, we'll get you a massive bottle of aspirin you can't take the lid off, and a dildo to help you turn the steering wheel', I was reassuring the West Coast that if James's arm came back from the shoot a bit worse off than when it started, he wouldn't sue. He'd just moan about it endlessly. To me.

One film in the can, albeit with only five working arms, energised us. Then things went up a level in Portugal, specifically at the Autódromo Internacional do Algarve, where we filmed our Holy Trinity shootout of the three hypercars of the moment: the McLaren P1, the Porsche 918 and the LaFerrari. For this shoot, Amazon sent along John Holmes, their Head of Production. John's job is to make sure that the technical scaffolding is all in place, so that what we've promised Amazon will get to Amazon in the shape and spec they require it. We were now, for example, shooting for the first time in 4K. And before you say anything, yes I know your camera is 4K but back in 2015 it was frontier stuff. On the shoots we now needed to have a dedicated team of nerds who would take the 4K cards from the cameras once they were full of smoking-tyre footage and download that data so that it could be uploaded into something called the Cloud. As Amazon John explained all this to the four of us, I swear we actually looked up into the sky, expecting to see one of the white fluffy objects above us swell a bit.

Anyway, the Holy Trinity shoot was a bit of a turning point for the *Grand Tour*. For starters it was one of those shoots where we'd all brought our A Game. When you have a window of just two working days at a race track – i.e. nine-to-five track permitted times – in which to gather the material needed for a thirty-minute plus film, exceptional planning of the military sort is required. We need to shoot runs with the presenters talking in car, runs just for beauty – slow mo, smoking tyres, etc; runs with a tracking car, which means the cameras at trackside have to down tools; then runs with external cameras mounted all over the cars, which in turn means no other big cameras can shoot the cars. Then we need to film the runs with the helicopter, which means you can't do any runs with sound or talking, and so on and so on. Phil the director is untouchable when it comes to orchestrating this kind of schedule, and that's before we get to how aesthetically match fit and creative he and his team are.

Amazon John was now a witness to all this A Gamery. In the pit lane garage, in his safe space next to the 4K nerds, he was bowled over not just by the beauty of the rushes, but also by the sheer speed at which we were creating them. American film crews can faff. We, for the reasons listed above, do not.

John was also witnessing not just the speed of the film crews, but the dexterity of the presenters' minds, as they riffed away with no script, all the while with Jeremy concocting new scenes on the run, such as the forfeit, should he lose the lap shootout, being the detonation of his house.

There's a line in *Butch Cassidy and the Sundance Kid* where Robert Redford, when being asked to prove how good he is as a sharpshooter, asks: 'Can I move? I'm better when I move.'

I definitely think that's us. And that's what Amazon, through gentleman John's eyes, started to see.

Canvas City

2015 rolled into 2016 and the September launch date approached at an alarming velocity. In fact the only thing speedier than the disappearing days was the rate at which we were spending our money.

Whilst we'd been filming, Chris, one of our senior producers, together with Brian the studio director, had been crunching the numbers on the tent. And sure enough it was now a very, very, very – actually sod it I'll add another 'very' – long way from Jeremy's *True Detective* tent. Once Brian and his team had collated all the technical requirements it was clear that the tent would have to be weatherproof and also soundproof, not just from, say, passing traffic, but also from rain on the roof, which would require a double roof. In addition the floor would have to be purpose-built in order to be completely flat, so that the cameras on wheels could roll across it without jerking. As for the big window thing behind the presenters, that couldn't be any old polythene tent shit you get in a normal camping shop. In order for there not to be reflections or something else undesirable to directors as the light faded, the window would have to be made out of – I don't know – fucking diamonds and space dust.

Then, in order for it to accommodate an audience of 200 and have room left over for the presenters to move around and for the camera crews to do their thing, its dimensions would have to be just shy of the Albert Hall's.

In fact two giant artics, plus an army of orcs, would be needed to transport it and assemble it.

Bottom line, our tent would have to have the characteristics of a building made out of bricks and steel and glass, such as, say . . . a normal TV studio that already existed.

I'm not finished. Because we were now committed to globetrotting, our schedule of studio records was too tight to allow us to take the tent down, get it to another country and put it up again in time for the next show, which meant that we would need two of the bastards.

Still not finished. Every studio recording requires a small army of technicians with all their banks of monitors and recording desks full of switches and winking lights, and they too would need their own, extra tent.

Still not finished. Because we were recording in 4K we would need a studio crew specialising in this new form of TV witchcraft, and the only team that would do the job was based in Holland, which would mean flying them to wherever we were each week.

Honestly, if you've not seen that episode of *True Detective* – I just can't watch it – pull up a picture of a shack in Haiti after a hurricane, then another of the Taj Mahal. That's what I'm on about.

When Chris and Brian finally reached the bottom of the list of heartbreak, I asked Chris if we could do all this for £2 million, which is what we'd kind of budgeted. He took a while to answer – understandable, because lying to your boss is a precise art – then eventually said 'yes'. And, with all of us having bought into this blatant untruth, we pressed 'go' on the tents.

I Can See Clearly Now . . .

Whilst our pension pots were being turned into canvas, Jeremy had been sketching out what would become the famous *Grand Tour* huge opening. With his tabloid brain fully on point, he believed our 'Hello, World' should be a proper statement, with a narrative – not one that said: 'Fuck you, BBC, we've got another job' (okay there was a bit of that) but one that said to all our audience, 'Don't worry, we're back and back with a bang.'

The opening would start quietly and sombrely as he exits the BBC, then there's the flight to America (at first he suggested he should be in Economy but we were like: 'You're probably milking it there, mate') – then he picks up his Mustang in the airport car park, which cuts to him driving on a classic American highway where he is joined in their respective Mustangs by Richard and James. Affirmation! The trio are here!

The most important component for him though was the song. He'd structured the whole opening around the iconic 1970s song 'I Can See Clearly Now', but not the original recording by Johnny Nash; more specifically the Hothouse Flowers version. In comparison to the Nash original, the Hothouse Flowers recording – especially the live version – starts very quietly but then turns into a full-on barnstormer, building and building with unstoppable force, like a 747 landing on your head.

Then, by the time we cut to the drive across the desert flats, with the three Mustangs bursting through a Praetorian Guard of hundreds of like-minded petrolheads in their weird and wonderful cars, the song has absolutely detonated. Given he had his heart set on the live version, it was a no-brainer that as the three of them finally pulled up amongst a few thousand *Grand Tour* fans, the Hothouse Flowers themselves should be there, playing live on stage.

There were other, smaller messages in that opening too. The hordes of cars, for example, were deliberately eclectic – from Mad Max to vintage to cheap to costly – because we wanted to emphasise that we were still a car show that embraced every type of petrol head. As for the desert setting, it wasn't all just meant to shout: 'Good morning, America!' We were also making the point that now we'd embraced the new frontier of streaming, we would be everywhere and nowhere all at once. It was, in the end, pretty damn perfect.

On the day of recording in the desert, we all simultaneously received an email from Jeff. The Jeff. Our boss Jeff. It would be the one and only time we ever had direct contact with him – fair dos, he's hardly running a corner shop – and he warmly wished us well for the future and generally said nice boss things.

Jeff had also said, along the way, that we'd been a 'very, very, very expensive' signing. Three verys no less. If he'd seen the invoices for the Big Opening though, he would have at least consoled himself that his money was going onscreen. By the time we'd hired the patch of desert, paid for all the car owners to ship their cars out, put them all up, bussed in a couple of thousand fans, fed and sheltered them, hired the Hothouse Flowers, flown the Hothouse Flowers over, paid for the song, built a stage, shipped in our film crew and drenched the place in security, Zoe, our Head of Money, was looking at bills for more than £2.5 million. But, it was necessary for such a juggernaut opening heralding a return full of intent.

As for which opening film to usher in our new era, we'd gone for the Holy Trinity hypercar shoot, a choice which surprised us all because when we'd shot it at the time, it didn't scream 'launch pad'. Instead it felt more like a solid mid-series number, and too petrolheady for the launch of a new show where we weren't sure who would be watching.

Apparently though, when people go to a dogs' home to pick a dog and they don't know which one to choose, there's this popular belief that you shouldn't worry, because the mutt you're meant to have will come up and pick you. It's kind of the same with films, once you get in the edit. You start piecing them together and they then start to come alive as their strengths and weaknesses, hidden until this point, make themselves known. Such was the case with the Holy Trinity. It wasn't just that it looked beautiful and exciting and the footage was the sort of material that 4K was born to be with, more importantly the film was completely sure of itself. I know that sounds a bit like film-school wank, but it's a real thing: if the content is comfortable in its own skin, if nothing is forced and nothing seems like it's trying too hard to entertain you, then a viewer will 100 per cent feel that. Such was the case here: just the right amount of sexy driving, just the right amount of banter, just the right amount of story arc, coupled with just the right amount of petrolhead passion.

On top of that, Jim Hart the editor – another *TG* veteran of immense skill whom I'd worked with for years – had toiled hard with me to give the film a seductive opening. We looked in particular for the shots where the cars had just driven past the cameramen out on the open roads, so *not* taking the shots with the cars in, but instead the couple of seconds or second just after the car had left frame. You would see at best the tiniest glimpse of something that had exited stage left, but you wouldn't know what it was. And nor would you hear it, because we also took all the engine sounds off.

I can't claim originality for this idea. I stole it from an amazing film called *Climb Dance*, made to celebrate Ari Vatanen's incredible 1988 record breaking Pike's Peak run in a Peugeot 405 T16. Google it and you'll see how the opening images are a cluster of tantalising shots of dust – dust that's been thrown up by a car that's just passed out of sight a second or two earlier. It's an ethereal and slightly disturbing piece of calm before the storm cinematography, and, once stolen, added a bit of intrigue to what was round the corner in our Portugal outing.

Once Jim and I had finished cutting the film I sent it over to Jeremy, who likewise quickly came back with a 'Bloody hell, wasn't expecting that!' type response.

And so, with everyone in agreement, the Hypercar film got promoted to first position on the gang plank.

The Flight of the Phoenix

With Show 1 stitched together, on 18 November 2016, we launched. Our newly repaired plane, with 'Grand Tour' painted over the bit where it had once said 'Top Gear', lumbered down the runway and rose once more into the air, carrying enough fuel for a three-year flight, and hopefully enough ideas in the cargo hold to see us through thirty-six episodes.

When I say 'launched', I mean 'dropped' – the parlance of streaming that we'd now have to get used to. Obviously it's a familiar part of TV grammar nowadays, but back then a show being dropped was an odd sensation. Having come from a terrestrial TV background, where *Top Gear* had a specified slot, there was a sense of a connecting thread. We could enjoy imagining, as the clock ticked towards 8 p.m. on a Sunday, that families would be finishing their meal in preparation for the sofa, and that parents up and down the land would be shouting: 'Get your school books ready for the morning, or no *Top Gear*!'

By contrast, a 'drop' felt like an underwhelming nothingness. And nor would there be any viewing figures to pore over, because neither Amazon nor Netflix gave them out.

Our barometer, therefore, was social media – Reddit, Twitter, IMDb, etc. – and phew! The fans loved episode one.

This was lucky for us, because boy did they hate episode two. Apologies if you've spent time in therapy trying to expunge it from your mind, but this was the one where the guys played soldiers in an army base in Jordan, doing our own version of Tom Cruise's *Edge of Tomorrow* film, when he keeps getting killed and then comes back to life again.

I don't know why people despised it so much – maybe a thirty-minute film with two minutes of car content was a bit of an ask, maybe the whole live/die cockabout was likewise a bit much, but yep, wherever you look on those 'Best and Worst *Grand Tour* Films' polls, there it sits every time, plumb at the bottom.

I feel I must add that although many of you clearly think we laid a big brown curly one with that film, we really liked it, and still do. I mean, *The Shawshank Redemption* bombed when it came out, and now look at it. The same could well happen with the Jordan film. Maybe.

Mercifully, in the pendulum that is our creative lives, we swung back to popular acclaim with a fistful of films that followed, including Grand Touring in Italy/ Hammond is a yob, the Namibia Special, and the sports cars in Morocco, where yes, the collapse of the giant scales was an absolute gift of an unplanned moment.

But, whilst we'd quickly found our rhythmic mojo with the films, the combination of the speed with which we were having to come up with new segments and the legal loopholes we were then having to jump them through, meant that we were inevitably screwing up elsewhere.

Guests, for example.

We'd always known from the get-go with *The Grand Tour*, that guests would be our Achilles heel. On *Top Gear* the whole celebrity guest setup had worked like a dream because our timetable was user friendly for pulling in the big names. If Hugh Jackman's new film is due to be launched on the Friday and our show goes out the same weekend, he'll happily give us half a day on the Wednesday.

Sadly though, with The *Grand Tour* there was no such harmonious link-up because, for a load of reasons to do with re-versioning the shows for other countries, the time between us recording a studio and the show itself going out was a whole month.

The only option then was to pay guests more money to compensate for the lack of a plug they'd be getting. And so back into the war chest we went, scrabbled past the empty space where the Big Opening cash had once been, moved aside the skipload of notes the tents would need, and pulled out a decent amount for guests – around £5,000–£10,000.

Still, cost aside, at least we had a logical plan. And then we went and spoiled it all by having one of our 'should have left it in the pub' moments.

These instances, as the name suggests, occur usually in the pub, where somebody has an out-there idea, everyone laughs like a drain, we then go ahead and do it, and only after it's gone out does the penny drop and we're left asking: 'Why the hell did we do that? Should have left that one in the pub.'

Such was the case with the *Grand Tour* guests. From memory the meeting had been relatively sane throughout, until we came to the practical issue of how the celeb should arrive in the tent. Should they, for example, do a conventional walk through the applauding crowd or would that be too much like the *Top Gear* format and the lawyers would send us to prison forever?

Next suggestion then: how about we first see the guest through the big window behind Jeremy, Richard and James, approaching the tent from a distance? It was at this point that Porter – I remember it clearly, bless him – suddenly said: 'Tell you what, wouldn't it be funny if we see the guest approaching, but they never actually make it to the tent?' Much laughter all round, quickly leading to the idea that each guest would suffer a terrible comedy death before they actually reached the tent door. Cue even more laughter and back-slapping. 'I mean, come on! Show us another chat show out there that's doing that with its guests!' Obviously the answer was none, for good reason, but that detail troubled us not a jot as we left the pub, with the Celebrity Death idea merrily skipping down the street alongside us. And then over the course of the entire first series, it merrily kicked us in the nuts each and every week.

I mean, where do we begin? For starters, the number of guests wanting to give up a day of their time so they can die a grisly comedy death is fewer than the number of guests who actually want to come on a show and talk. That reduced the pool somewhat. Secondly, dead or alive, the guests still wanted paying for their time, with some of the big American stars wanting to be paid handsomely. So, Show 1; Jeremy Renner standing up in a plane with a parachute on, going 'Aaaaahh' and pretending to jump out to his death – fifty grand. But it was Show 1 and we had Show 1 fever.

Back in Europe the prices dropped a bit but we were still paying fair dollops of cash. On top of that, the act of killing all these celebs didn't come cheap either. Mincing Daniel Ricciardo in a hovercraft was an expensive piece of stunt work, likewise dropping a container in Rotterdam on Golden Earring.

And on top of all this . . . no shit Sherlock, the audience in the tent and the viewers actually wanted to hear the guest come on and just . . . be a guest.

We had plenty of time – eleven episodes in fact – to repent at leisure over that wallet-chewing folly.

However, we were all still waiting for the big one, the Godzilla of invoices, and as Series 1 came to an end, we knew the tent bill would soon be upon us.

The night before we were due to shoot the tent records in Scotland, Jeremy and I were walking back from the pub in the nearby village, and stopped on a little stone bridge that overlooked our site. Basically we were now building, wherever we went, Glastonbury. Tent after tent after tent – all admittedly serving some useful purpose or other – clung around the sides of the main *Grand Tour* edifice. 'You know what that is?' said Jeremy. 'Our kids' inheritance, all going on tent pegs.'

A month or so later, once everything had been totted up, it finally arrived.

As I said earlier, we'd all hoped it would come in at around £2 million, whilst admitting secretly to ourselves that that number was a fantasy. It would definitely be closer to three.

What we weren't prepared for, though, was the number that was actually written at the bottom of the page. Which was '5'.

That settled it. We immediately re-examined the contract, decided that the clause requiring us to make a show 'of first-class quality' didn't need to include mass canvas transportation, and set the tent up permanently at its new home in the Cotswolds, about three yards from Jeremy's front door.

Other changes for Series 2? Guests would now no longer suffer death from having a camel dropped on them, and instead earn their fee via the radical method of coming on the chat show section to do some chatting.

Also our tame racing driver, the American, played so gallantly by Mike Skinner, had to go. Not his fault in the slightest – he did absolutely everything that was asked of him. It was more that 'The American' character had been likewise too hastily conceived in the legal whirlwind.

However, every cloud, etc., and enter Abbie. It was Jeremy who'd championed the idea of a female driver, and hells bells was Miss Eaton a good call, because from the moment she went on air, social media loved her as much as they'd hated 'The American'.

Maintaining Altitude

The bottom line here is that from Series 2 onwards we were ironing out kinks and finessing. The days of surprising ourselves by accidentally discovering new and exciting strands of films: builds, races, etc., were no more. Our armoury of creative weapons was fully stocked and the job was to keep the plane in the air by turning out shows of 'first-class quality'.

In the main then, that's what we did for the next two series of the *Grand Tour* – shot films, recorded studio segments, stitched the shows together, and put them out. If I'm sounding perfunctory I don't mean to, but in a book like this where the main focus is to tell you about what's going on behind the scenes, there simply isn't much to report.

Having said that, even with the tent globetrotting now behind us, we were still capable of the odd flash of fiscal lunacy. One day, for example, the four of us decided that we should all have matching company cars and duly bought four Reliant Robins. We thought they'd look good alongside each other in our 1970s 'Reserved for the Managing Director' parking spaces outside the office, and that occasionally we could put one on its side and Instagram the photo, with a humorous caption about Richard having arrived at work in his usual manner. Modern-day publicity no less.

The Robins weren't cheap to start with – I guess Jeremy's *Top Gear* film was the petard that had hoisted us – and we had to spend a good few thousand more on top having them mechanically reconditioned. Then, one evening at the end of a day's toil, Hammo set off in his Robin, heading back to his place in South London. About twenty minutes later I got a call. Had I left work yet? No. Good. Could I come to his aid, because he'd broken down in the middle of the big junction on Cromwell Road. Now if you happen to know that junction, you'll know how busy it is at rush hour. If you're not familiar with it, imagine that famous one in Tokyo where thousands of cars and people criss-cross it like ants. It's that.

I told him I was a bit busy; couldn't he ring Jeremy

for help? He said he'd already done that, that Jeremy had indeed leapt into his Robin to mount a rescue, but his car had packed up after ten feet.

Sweeping up my keys I leapt into Thunderbird 3, which duly started first time. Ha! Then I grabbed the gear lever to slot it into first, and the whole ensemble – gear stick, housing, the lot – came away in my hand. I rang Hammo to give him the bad news, as he was receiving help from kindly commuters to push his heap out of the way. Out of our fleet of four Robins, three had given up the ghost in one evening. The love affair with triangular transport was over.

Swiss Roll

I may have implied a few paragraphs back that the making of the second and third series of the *Grand Tour* was a steady process. In the main it was, but that didn't stop the occasional gremlin from our *Top Gear* past swinging by to say hello.

What we didn't expect was for it to pay us a visit in Switzerland, at the climax of the Past, Present and Future road trip.

The past, you may remember, was championed by Jeremy in a Lamborghini Aventador, the present by James in the latest Honda NSX, and then there was the future, with Richard driving the all-electric Rimac Concept One.

Let's just break with the tradition of my brain and get car-y for a moment. This Croatian hypercar, with its 1200 hp motors and 1,180 lb ft of torque – your Golf GTI has 273 lb ft – could cover a standing quarter-mile in under ten seconds. You probably saw the evidence of that when it not just beat, but gave an absolute automotive bending over in the prison shower to the other supercars.

The sensation of speed it conveyed, even to a seasoned wheelman like Hammond, was akin to what a medieval peasant would have felt like doing 60 in a Nissan Micra.

It's not totally unsurprising then that at the Swiss hill-climb he misjudged his braking on that last run up the hill and plunged over the drop.

Richard has spoken at length about his recollections of the crash itself and us being us, we quickly made fantastic comedy currency out of his injury in the following episode, with the race against Jeremy in the new Ford GT.

But when I think back to that accident it makes me shiver much more so than his jet car accident.

With the jet crash everyone was on high alert, prepped for something to go wrong, with medics and ambulance ready to shoot down the runway in an instant.

Obviously there was medical support on hand at the Swiss hill climb because, well, it was a hill climb organised by the Swiss. But from the second Richard speared over the edge and started tumbling and tumbling, falling for 360 feet, he was getting further and further away from help with every foot he fell.

He remembers the tumbling, he remembers the moment his knee went bang, and then when the car came to rest at the bottom. Even though he was upside down, he didn't panic but, as he told me, instead took stock: 'I knew my knee was fucked, but I was conscious, so I thought, okay, just wait here until help arrives to get me out.'

But then, when he started to smell burning, he knew he couldn't hang around a second longer. Trying to extricate yourself from an upside-down claustrophobic supercar by smashing and then crawling through a letterbox-sized window, when you're one knee down and you have no idea whether it's ten minutes or ten seconds before it becomes a fireball – that whole situation is capital P panic.

Fortunately though, Richard has a fast brain when under pressure. Out of the three of them, he's the one you'd want next to you in a First World War trench. James would literally be polishing each bullet before putting it into his gun, even with the enemy coming over the top. Jeremy would be running around shouting: 'We need to shoot the Germans! Everybody shoot the Germans!', whereas Richard would be firing and reloading with precision.

Once again though our fate had spun on a coin, because it could have been any of them in the office who'd said: 'I'll take the Rimac.'

Hopefully though, Fate wouldn't get in the way anymore. Because surely, to God, we'd now paid our dues with crashes.

A Feature-Length Future

Series 2 and Series 3 proved, with some relief, that we were still capable of producing the odd barnstormers. Without question the Mongolia adventure and Funeral for a Ford film, the trio's extremely poignant requiem for the Ford saloon, stand alongside any Special or any film we'd made on either show.

With this warm and fuzzy feeling in mind as our thirty-six-show contract came to an end, we started to lower the landing gear of the *Grand Tour* plane and look for somewhere pleasant to touch down, preferably with palm trees either side and a nice big Duty Free shop.

It all made complete sense. We would now be able to call it a day at a time of our own choosing, rather than when the BBC said so. More importantly we could bow out before our audience tired of us, taking aim at our plane with rocket launchers and unleashing missiles of Boredom and Indifference.

Also – small but important point – we'd heard nothing from our Amazonian paymasters about any future contract renewal.

'Right, let's tell them we're done then,' said Jeremy. 'At least it'll save them one of those embarrassing calls where they give us the boot.'

I made the call and – bugger me – Amazon were actually very much in the mood for some air-to-air refuelling and wanted to renew for another twenty-four episodes.

The four of us talked this flattering offer through and then declined it. Our refusal was fit to bursting with high-minded principles: don't just do things for money, quality is all, respect our legacy, respect our audience, leave a good-looking corpse, etc.

'Okay,' said Amazon. 'Would you do some more *Grand Tour* if . . . we each gave you your own solo series?'

Bastards! What a cunning move! If there's one way to seduce four egos trapped inside the same show, it's to give them each their own show.

In the end we held firm that twenty-four more *Grand Tours* would be too risky, but agreed to make more feature-length Specials – plus, naturally, the solo projects.

Amazon then enquired about whether we had any ideas for the solo outings and Jeremy said he'd like to do a series about life on his farm. It still makes me chuckle how many execs then asked me if I could talk him out of this idea so that he might do something a bit more . . . exciting.

Luckily for all, he stuck with the unexciting option.

Today's Special . . .

Our new careers in the movie-length monsters business kicked off with 'Seamen', the aquatic adventure in Cambodia and Vietnam that featured boats instead of cars. Internally there were a few nerves that our petrol-head viewers might be bored with a film that swapped tarmac for water, but they needn't have worried because the climactic ride on the South China Sea nearly killed us.

I was on the camera boat filming James when a wave picked up his wooden river cruiser and slammed it into the stern of our camera boat so hard that I was sure one vessel or another was going down. On another camera boat, as you saw in the film, they actually had begun the process of going down. Without question it was the riskiest situation as a whole crew that we'd ever been in, with every element beyond our control. But on the plus side our pain was everyone's gain, because 'Seamen' went down, literally, a storm with the audience.

Our next film, however, the treasure hunt in Madagascar, less so. Just like that insanely terrible road that we had to travel along, the finished film seemed to go on and on, and on, in the most uncomfortable and irritating way, without ever letting up. And pirates? Looking for pirate treasure? What the fuck were we thinking?

Fortunately our disappointment with ourselves matched the audience's disappointment with us, so at least we were still on speaking terms.

But the mediocrity of Madagascar also caused us to realise how vulnerable we had unwittingly made ourselves now that we'd stopped having any kind of studio.

The thing is, whether it be Conversation Street in the *GT* tent or the News in the *TG* hangar, those weekly slots where the trio had nattered about whatever motoring things were going on across the globe had meant they'd been looking outward. They could be commentators, they could show attitude, they were connected to the outside world.

Now we were just making Specials, we had enclosed ourselves in our own little bubble, which in turn meant the only trick we had up our sleeves was to be entertaining. That was fine as long as we kept doing just that, but this state of affairs also made it easier for our plane to be shot down.

With this in mind we resolved to erase the Madagascar misstep by basing our next Special around a thrilling adventure in the icy wastes of Russia, in machines that would be an absolute firm favourite with the viewers: rally-bred sports cars.

As we set about our preparations, we didn't pay much attention to the news stories about a flu bug that was making its way out of China. We did recces in Siberia, bought the cars – a Mitsubishi Evo for James, a Subaru Impreza for Richard and an Audi quattro that wasn't a Quattro for Jeremy, and worked out a route. As fast as we worked though, the virus from China was travelling much faster and – as I'm sure you all have the equivalent memories to match, the moment came when we had to down tools, shut the office and go home.

The whole *Grand Tour* team then joined in with the national pastime of breakfasting on red wine whilst watching Joe Wicks. Then several months later, when restrictions on domestic travel started to ease, we regrouped to shoot two UK-based Covid Specials.

With the first one, 'Lochdown', we actually felt quite chuffed about our smart, creative thinking in heading for the remote Outer Hebrides. Sure you didn't need a passport to get there, but no matter, because this part of the British Isles was certainly dramatic and wild enough to give a damn good *Grand Tour* feel to proceedings.

Only when we arrived did we realise that every other TV show had had the same idea. In one tiny village alone we ran into the camera crews for Bob Mortimer and Paul Whitehouse's fishing programme, *Top Gear*, some cookery show I can't remember the name of and *SAS: Are You Tough Enough?* Then when we walked into the local hotel to get out of the London camera crew melee, we found Joanna Lumley with her team. Basically if a bomb had dropped on that tiny hamlet, your screens would have been blank for the next ten years.

Scandi Flick

In the end I was quite proud of our two lockdown Specials. I think 'Carnage à Trois', the surreal French-car based number, had the edge over 'Lochdown', but now the world was opening up again we could finally get back to Grand Touring proper.

There was, though, a definite air of paranoia wafting through the office, because the last time we'd had what one would call 'a hit' was 'Seamen' in December 2019, and from where we stood right now the earliest we'd be able to get something on air would be Winter 2022. In telly land, a gap of three years – you're getting into carbon dating territory.

However, to borrow a phrase from therapists everywhere, the only way through it is through it, so we set to work.

The most logical plan was to revive the film we'd been working on just before someone dropped a test tube in Wuhan. This was the story involving road-going rally cars and a journey based around an 'escape' from Russia. Jeremy and I had both read an amazing thriller called *Kolymsky Heights*, centred around a spy stealing secrets in Siberia and trying to get to safety across the Bering Strait, pursued by loads of baddies. (If you're Russian and you've bought this book, feel free to change that to 'pursued by loads of goodies'.). *Kolymsky Heights* fired up our respective, ever present Delusions of James Bond-o-meters and soon we had a road trip based on Jeremy, Richard and James escaping from the Solovetsky Monastery – notorious as the first Soviet gulag – in the frozen White Sea, then, in their three rally-bred sports cars, a perilous journey to Archangel before finally reaching freedom in Finland.

However, just as we were dusting off our old research notes and pumping up the tyres on the star cars, Putin decided he'd help himself to Ukraine. So that was the end of that.

Instead, we turned our sights on Scandinavia. A road trip across Norway, Sweden and Finland, way up in the north inside the Arctic Circle, meant we could keep the snowy wasteland vibe and, equally important, still use the cars.

Another bonus for me was that because I didn't have anything to cut in the edit, I could go on the recce. And looking back, James May will certainly not thank me for doing so.

A couple of days into our story safari, we found ourselves scouting out a Norwegian Cold War submarine base. It was me who, as we walked down the tunnel, noticed that the overhead lights were activated by movement. From there it was a short step to dreaming up the sequence where each presenter would have to play a game of chicken by driving as fast as possible down the pitch-black tunnel, activating the overhead lights as they went, to see whose car could achieve the highest speed, then braking and stopping before hitting the solid rock wall at the end. With that scene tucked away, we then headed east through Sweden and into Finland, eventually arriving at the Finnish ski resort where (I'm assuming if you're reading this book you've watched the film) all the high jinks with burning sheds, etc., would take place.

I also think that if you're a keen student of our output, you'll have worked out that some of these stunts don't happen by accident. We could not, for instance, just pitch camp on a slope at a working ski resort and proceed to cause mayhem. One does need to have a word with the owner first. I mention this because I sincerely wish everyone could have the opportunity to work with the Finns in the way we did. The joyousness of it comes from the fact that the Finns are the Mr Spocks of the human race. They do not do hyperbole or randomness. If you tell a Finn you'll be 'back in a minute', he'll start looking at his watch after sixty seconds, wondering what's happened to you.

Naturally with this outlook, Finns are not predisposed to the joys of nonsensical humour, and this thought was very much front of mind as the *Grand Tour* recce team – Phil the director, Dave the producer and I – sat down with the ski resort's owner. Outlining a request that is basically juvenile drivel to a serious business person is hard enough at the best of times, so the trick is to convince them that taking part in *Grand Tour* nonsense is the most important thing that's ever happened to their lives. One must sell with the force and conviction of Jordan Belfort, which in our case meant pumping in all the children's entertainer phrases one could muster: 'Hey, just think . . .' 'You're gonna love this! Here's the really good bit!' etc.

However, when this kind of hyperactive sales pitch has to go through a translator, especially a Finnish one, you are somewhat on the back foot.

Consequently I turned up the wick to eleven, actually twelve, as I started selling, but I just knew, as the Finnish translator passed said request on, that there was no way in hell he would be conveying any of my hyperactive bonhomie. I just knew that: 'So, because the guys have this way of pranking each other – which all our audience REALLY loves! – Jeremy will push Richard's shed down the slope . . . WITH RICHARD IN IT! And his shed will smash to pieces! IMAGINE THAT!' would arrive in the resort owner's ear as: 'One of their men wants to push another man, in a shed, down one of your slopes, and it will hit the bottom and break up.'

Likewise: 'And then for the big one! Jeremy tries to drive his shed down the slope but because he's fitted this crazy exhaust that shoots flames and it's been a running joke for the whole film and it's a joke everyone will love (gasp of air), his shed then sets alight and so we have a car driving down the slope towing a shed that's totally in flames! And that's gonna be watched – IN YOUR RESORT! – by millions!' That went in his ear as: 'The other man then wants to set fire to his own shed and drive it down the same slope, towing it behind him.'

The translator finally finished translating my words. Given the amount that his Finnish brain had stripped out as surplus to requirements, it hadn't taken him long. There then followed a never-ending pause as the resort owner stared silently at the table, his face completely expressionless.

'Oh shit,' I thought. 'We really need this slope. Here it comes via the translator: "Get out of my office, you clowns."'

Finally the resort owner leaned forward and, with his face still set like a glacier, pointed at an area on the map of the resort and spoke in a monotone to the translator. The translator then said: 'You can use slope no. 23.'

And that was it. Sorted.

A couple of months later the *Grand Tour* team, surrounded by racks of dried fish and assembled at the Henningsvaer football pitch, the most bizarrely located soccer ground in the world, began shooting 'Scandi Flick'.

All went swimmingly for the first couple of days and eventually we arrived at our spooky Norwegian Cold War submarine base, to shoot our 'Race Down the Tunnel in the Dark as Fast as You Can Whilst the Lights Only Come on as You go Without Hitting the Rock Wall at the End Challenge'.

Once Jeremy, Richard and James had filmed their introductory walk chat we then prepped to shoot their actual runs.

Now at this point I actually had to scuttle off to find a quiet office, because I had a Zoom meeting scheduled with the owner of the huge transport plane that we hoped to use for the climax of our next film, the Eastern European outing that became 'Eurocrash'. Having duly found an empty office I fired up the laptop and began Zooming with the Ukrainian plane owner. Naturally, as a pilot with a military background, he too, like the Finnish ski resort owner, had little interest in the narrative of our pre-school editorial. He just wanted specific and detailed information: where, when, how many cars, how many crew, etc. Eventually the conversation turned to the issue of safety and I kid you not, just as I was mid flow, telling him – with my face on its most sincere setting – that 'we go to bed thinking about safety and wake up thinking about safe . . .' the door behind me flew open and one of the team burst in, shouting: 'Andy! James has just had a fucking big one! He's gone into the wall.' Since the door was right over my shoulder, the plane owner had caught every word and seen the delivery. He stared at me silently, clearly wondering where I was headed next with my now rather suspect speech. I said I'd call back and headed for the tunnel.

Mr May's crash had indeed been a big one.

Later on when we reviewed the in-car cameras, the editor and I looked for James's commentary – given that that's what presenters are paid to do – but there was none. He didn't say a single word during the run, and the look on his face clearly says that, never mind the power deficit of his Evo to Jeremy's Audi, he was shooting for victory.

Luckily, when he realised his tyres were simply not going to stop in time on the shiny tunnel floor, James did manage to get the car turned before he made full contact with Norwegian rock. If he'd gone into the wall head on . . . doesn't bear thinking about.

In the ambulance the medics reckoned some rib busting had occurred, but primarily they were concerned about James's head, what with the wallop he'd given it against the door frame. As for the rest of us, we were obviously relieved that our friend was more or less alright, but inside I was thinking: 'Okay, that's another one we got away with. How many more before we don't?'

As we watched the ambulance speed off down the tunnel, we turned to James's car. The conversation that followed may have sounded callous to a stranger, but we'd all been doing this together for so long that we'd worked out our own way of balancing concern with pragmatism. It was a case of: medical people will take care of James, what do we now do about the film? And indeed the Evo? Never before had we had to contend with a star car in such a smashed, critical condition, and crucially never so early on in the filming.

Obviously we had the forfeit car waiting in the wings – a Volvo that had been born wretched and lived a desperate life – and as comedic as we try and make our forfeit cars, I ask you as a viewer: when have you ever actually wanted to see one of them come into play? No, us neither.

Two hours later, the car was on a ramp in a workshop in town. The attending automotive medics included Max, our long-standing veteran mechanic, the workshop owner and our newest member of the GT spannering team, a young Finnish kid called Elia. We'd hired him because our star cars were much more the children of the engine diagnostics era, and twenty-something Elia was handier with modern Audis than Max.

These three finished their inspection and gave their verdict: without question the car was a write-off. It wasn't just the damage to the suspension components and the brakes, more crucial was the fact that the chassis was bent. 'Look there,' said Max and Elia, who had now somehow formed The Mechanical Misery Brothers double act. They pointed at a part of the chassis that clearly was bent, and at this point, realising our future might very well feature a shit Volvo, I decided my only option was to bring my entire fifty-nine years of engineering ignorance to bear. 'Is that it?' I scoffed. 'That looks fine! It's a ding!' Whilst Elia stood back, clearly thinking: 'Is this the man who runs *The Grand Tour*?' Max then patiently explained how the chassis damage ran much deeper than just appearances. He spoke of suspension geometry and misalignment and handling issues, and then Elia chimed in, adding for good measure that the Evo was most likely no longer road legal. I was stuck in a Mechanics Sandwich, but without any logical means to argue back.

So instead, I turned to Elia and the workshop owner, took a deep breath, and began. 'When you were kids,' I said – slowly, and with as much pomposity as I could muster – 'did you watch *Top Gear*?' They both replied that of course they did.

'Wonderful. And did you enjoy, for example, the Botswana Special?' Yes, they both nodded, one of our best. 'Absolutely. It was. And were you sad when Oliver was down and out, flooded to death by the river crossing

372

Hammond had driven it into? And . . . were you then cheering on the sofa when you heard, then saw him coming round the corner, not dead after all, but alive?!'

Both of them agreed enthusiastically; for sure, what a moment.

'Well,' I thundered, 'now the time has come for you . . . to do the very same! To join that long line of mechanics who turned everything around and snatched victory from the jaws of failure.' My speech was really building, I could feel it, I could see it in the rapt eyes of my audience of two. I say 'two' because Max had turned away to light a fag, rolling his eyes at having to listen once again to this poor man's Churchill speech.

'Tonight . . . a *Grand Tour* film will live . . . or die. And this . . . is not the time to let defeat rear its wretched whining head. Greatness is now required from everyone in this workshop; a whole vast global *GT* audience is now looking at us – you – to save the day!'

For good measure I then threw in a bit of Mel Gibson from *Braveheart*: 'Dying in your beds many years from now, would you be willing to trade all the days, from this day to that, for just one chance – one chance! – to come back here and say, they can take our . . . thing . . . but they can never take our EVO!'

My speech was done. I was done. Elia and the Norwegian mechanic man stared at me, a bit dumbstruck. From behind I heard Max mutter quietly: 'Fucking Norah.' Nevertheless, I had turned the room. There was no turning back now for our little Scandinavian elves with their spanners and hammers. They would do what it took or die trying.

As it happened the closest they came to dying was from the amount of fat in the bucket of takeaway burgers they consumed, to propel them through the night. But, as the contents of 'Scandi Flick' will attest to the fact, a battered, rather offset and probably illegal Mitsubishi Evo, driven by a bruised and slightly concussed James May, did appear over the horizon twenty-four hours later. And made it to the very end.

'Scandi Flick' dropped in September 2022. We'd all done the best we could, we (well, Amazon) paid Duran Duran a small fortune to use 'The Wild Boys' as the soundtrack over a banging trailer, and now it was crunch time. Had we become yesterday's men during Covid?

Mercifully it seemed not. Even though we still couldn't get any numbers out of Amazon, we learned enough to know that the film had gone to No. 1 in many countries, and the comments of support on social media were backing that up. We had – phew – kept the plane up in the air. But there was no time for high fives, as we dived without a break straight into making the next one.

Sadly there's not much to report about 'Eurocrash'. The chaps had picked their cars for the film over beers during one of the overnight stops in Scandinavia, with James absolutely unprepared for how shit that Crosley would be, and the shooting of the film happened as you saw it.

Our little jaunt across Eastern Europe on a journey nobody would have thought of, in cars nobody would dream of, certainly didn't have the visual wallop or excitement of 'Scandi Flick', and selfishly none of the presenters thought to pump up the ratings by having a massive crash. Jeremy even had a bit of a downer on it when I sent him the first cut, worried that it was all a bit drawn out. The guys who make our trailers were also more polite than enthusiastic and the 'bit of a downer' infection started to spread. Maybe now was the moment when the viewers' Missiles of Indifference would start to lock onto our heat signal.

The thing is though, as the great screenwriter William Goldman (*Butch Cassidy and the Sundance Kid*, *Marathon Man*, *All The President's Men*, *Misery*, *A Bridge Too Far* ... need I go on) once declared of people in the film world: 'Nobody knows anything.' The great man could say this with some conviction, having had to suffer endless Hollywood execs tell him that *Butch Cassidy* would absolutely fail because there wasn't enough shooting in it for a Western.

Luckily, such was the case with 'Eurocrash', because although the film may not have been a provider of immense spectacle, the viewers found it really funny, in particular the world's worst waxwork museum and the theft of Nigel Mansell, who then temporarily became a fourth presenter until his catastrophic speed run. The fans also loved the nerdy Eastern Bloc Formula 1 stuff, and as for that ending – the boarding of the big transport plane on the never-ending *Fast and Furious* runway – any member of the audience old enough to tie their own shoe-laces knew that that was bollocks, but because it was so tongue-in-cheek it was accepted for what it was.

A mention in despatches here must go to Clarkson. It was he who campaigned for the punch line that the plane shouldn't take off at the end, but instead should have actually just landed. We all disagreed, saying that since we'd paid for the fucking thing, we needed a big triumphant take-off, but he insisted that the disappointing lameness of a plane taxiing to a halt, following on from all the drama of the three of them boarding it, would be the perfect misdirect of a punchline. When we cut it together in the edit – you often never know until that moment – he had clearly been right.

Then – as a personal little bonus for Jeremy, James and me – a few months later, at a memorial for Stirling Moss, Richard had to sit next to . . . Nigel Mansell.

Mauritania

After the short-haul flight distance of 'Eurocrash', we went properly Grand Touring again with our Paris–Dakar based journey across Mauritania and Senegal. Of the two

376

countries, it was Mauritania that we found so bewitching. For starters, it had the vibe of a destination from one of our older *Top Gear* Specials – a place that nobody knew a thing about. Indeed the whole running joke of Hammond thinking it wasn't a real country but somewhere you got to through the back of a wardrobe, came about because in the run-up to going there everybody, when we mentioned Mauritania, went 'Where?'

Colin, the lovely British ambassador who popped up in the film, told us that even some of his government colleagues often said how jealous they were of him for having a posting featuring white sandy beaches surrounded by endless aquamarine water. 'I think you'll find that's Mauritius,' he had to point out.

It was no surprise that nobody knew anything about the place, though, because nobody goes there. The latest statistics we'd been able to find for tourism stated that a mere 4,000 people a year visited – basically the occupants of a mid-sized concert hall – set against the 40 million a year that visit the UK. And on top of that, the country itself is four times bigger than the UK.

Likewise with regard to its own population, it's more or less empty: 12 people per square mile, compared to 715 per square mile in Britain, with hardly any infrastructure of any kind. Remember that amazing two-mile-long train we featured? The iron ore that it carries to the port accounts for 55 per cent of Mauritania's wealth: one product, one railway line for the whole country.

Mind you, it's not a place where one actually gets the urge to run around being productive. On the day we filmed in Chinguetti, the town being swallowed by the desert where Richard and Jeremy filled James's car with sand, the temperature climbed past 60 degrees. In their spring.

But there was so much that was captivating, be it the mind-blowingly immense landscapes that even a fleet of drones couldn't scratch, or the towns filled with the absolute best examples of unstoppable, valiant old shitters we've ever seen.

But although we were filming in an 'old school' *Top Gear* Special location – harsh, beautiful, unknown, mysterious, empty – we were definitely making a 'new school' film.

By that I mean we didn't merely set off, as we would have done in the early 2000s, and hope that entertainment would come from the cars breaking down. No; in Mauritania, we brought the kitchen sink. Modded snowmobiles, cars winched down a mountain, cars turned into boats, and obviously, a joke you could see coming from the farthest distance ever in telly history: the fuel bowser that the chaps were trying to prevent from being blown up.

Eventually, as you all saw, the fuel bowser was sent to fuel bowser heaven in a massive explosion when, in a moment of impeccable *cinéma vérité*, Jeremy's snowmobile that had escaped two days earlier somehow rejoined us and ran into it.

That was, without a doubt, the biggest explosion we ever exploded in our entire twenty-two-year reign as nine-year-olds. It was so big in fact, that when the military colonel in charge saw the amount of C4 and kerosene being hauled into place, he made us go house to house, door to door, in the nearby town. Mauritania was, he reminded us, a country that had not yet settled on its foundations. The last military coup had taken place as late as 2007 and no locals were watching the *Grand Tour* on Prime. If the nearby residents suddenly saw an explosion this huge they wouldn't think: 'Oh what's Jezzer up to now?', they would more likely start loading up their possessions and soon there'd be a town exodus in a shagged Mercedes.

What a place. I've been to more beautiful countries, I've definitely been to more relaxing countries and I've also been to countries where you can get a drink. But out of all the locations in our massive *TG* and *GT* global address book, it's Mauritania that I have the most fondness for. It's a place that needs a break. The locals need a break – with some of their vast untapped wealth getting tapped, and then coming their way.

Curtain Call

Mauritania was well received and watched in great numbers but . . . we now knew one thing for certain. Whatever film we shot next would be our last.

This time there would be no more changing our minds, no more spouting high-principled statements about protecting quality control and then crumbling at the sight of Jeff's cheque book. This time, these four ladies would not be for turning.

In truth the list of reasons was large enough by this point to make it clear even to my dog that this decision was the right one.

Firstly, age. At thirty-eight every physical challenge is a bit of a laugh, great material for a pub anecdote. But at sixty, which three of us were now on the wrong side of, hours of back-breaking torture on a Madagascan road, or dinner yet again being a midnight KitKat, becomes something you want to watch, not do.

Jeremy was also about to become a grandfather and had no desire for that experience to be a series of WhatsApp photos that he couldn't open on account of being in a jungle. On top of that, we all wanted to have a crack at other things whilst we could still feed ourselves without assistance.

Age, I guess, dovetails into the issue of luck. We'd been lucky, given the risks we'd taken, for twenty-two years now but how much longer could we keep pushing it? Richard had already survived two killer crashes; what would happen with a third? And James's argument with a rock wall in Norway had proved that crashes were still very much on the table. Likewise our little boat trip on the South China Sea. It's hard maybe for a viewer to separate entertainment from real danger on our show, given how skilled those three are at delivering quips for the camera in any condition, but the South China Sea – we were not in control. Then, from the archives: Argentina. If luck is a finite resource that we are all allocated only so much of, it was unlikely we had enough left in the bank to get into another one of our pickles and bring everyone home.

Maybe a smaller point but still a powerful one, the veterans who'd been there since the beginning – people like us four, Ben and Casper the cameramen, Russ the soundman, Phil the director, we all missed the smallness and the simplicity of how life had been. In Mauritania our crew had been so vast, what with the medics and the security and the DIT operators and the drone specialists and whoever, that it had been cheaper to charter our own plane to get us all to the start line. The shooting convoy was now north of thirty vehicles, and even though none of that immense infrastructure is in shot, it can't help having an effect on what actually is shot. When we'd made the Botswana Special sixteen years earlier and our crew had numbered just ten, that leanness absolutely complemented the tone of what we were trying to convey on screen: three blokes bumbling about, having mishaps and making shit up as they go along. For sure our recent films still gave off that 'three fuckwits falling over' vibe, but with an army of personnel hovering in the background, it gets harder and harder.

Now I'm well aware that, as problems go, this one is hardly up there with Israel versus Palestine, but nevertheless we really missed the simple days, and we knew there was no way we could ever get them back.

By far the biggest reason for calling time, though, was the one I've mentioned throughout: namely our desire to land our plane on our own terms.

It really is one of the absolute greatest goals you can achieve in the TV world – to end your show whilst people still have a desire to watch it. But unfortunately such is the nature of television that it rarely happens. If something is popular you make just one more, then just one more, until you've made just one more too many.

Obviously the longer you go on the greater the risk, and my God had we gone on for a long time. For sure brilliant shows like *Have I Got News For You* had clocked up more years than us, but that's a current affairs comedy quiz, fuelled by a never-ending supply of fresh weekly news. We, however, had been keeping ourselves going on a diet of our own home-grown nonsense for twenty-two years. For a show such as ours – one with very little format, needing to constantly generate ideas, we were now off the map in uncharted waters, and had been for a while. If there was a mountainside awaiting us to plough into it, it wasn't on any radar.

So yes. No changing of minds. This time we would land the plane.

Set Your Controls for the Heart of the Sun

The *Grand Tour* team duly convened to discuss our very final film shortly after we got back from Mauritania, and there was a definite sense of 'this is it' in the room. Also, more than a few nerves. Part of us wanted to jump ahead to the moment when the film – hopefully a good one – would be in the can, so that we would no longer have to look over our shoulders.

But, once the mugs of tea had been made and the usual snacks and confectionery carousel had come to rest, it quickly became like any other brainstorm.

As I explained earlier, the genesis of a Special usually comes from either the location, the cars, or a storyline. This time it was the storyline and it was a no-brainer: 'It's you three saying goodbye,' I said, reaching out gently to pick up the No Shit Sherlock award. 'That's what we have to do properly for you and the viewers.'

With that peg in the ground it followed that the location, the cars – basically all the main elements, would be based around what Jeremy, Richard and James wanted to do at a gut level, rather than what we felt the show *should* do.

That meant the location would be Africa. It didn't matter that the last Special had taken place on the same continent: Africa is their favourite place. We then refined that thought around the fact that their most cherished location from any Special ever had been Kubu Island in Botswana.

'Botswana always felt like my favourite Special,' said Jeremy, 'and also, strictly speaking, it was our first proper one because "Florida Fly-Drive" was kind of an accident. So there's a closing of the circle going on there. And then Kubu . . . we all love Kubu.'

James and Richard concurred wholeheartedly. Then, two of the younger members of our team, Rachel and Chris, also chipped in. 'We always used to talk about last night's *Top Gear* on the bus to school on Monday morning, and Botswana – Oliver, the salt flats – it was just, everything.' We hadn't really needed any more persuading, but this affirmation from our former child viewers . . . yes, Kubu it had to be.

Next, we needed a start point, and since we couldn't just retrace the Botswana film in its entirety, new turf was needed. Zimbabwe quickly made its presence felt. We'd never been allowed to go there when we were at the BBC, and as a destination it felt like it had a bit of an edge, a bit of unknown to it.

Then the cars. Since this film was about the three of them saying goodbye, we all agreed they should have special privileges, in that the cars didn't have to be confined to any 'category': three convertibles, three cheap 4x4s, etc. Instead they should take cars they had always wanted to drive but had never had the chance to. After a flurry of blather Jeremy settled on a Lancia Montecarlo, because besides being a complete Lancia-phile, he also wanted to tip his cap to the way his Beta in the original

Botswana film had confounded every cynical expectation by reaching the finish line.

As for Richard, he wanted a Capri, the first car he'd ever pined for as a teenager.

Finally, James, and we all knew what he'd go for because he'd been trying to shoehorn it into films for years.

'I want,' he declared, 'a Triumph Stag.'

'Nice one! Good choice! You finally get your Stag,' we all declared.

'And,' he added, 'it must have the original V8.'

'And you're fucking kidding!' came back the chorus.

Even I knew that the original Triumph V8 is one of the world's most unreliable engines, but James was not for turning. Dave, our series producer, quickly phoned Max the mechanic to get an instant expert opinion on the matter.

'Max will be on my side,' said James. 'He knows these engine stories get overhyped.'

'Christ. You're fucking joking,' we all heard Max exclaim over Dave's phone. 'That'll never make it.'

With Max's clear vote of confidence added to the minutes of the meeting, we moved on to the next order of business, which was to work out any big budget crash-bang-wallop moments.

What should we do this time? Celebrate our swansong by throwing an even more spectacular Mauritania-type kitchen sink at it, or . . . not?

Very quickly the presenters stated that no, they didn't want to sign off by dropping an aircraft carrier from a space shuttle. Instead, if they were closing the circle, they would logically be going back to where the circle began, which in turn meant evoking the simple, unplugged spirit of the early Specials. For sure there would be the odd bit of malarkey but overarchingly the film would be about taking old, charismatic cars into an environment they weren't built for, and seeing what happened.

As noble as this intention was, and as much as I wanted it too, part of Producer Me – best fruit and veg at the front of the stall – was worried that after twenty-two years we'd simply come too far from the days when a boiling radiator counted as entertainment. The other half of me, however, approved: partly because their instincts were probably right, and . . . if we weren't borrowing the Eiffel Tower to use as a bridge to cross a river, then that meant more money for me to spend on quality music in the edit.

(I kept this last bit to myself. No point bringing up grubby fiscal wins in such a noble-minded meeting.)

In the end, to blow shit up or not blow shit up was a moot point anyway. This was the film Richard, James and Jeremy wanted to make. We would hold back Kubu Island as a surprise, hope that the cars would give grade 'A' breakdowns, and likewise their drivers would deliver grade 'A' banter.

The Grand Finale

Zimbabwe was not an easy place in which to get permission to film. The turbulence of its past and its toxic relationship with the BBC meant we had to swim against a hefty tide of paranoia-fuelled reluctance, but fortunately we had the help of the Mavros family. They're friends of Jeremy's, a dynasty that's lived in Zimbabwe for generations, and people whose love and loyalty for the country meant they were trusted by the government. Hanging onto the coat-tails of their persuasive pitching, we finally got our film permits.

That didn't mean, however, that a beady eye wouldn't be kept on us, and this monitoring manifested itself in the most charming, quirky ways: our drones, for example. Getting permits for drones is actually a nightmare in most countries, naturally so in Zim, but this time the permission came with an extra theatrical flourish.

'They're sending a guy to be with us all the time,' Lec, our main drone operator, told me.

'Yeah but that's happened before, you know how to work with that.'

'No I know, but the bloke who they're sending – he's from the Zimbabwe Space Agency.'

'Blimey. You only go to 500 feet, don't you?'

Spaceman, when he eventually joined us, was actually a lot of fun and extremely charming. But then again, many spies usually are . . .

And so, in late September the *Grand Tour* crew assembled at our start point in the Eastern Highlands of the country, and set about, for the last time, turning ourselves from global movers of luggage mountains into a filming convoy. Amongst all the activity I got a sharp reminder of how long we'd been doing this, because there in the thick of it all was Noah, my son. As a toddler his first ever attempt at a sentence, after watching the Winter Olympics, had been: 'Jeremy eat snow wee.' Aged six he'd decked the Stig in the plums. Now here he was, twenty years old and running around being a Runner.

Shoot day No.1 dawned and once camera cars A, B and C, the Dronemobile, the tracking car and every other vehicle with a job had taken up battle stations, our old star cars, piloted by our ageing stars, fell into line and set off on our final journey.

Again, I won't take up your time by repeating here what you actually saw unfold, but I can report that off camera, the shoot was absolutely as much fun as it was in the lens. I guess – what with this being the last rodeo – if we didn't take a moment to appreciate our itinerant dysfunctional family now, we knew there would never be another chance. Hence the evenings featured more laughter and drinking than normal, and as for the film itself, we all genuinely enjoyed that our show had gone back to being analogue: no outlandish props (okay okay, there were the trains), instead just lots of fun with roadside breakdowns of a 2007 vintage.

We even took the opportunity to poke fun at our own tropes. That last *A-Team* sequence, which featured them painting tiny car wheels and dismantling a kiddie trike in place of the usual montage of welding torches and big girders, was a deliberate thank-you to our regular fans: 'We know that you know that we never really turned a car into a spaceship overnight with whatever was lying around, so thank you for playing along with it. Thank you for indulging us.'

What I absolutely enjoyed most though was the banter between Jeremy, Richard and James. As promised they had brought their A-plus game and each three-way chat just sparkled with inventiveness and wit. Best of all for me were the moments when they were addressing their imminent demise as a TV trio. 'Do we all have to live in the same old people's home?' 'James has said he's deleting our numbers as soon as this is over . . .' Once again, as they'd done with the return of Hammo after his big crash, they were masters of juggling the tone, making light of their impending retirement just enough to give any viewer who might be sad a bit of a lift.

This happy happy mood spirited us from one side of Zimbabwe to the other. Then, at the border it suddenly stopped in its tracks, stayed there and watched us leave.

Because when we crossed into Botswana it hit us like a hammer. We really were near the end.

2 October: The Final Day

Camera Car C thrummed along across the salt flats. Jeremy, Richard and James, in their now doorless star cars, were a couple of miles away off to the left, but because the ice-white ground we were driving over was billiard-table flat for some 6,000 square miles, we could easily see them. The three of them were being filmed by the *Grand Tour* tracking car, a bespoke machine featuring a camera mounted on the end of a crane, operated from inside the cab via a console bristling with joysticks, levers and screens. It gave the cameraman and Phil the director an infinite number of shots, and by comparison our setup in Camera Car C was now Stone Age.

In unison with the tracking car a drone was flying overhead, hoovering up the aerial shots. Our drone guys were now so skilled that the operator could control his eye in the sky from the passenger seat of a car whizzing along at 50 mph. If you could plot a graph showing the increase over the years in our ability to capture footage, and another showing how much our hair had greyed and our girths had expanded over the same period, the two would lay over each other like tracing paper.

But no matter. Camera Car C would become useful again when we all eventually pulled over to shoot the next scene, which this time, would also be our very last scene. Not one of us – not Casper, not Joey, not Marc, not me – could bear thinking about that.

For a while we tried to take our minds off the situation by talking about getting a Camera C tattoo, knowing full well it would never really happen.

Then I had a bit of a brainwave and came up with an important task to distract us all:

'Right, they're now doing their final drive to their final destination. In the edit we're going to need a properly special bit of music to go over that. We're the camera car with the best music taste' – much agreement from everyone on board – 'so let's have a think. Let's crack that nut.'

There then followed a flurry of competitive phone scrolling as everyone thumbed through their music libraries:

'Fleetwood Mac, second half of "Oh Well".'

'Fuck offff.'

'Alright then, "Albatross".'

'Nah, not mournful enough.'

'Pink Floyd, "Welcome to the Machine"?'

'That goes on for a week; everyone watching will have died of old age.'

'"Gimme Shelter".'

'Now you're talking.' (this from me)

'Disagree; way too much going on; tempo's wrong.'

'Blur: "To The End".'

'Too obvious.'

Whoever suggested 'To The End' then got a good staring at from the other three because in Camera Car C, being obvious with your music choice was absolutely the worst offence.

Then, someone – I can't say who – suggested Dire Straits, 'Brothers in Arms'. This immediately unleashed more protests about songs being too obvious, but we played it anyway. Luckily for us, we were in the exact location where the final driving scene would be shot, and out here, amongst the very images the song would cover, all concerns about being 'obvious' evaporated. Knopfler's mournful guitar was perfect; the sense of portent was also perfect, and when the lyrics came, all of us thought sure, maybe a bit on the nose, but those three have definitely earned those words.

Our search for a song was over. And the reason I can't say who suggested it is that back in England all four of us – as is the way of C – would separately claim the credit.

The only problem was, hunting for the right music track was meant to have taken our minds off the sadness of the day, but because 'Brothers in Arms' was so perfect, we just felt more sad than ever.

Then Joey made things a bit worse by reiterating how much he was going to miss not just Camera Car C, but the whole *Grand Tour*.

'There's no show like it,' he said specifically to me. 'You wouldn't know it cos this is the only show you do, but trust me on that.' Marc then added his agreement, saying how on other shows at mealtimes, the soundmen sit with the soundmen, the camera assistants sit with the camera assistants and so on, but with this show, everyone just . . . mingles . . . like a family.'

Joey was absolutely right. This – and *Top Gear* – were really the only shows I'd known, certainly the only ones I'd run, so yes, I had nothing to compare them to. What he was now saying did choke me up a bit. And he wasn't done:

'Honestly, mate, I can talk to Jezzer about Chelsea, I can talk to us lot about music, we all talk about anything. I'm on these other shoots and I'm with the assistants and they're all reading *Lens Monthly* and I just sit there thinking: "Will someone just *please* call me a ginger cunt?"'

I mean, naturally, we obliged.

Then, Kubu Island started to grow out of the horizon. As we approached it – our final ever drive to our final ever scene – Marc said:

'Andy, you know what, your driving's actually starting to get a bit better.' Everyone cracked up, I nicked his last chewy mint and the laughter took us the final few miles to our destination.

Kubu Island. Its party piece is 'age'. The giant baobab trees are reckoned to have been there for more than 2,000 years, and as for the granite rock around them, that's been sitting there for 2 billion years, or half the time that earth has existed. They've seen a lot. We'd last been here seventeen years earlier, Jeremy, James and Richard had routinely stated that Kubu remained their favourite ever location, but nevertheless a couple of days earlier Jeremy had wondered briefly: 'Oh God, what if it's all just rose-tinted spectacles? I mean, look where we've been since. Syria, Mongolia, Burma, Chile . . . what if it's not that special anymore?'

As we all dismounted, those worries evaporated. Obviously a two-billion-year-old island doesn't change much in seventeen years, but that wasn't the point. It still had the same air of total serenity, the same stoic charisma, just sitting there, standing proud in a vast salt lake saying: 'You're most welcome to wander around, you're not disturbing me, I'll just sit here sleeping while you do.'

This was still, without question, their favourite place; the right place to close the circle.

The camera crews got into position and nobody wanted to shout 'Action!' But, as had been the case for the last twenty-two years, the sun was looking down, tapping its watch impatiently, saying: 'Guys, I'm really sorry but I've got other places to be.' So 'Action!' it was.

The BBC had kindly sent us the old footage from the Botswana Special, so we knew that in the final film we could choreograph the trio's moves to match how they'd pulled up, got out and walked around nearly two decades earlier.

Phil had the footage on his laptop and it was a bit chilling, and not a little sad, to watch the Jeremy, Richard and James of today replicating their moves. It was absolutely nothing to do with grey hair, or lives lived, it was more: 'We're really doing it. We're really filming our last moments.'

Jeremy unplugged his mic and they shook hands – the final onscreen full stop – and we were done. There then followed, as you saw onscreen, a spontaneous bout of hugging and selfie-ing, then with the cameras off we all passed around a clapperboard bearing the date and time and title of this last scene, had our photos taken with that, and as the sun set, piled into our 4x4s and set off back to camp.

It would be a fair journey, at least two hours, and none of us wanted to get bogged down at night in the salt flat mud, so our local guide said that foot to the floor was the order of the day. Nobody needed telling twice and as we blatted along we were quite the armada, like a scene from *Sicario* on steroids. Either side of me was a phalanx of headlight beams, and in front, a huge switchboard of taillights, all bathed in swirling salt dust. Honestly, you could have put it on a car show.

In Camera Car C, all was silent once more, and this time nobody made any effort to break it. That was fine by me because now, after Kubu, loads and loads of thoughts were coming tumbling down the stairs in my head. They were snatches of memories from twenty-two years of doing our thing, and I went through them at speed – Tom Cruise swiping those boards in *Minority Report*. 'Powerrrrr!' 'Clarksonnnn!' 'I am a driving God!' 'In the plums!' 'Some say ...' 'Now we're alone, viewers'; 'That's not gone well.' 'Buffeting!' 'How hard can it be?' 'Oliver!' 'Jaaaaag'; 'Good news!' 'Let's not get bogged down ...'

I thought about how far we'd come with our day jobs, from taking baby steps with our new *Top Gear*, then learning to run as we made bigger and bigger films.

I realised – I mean I knew already – that the cycle of our existence in all this had been one of work, nerves, relief. We shoot something, we worry about it, it works ... relief. Then the cycle immediately starts all over again. Very rarely had we ever slotted in a fourth element: 'savour'.

Our *Guinness Book of Records* plaque, for instance, had just sat in its bubble wrap on the floor against a filing cabinet for months. None of us had even popped a cork, because there was always work to do. Metaphorically, that had been us. I was okay with that because that's how I'm wired, but now, as we drove back in the dark, never having to prove anything to anyone ever again, the shackles started to loosen. And I allowed myself to have a huge, alien thought; a compliment, I guess. And that thought was, that for certain, nobody would ever see the like of us again.

It was such a strange feeling that I didn't know where to put it.

What still puzzled me though was why we'd managed to stay on this pedestal for so so long. Sure we'd worked devilishly hard to entertain, sure we had Jeremy's tent pole brain, sure our trio had been lightning in a bottle, but there was something more than that.

The soft salty mud snatching at the wheels, pulling at us to bog us down and making the car skittish, kept bringing me back to our surroundings. That in turn brought me back to us four in C, sad that I would miss all our random, aimless chat, and proud that we'd cracked that most important music puzzle: 'Brothers in Arms'. C and music: they'd gone together like butter on hot toast.

Music. Music. Musicmusicmusicmusicmusic. It was music.

Jeremy had once told me quite excitedly that he'd been invited to a shoot (a shotgun shoot) and found himself – a proper Bedder Six moment – in the company of Nick Mason, Roger Taylor and Eric Clapton. At one point, while listening to all these rock gods as they swapped tales, he'd remarked: 'Jesus, it must be brilliant to be in a band.' And Clapton had replied: 'What? You don't think *Top Gear*'s a band?' The way he'd posed the question was fully rhetorical. He was saying to Jeremy: 'Of course you are.'

Oh my God. Slowhand was right. All this time we had never been TV makers, putting out TV shows. For the last twenty-two years, we'd been a band. Each series had been a new album and all the episodes on each one had been the tracks. Some were No.1 hits, some were solid, satisfying album tracks, some were experimental failures, and a few were shit.

As with all bands we had a recognisable sound, but the point was that – come the next series – we wouldn't be giving you yet another run of the same format show where the only change was new contestants. Instead, just as with records, our latest material had the potential to contain new and exciting things. As a viewer you might be thrilled, or you might be disappointed, but you didn't know what we'd do next. All our discoveries and change-ups: cheap-car challenges, Big Races, silly stunts, the improbable builds, Mr Needham tests – these had been new music on successive albums. Then, with the Specials, we started releasing double albums containing twelve-minute epics, à la Zeppelin or Pink Floyd.

You had Jeremy, the arrow tip, the member who came up with most of the tunes, on lead vocals, then James and Richard on guitar, bass, drums and keyboards, making those tunes into songs, shooting off solos, adding layers and providing the backbeat. At one time I guess we'd had the Stig on the triangle. The *TG* and *GT* team had been tour managers, roadies, set designers, sound, lighting . . . everything that made those three come to life.

And as for me, yeyyy! I'd finally got to be in a band. This time though I'd been the producer – not a telly producer but a music producer – in the edit/recording studio, mixing and shaping their material.

The name of the group could change from *Top Gear* to *Grand Tour*, the record label could change from BBC to Amazon, but in the end it was all about the band. That . . . had been the secret of our longevity.

Back at camp we all got blackout drunk and I made a speech. It's a running joke how shit mine are, but this time I'd dug deep and composed this one with the help, yet again, of the Swiss army knife that is Car C, and I knew the point I wanted to make. I reeled off some mind-boggling back-of-an-envelope stats relating to what we'd done over the years: how we'd covered enough miles to go to the moon and back forty times, how on the shoots we'd spent five noughts on crisps and soft drinks alone, how it would take around five years of non-stop twenty-four-hour viewing to get through all the rushes we'd shot. But those were merely large numbers. The more important and amazing numbers were the small ones: how in twenty-two years we'd had the same five main cameramen, the same five main soundmen, and so on, and so on. Tiny numbers in an unbreakable dysfunctional family.

'We know the fans will miss the shows,' I concluded, 'but all of us here, in this tent, we . . .' and I saw Hammo mouth exactly my words, 'will miss "this".'

'Boss! The Plane! The Plane!'

Although the hurricane of emotions that was our last day had brought the curtain down on our shooting lives, the job wasn't quite over, because we still had to cut the film together. Back in England, we assembled at our edit house in central London. The editors on this would be Dan, who had worked with us since 2004, and Robin, who'd come across to us from the Flintoff-era *Top Gear*. As with all my favourite editors, there was a charming air of special needs about them both. If you moved any of Dan's highlighters or a pen holder on his desk, he'd immediately move it back. When he brought in his huge giant Schnauzer, Alfie, he'd look at me semi-sternly until I got off the people sofa and gave it all over to the dog.

Robin, once he started working with the rushes, would disappear into his own world. He loved the melding of pictures and music in the same way that I loved moving story beats around on my internal washing line.

In the hands of Team Zimbabwe the film came together over the following weeks in a reassuringly easy manner; reassuring because if you're not fighting with the content it usually means the 'whole' will work.

And yes, because we'd left the dynamite at home, we had money to spend on good tunes. The Who for the rousing opening drive through the Eastern Highlands, Einaudi for a quieter, more reflective moment, Doves for the trucking-along bits. We could afford to pay Struggle Jennings for Jeremy's 'Monte Carlo' and other songs just 'presented' themselves. When I saw James was wearing a Joy Division T-shirt on the drive out of Harare, 'Love Will Tear Us Apart' suddenly became the natural choice.

Finally, it was time to cut together the film's closing moments. Dan, as editor of longest standing, had the honour, and I left him to it. He took 'Brothers in Arms' as his foundation, and then built simply the most evocative sequence of Jeremy, Richard and James making their final drive to Kubu over the top of it.

All three of them had said quite a few words in their cars, but we stripped those back to the 'thank you for watching' from Jeremy and the small, gentle comments of reluctant portent from James and Richard – the 'we're finally here, but part of us doesn't want to be' comments.

As for the walk over the rocks and up to the giant baobab tree, where we matched the shots with the ones from the original Botswana films, Dan had chosen, as the soundtrack, total silence.

That took us to Jeremy unplugging his microphone, then into the aerial shots of the cars driving away from Kubu, splitting off to go their separate ways. On paper that too read like a maudlin moment, but we instinctively felt that enough was enough. Once the guys had shaken hands, the sad part was done. So for the driveaway I went for 'My Sweet Lord'. Harrison's song still had enough gentleness in it to compliment the moment, but the song also had a strong beat and an uplifting chorus. It would hopefully say to the viewers: 'Look, we know this is sad, we're sad too, but it's been great. Just think of all the good times.'

Then there was that little moment where James deletes their numbers from his phone. We put it in, we took it out, we put it back in again, we took it out again, and so on, not sure whether it ruined the moment or added that perfect touch of Jeremy, Richard and Jamesness – gently popping the balloon of all this emotion. In the end we made the right call and went for the latter.

Nigel the scary director once said to me: 'You never really finish a film in the edit, there just comes a point when we have to walk away.' He was certainly on the money for this one. We wanted to tinker forever – maybe because after this there'd be no more – but finally we had to let it go out the door.

With the film getting ever closer to its birth date, what we needed next was a name. The team at Empire, a specialist outfit who cut all our trailers, are masters of this. They were the ones who'd come up with 'Seamen' and 'A Massive Hunt'. This time they came back quite quickly, offering up 'One For The Road'. Jeremy messaged me: 'That's just perfect', and we were good to go.

'One For The Road' was released on 13 September 2024.

We were absolutely at peace with the decision that our final offering should be such a gentle canter into the sunset, but nevertheless I was certainly still paranoid about how people might react to it: would they enjoy the gentleness as we'd intended, or see it as a sign that our well had definitely run dry, and that it really was time that we got our coats?

I made myself wait until the show had been available for a good half a day and then, like a fox going through the bins, started snuffling around for reactions.

The first comment I read was just what we'd hoped for. It was someone thanking us for all the years of entertainment, saying how much they would miss us. Then I scrolled down, devouring more and more, and they were all of the same mind, with people saying that 'One For The Road' was the perfect way to wrap up and how much they'd enjoyed what we'd served up over the years. But also – and I welled up at this – there were many more, not just saying how much they would miss us, but how much we'd meant to them. They talked about how we'd been part of the soundtrack of their lives from teenage years into the forties. Dads recounted how they'd sat down with their young kids to introduce the show to them; a few people even said that our antics had helped them through dark times. The comments are all out there on IMDb and elsewhere, thousands of sixty- to seventy-word thank you notes that I could never have dreamed would exist.

And at that moment I saw them as more than just comments. Each message, when it popped up on a thread, was a runway landing light, switching itself on and guiding our plane in, so that finally, it could touch down safely.

Postscript

Oh the irony. As I scour through this book on my laptop, making corrections and fiddling here and there, I'm sitting outside Court Room No. 2, at Lavender Hill Magistrates' Court in South London, awaiting news of my fate for racking up twelve speeding points. A six-month driving ban is definitely coming. So if you're reading this, Texas Highway Patrolman, treat yourself to an extra beer at the bar tonight, because justice was finally served.

Acknowledgements

I'd like to start by thanking Rowland White, the publisher of this book. Our paths have crossed gently over the years, but this is the first time we've worked together, and what a pleasure it has been. He gets into your head so that he can critique your scribbles with great insight and empathy, but once he's in there he knows instinctively what you're trying to achieve and what matters to you, so he never moves the furniture around for the sake of it.

I'd like also to thank the rest of the team at Penguin: Ruth, Hayley, Nick, Beatrix and Gaby, for their skilful copy-editing and publicity management – all the stuff that got this book out of my head and onto a bookshelf, safely and securely.

Throughout the book I tried to namecheck as many people as possible who were in the trenches and at the coalface throughout the *Top Gear* and *Grand Tour* years, but I couldn't get everyone in, so thank you to Chloe and Jess, without whose post-production skills our shows would have just remained a pile of rushes on a big computer somewhere. I'd like also to thank, in no particular order, Stuart Snaith, Kit Lynch-Robinson, Grant Wardrop, Adam Waddell, Greg Vince, Dave Morgan, Lillie, Bex Robinson, Toby Wilkinson, Ren Ferrari, Kiff McManus, Will Churchill, Gav, Kenny, Tom Carling, Peter Richardson, Eve Swayland, Stu Fennimore, Amy Gaunt, James Longley, Marguerite Poupinel, Guy Savin, Lauren Stacey, Emma Garvie, Jon Shepley, JD and Andy, Emma Carter, Emma Little, Jerome Lyte, Sara Hulme, Karl Trunk, Adie and Steve the medic for all the help with injuries and hangovers. There are more, obviously: more crew and studio crew, Hadrian the builder of things and the people driving ambulances, who it turned out we did need. Thank you to everyone for your immense skill and dedication, and thank you and sorry to anyone I've forgotten. Those two shows we made may look quite grand on the screen, but they were also in fact big toddlers that needed feeding, dressing and nurturing, and without all of you, they would have just fallen over all the time and cried.

I'd also like to thank Elaine Bedell, who was our boss at the BBC for a good long shift, and who taught me a heck of a lot about television once the Pebble Mill ties were severed.

Thank you to Amazon and its crew: John H, Jay, Helen, Dan, Anna, Fozia, Tara, Harj for giving us a new home and, once we'd moved in, letting us decorate our bedrooms how we wanted to.

Once we left *Top Gear* we also left its theme tune, *Jessica*, behind. Enter Matt Clifford, a brilliant musical composer and keyboard player for my favourite band – you can probably guess which one – who composed and recorded *The Grand Tour*'s fantastic theme. Thank you, Matt.

Staying with music, I'd also like to thank Jay Kay for always being there for us. Like I say in the book, famous people are reticent to come near a new show, but Jay had no such qualms.

Fleet St. We had some ups, we had some downs, but the sparring was enjoyable for the most part and obviously we'd have secretly had our bottom lips out if you hadn't taken any notice, so thank you for all the Fleet St fun and games. In particular though, a big thank you to Nick Rufford at the *Sunday Times* for all our dealings together over the years.

As much as we liked to be in the thick of it, we didn't just deal with the press on our lonesome. In the *Top Gear* days, the hectic days, we also had Tara Davies by our side, the smartest, wittiest and most empathetic of BBC Press Managers. She got us, and thank you for that.

Finally, I'd like to thank Lance Klein and Mark Devereux for so brilliantly compensating for the complete and utter lack of financial and business skills shared by the four of us.

Mauritania.
Blowing the budget.